WAYNE HUDSON is Associate Professor in the Faculty of Humanities at Griffith University and Director of the National Institute for Law, Ethics and Public Affairs.

GEOFFREY BOLTON is Professor of History at Edith Cowan University.

CREATING AUSTRALIA

Changing Australian history

Edited by

Wayne Hudson & Geoffrey Bolton

ALLEN & UNWIN

First published in 1997 by
Allen & Unwin
9 Atchison Street
St Leonards NSW 2065
Australia
Phone: (61 2) 9901 4088
Fax: (61 2) 9906 2218
E-mail: frontdesk@allen-unwin.com.au
URL: http://www.allen-unwin.com.au

National Library of Australia
Cataloguing-in-Publication entry:

Creating Australia: changing Australian history.

ISBN 1 86373 560 7.

1. National characteristics, Australian. 2. Australia—History. I. Bolton, G.C. (Geoffrey Curgenven). 1931– . II. Hudson, Wayne, 1945– .

994

Set in 10/12 pt Goudy Old Style by DOCUPRO, Sydney
Printed by South Wind Productions, Singapore

10 9 8 7 6 5 4 3 2 1

Contents

Contributors

Geoffrey Bolton is Professor of History at Edith Cowan University, Perth and a senior historian. His books include *The Oxford History of Australia 1902–1988* (ed.) (1992) and *Spoils and Spoilers: A History of Australians Shaping their Environment* (1992).

Ann Curthoys is Professor of History at the Australian National University, Canberra. She has written widely on questions of gender, race and ethnicity in Australian history, and is currently working on a history of the Freedom Ride of 1965.

Joy Damousi is Senior Lecturer in the Department of History, University of Melbourne.

Wayne Hudson is Associate Professor in the Faculty of Humanities at Griffith University, Brisbane and Director of the National Institute for Law, Ethics and Public Affairs. He has written an internationally acclaimed study, *The Marxist Philosophy of Ernst Bloch* (1982), and has edited books on contemporary German philosophy, postmodernism, aesthetics and republicanism.

Bruce Johnson is Associate Professor in the School of English, University of New South Wales. He is the author of *The Oxford Companion to Australian Jazz* (1987).

Bruce Kercher is Associate Professor of Law at Macquarie University in Sydney. He is the author of *An Unruly Child: A History of Law in Australia* (1995) and *Debt, Seduction and Other Disasters: The Birth of Civil Law in Convict New South Wales* (1996).

Marilyn Lake is Professor of History at Latrobe University, Melbourne.

Janet McCalman is Research Fellow in the Department of History at Melbourne University. She is the author of *Struggletown: Public and Private Life in Richmond (1900–1965)* (1986), and *Journeyings: the Biography of a Middle-Class Generation, 1920–1930* (1993).

Ann McGrath is Associate Professor in the School of History, University of New South Wales. She is currently working on a project on gender and the frontier.

Gregory Melleuish is Senior Lecturer in Politics and History at the University of Wollongong. He is the author of *Cultural Liberalism in Australia: A Study in Intellectual and Cultural History* (1995).

William Metcalf is Senior Lecturer in the Faculty of Environmental Sciences at Griffith University. He is the author of *From Utopian Dreaming to Communal Reality* (1995).

Peter Read is an Australian research fellow in the Department of History, Faculties, Australian National University. His most recent book is *Returning to Nothing: A Study of the Meaning of Lost Places in Australia* (1996).

Robert Reynolds has recently completed his doctoral thesis at Monash University, Melbourne on 'Sexuality, citizenship and subjectivity: the Australian gay movement 1970–74'.

Jan Ryan is Senior Lecturer at Edith Cowan University, Perth. She is the author of *Ancestors: Chinese in Colonial Australia* (1995) and has edited *Chinese in Australia and New Zealand: A Multidisciplinary Approach* (1995).

Geoff Stokes is Associate Professor in the Department of Government at the University of Queensland.

David Walker is Professor of Australian Studies at Deakin University, Geelong and the editor of *Australian Cultural History*.

McKenzie Wark is Lecturer in Communication Studies at Macquarie University, Sydney. He is the author of *Virtual Geographies*.

Richard White is Senior Lecturer in the Department of History, University of Sydney, the author of *Inventing Australia: Images and Identity, 1688–1980* (1981) and the co-editor of *Memories and Dreams: Reflections on 20th Century Australia* (1997).

Preface

The appearance of this book could not be more timely. In the closing decades of the twentieth century, familiar national and international cultural forms disappeared. Cold War rivalries yielded to a new world order, welfare capitalism to the vagaries of globalisation and deregulation, stable systems of meaning to a shifting play of simulacra, nation-states to contingent identities, nouns to present participles; hence the title of this book. During the 1980s and early 1990s, Australia seemed to negotiate this transition with greater confidence than elsewhere in the world. Strategically and economically, Australia was sensitive to change and yet resilient. Culturally, it found ways of managing diversity without ethnic recidivism.

Then, in 1996, this apparent new national settlement was thrown into doubt. In the space of a year the cuewords of public discourse changed—from Paul Keating's 'Big Picture' to Pauline Hanson's 'Asian Invasion', from Don Watson's anticipation of the 'first postmodern republic', with the principal values of difference and tolerance, to John Howard's assault on the 'black armband' view of history.

In speeches written by Don Watson, Paul Keating had reached back to familiar episodes—European settlement, frontier encounters, Gallipoli and the Western Front, the fall of Singapore and the Burma–Siam railway, postwar migration—to rework and enlarge an older national legend. He had told a story of a people who had triumphed over their tribulations and prejudices to embrace diversity and tolerance with an egalitarian generosity, enabling them to adapt to an open, globalised economy and engage with their Asian neighbours. They would do so by rejecting the imperial detritus, those 'old-world errors and wrongs and lies' that had made colonial Australians dependent, fearful and intolerant.

In speeches that commemorated the patriarchal figures of Alfred Deakin and John Playford and that drew their recurrent motif of the black armband from Geoffrey Blainey, during 1996 John Howard sought to attach present-day Australians to a different history. This was a story of heroic achievement, of prosperity wrought from wilderness, of democratic innovation, of the fair go. In contrast to certain unnamed revisionists whom he accused of making the national past 'a basis for obsessive and consuming national guilt and shame', he encouraged his compatriots to feel relaxed and comfortable with their heritage.

One common riposte to John Howard has been to observe that history, with or without an armband, is an endangered activity in this country. A diminishing proportion of young Australians study the subject in schools. Less than one-in-five senior secondary students take a history subject, while in the primary and junior secondary levels mere scraps of history are offered as part of the stew that is called Studies of Society and Environment. In universities, history enrolments constitute just one percent of all undergraduate studies. Only half of the universities sustain history departments and many of them are under intense pressure from the vocational emphases and entrepreneurial procedures adopted by university administrations: at the University of Queensland, a department with 27 academic staff in 1988 is now reduced to 19; Macquarie's department of modern history has been halved from 28 to 14; and at Sydney, there were 41 staff in 1988 and only 26 in 1996.

Perhaps, however, the problem is not neglect of history but neglectful historians. With certain conspicuous exceptions, the historical profession has not been prominent in the recent public debates over Aboriginal reconciliation or Asian immigration, much less the battle for custody of national identity. Nor do the works of academic historians figure in these disputes over Australian history. Again there are conspicuous exceptions, but on closer inspection these turn out to be distinctly atypical of professional norms. Manning Clark and Geoffrey Blainey both bypassed disciplinary conventions to reach a popular audience and were, in turn, regarded almost as lapsed members of the discipline because of their popularity. Perhaps the most effective rejoinder to the 'black armband' allegations comes from Noel Pearson, whose undergraduate study of history informs his incisive and generous contributions to what passes for debate on the continuing legacy of original aggression.

Why such reticence from the 500 or so practitioners who make up the academic historical profession? Many, I suspect, find it difficult or uncongenial to translate their expertise into the dialect of the three-minute radio interview. Media conventions do not allow for the complications and qualifications that hedge our judgments, or the framework of reference with which we normally formulate our interpretations. Most historians feel profoundly uncomfortable with the very terms in which the public discussion is conducted: they left arguments over national identity behind when they stopped setting Russel Ward's *Australian Legend* on undergraduate reading guides.

But culture abhors a vacuum, and the failure of historians to engage with such issues leaves the way open for the uninformed assertions that stand for want of better. For this reason alone a volume of essays that present the current state of Australian historiography under the rubric *Creating Australia* is a welcome initiative.

Wayne Hudson and Geoffrey Bolton, two highly engaged members of the profession, have assembled a team of informed, lively specialists to explain their fields and how they bear on contemporary national issues. In chapter one they present the quest for that elusive creature, the Australian identity, as yielding a multiplicity of identities. In place of the older argument between the triumphalists and the pessimists, they propose a process of challenge and response. In advancing these themes they seek to promote a re-reading of the standard narratives to allow for pluralism and to embrace inclusion and diversity. The first half of the collection suggests how a recognition of agency allows for new voices to be heard, the second records a variety of neglected achievements.

Here, then, we find eighteen scholars reaching out to tell us how their field of study contributes to an understanding of Australian history. The pluralism that characterises their reflections on *Creating Australia* permits a variety of viewpoints and assumptions. Disagreement between the contributors is left implicit.

Difference, recognition, inclusion. The claim to have one's separate identity inscribed in history is as powerful as the claim for cultural recognition in contemporary civic life. Peter Read argues eloquently in his essay on 'Aborigines Making History' that to understand our role in history provides us with the capacity to manage our present and future. He also explores the politics of such historical understanding with acute sensitivity, showing how well-intentioned non-Aboriginal historians cause resentment, and how dissident Aboriginal readings of the past also have unintended effects. The demand to be recognised for what you are seems almost by necessity to involve a particular characterisation of what you aren't, which in turn is irksome to those on whom it is conferred. Ann Curthoys suggests this in her discomfort with the category 'Anglo-Celtic'. What, after all, is a stereotype but an uncongenial role model?

One reason for the decline in the study of Australian history, I suspect, is that the subject has dissolved. History once served as a form of statecraft that inducted the governing class into their future responsibilities—thus nineteenth-century pupils learned how governors and explorers guided the fortunes of the colonies. With the rise of the nation-state and popular sovereignty, history became a story of the people—thus students learned about the convicts, the diggers, selectors, the AIF. Under the impulse of social science, it then sought to identify the structures, institutions and processes that shaped development. As early social movements challenged their subordination, popular national history yielded to a history of social contestation—thus class, gender and race. As new social movements arose, they too reworked the record, with results that are evident in contributions to this volume.

The legitimacy of such claims for recognition is irresistible, the historiographical effects more problematic. How is my story to be reconciled with yours? How is the full range of these versions of the past to be made comprehensively intelligible? In contrast to the old triumphalist narrative, the contributors to this volume suggest far more complex and conditional perspectives that are not easily drawn into an effective whole. And why should I know your story if it does not bear on mine?

Apart from the fragmentation of Australian history, there is doubt among many of its practitioners about the very grounds of historical knowledge. Historians seek to recover the past. They accept that their enterprise is necessarily interpretive, that the constantly shifting relationship between the past and the present, history and the historian, precludes certainty. More recently, they have taken on the scepticism of other practitioners of the humanities towards historical realism. Since all knowledge is constrained by discourse, the sceptics contend, knowledge of the past can only be a textual interpretation. It can never give us the past itself, only a reading of its fleeting representations. Again, this retreat from epistemological confidence weakens the capacity of the profession to speak to an audience seeking guidance. Against the historical simplifications of triumphal nationalism, it offers the decidedly unappealing advice that the nation is simply a textual effect.

The editors of this volume observe that neither naive realism nor the arcane excesses of textual deconstruction is adequate as a way of understanding Australia. The standpoint of the contributors varies, from the postmodernism of McKenzie Wark, here explicating cultural history, to Janet McCalman's affirmation of ordinary lives. Richard White revisits his influential account of *Inventing Australia* to clarify its purpose: it is not a nihilistic tract of endlessly differing interpretations but an exploration of multiple identities, not a denial of Australia but an examination of the uses to which it has been put.

In his campaign against the 'black armband' view of history, John Howard employs two recurrent arguments. The first is that historians have exaggerated the bad at the expense of the good; thus he says that he does not 'seek to obscure the failings of the past but to restore a sense of balance and perspective'. This argument is one that accepts that history is open to interpretation and allows for different judgments. His second argument is that certain persons have engaged in a 're-writing' of history as a 'systematic and deliberate' act of denigration. In this usage history is given, not made, and the historians who query or criticise the national story of achievement are vandals or trespassers.

Such arguments are played out in a number of areas of public policy. They can be discerned in the conservative outcry against the Mabo and Wik judgments, in the retreat from multiculturalism and in the attempts to stave off the republic. We can expect them to continue and to intensify the contest over Australian history. This book, with its insistence on critical affirmation and its demonstration that historians can illuminate the national past, is an important contribution to that debate.

Professor Stuart Macintyre,
University of Melbourne

1 Creating Australia

Wayne Hudson & Geoffrey Bolton

Over the years there have been many attempts to characterise that fabulous beast, the Australian national identity. Many members of the Australian public, and perhaps a few academics, still contend that the beast was best described in Russel Ward's *The Australian Legend* nearly 40 years ago (Ward 1958). The rough, honest, easy-going bushman, laconic, resourceful, loyal to his mates, uncomfortable with parsons and women, and facing adversity with a stoical joke, remains an appealing stereotype for a nation at least three-quarters of whom live in substantial cities; but even Russel Ward claimed to be writing a history of the national image, not offering a statistically verifiable portrait of the average Australian. Subsequently it has been argued that Australian national identity is entirely mythical, even a fiction promoted for their own good or bad purposes by scholars, politicians, journalists, advertising agencies and other conscious shapers of public opinion (White 1981). Geoffrey Blainey has sometimes written as if the beast once had an existence but, like a nobler version of the Tasmanian tiger, has been harried into extinction by the forces of multiplication (Blainey 1994). Many other attempts to characterise Australian national identity have been no more successful.

But the problem has been conceived much too narrowly. A better approach to understanding Australian achievement since 1788 is to emphasise the extent to which *multiple identities* have been available to Australians during the last two centuries.[1] The existence of multiple identities will occur to anyone sufficiently fortunate to retain one of Australia's current series of banknotes long enough to reflect on the personalities portrayed on them. Sir John Monash was arguably Australia's most illustrious soldier; but he was also an engineer, vice chancellor, Jew and upholder of civilian politics against dictatorship.

David Unaipon was an elder of both Aboriginal and Christian traditions, an inventor who theorised on perpetual motion and a folklorist. Mary Reibey was a pioneer of colonial capitalism, a matriarch and an early nineteenth-century female ex-convict who fits comfortably into neither of the stereotypes of 'damned whore' or 'God's police'. Given this diversity of background among prominent Australians selected as representative figures for our national currency, we conclude that it might be profitable to explore the multiple identities which have emerged in Australian society, particularly during the last half century with its conscious acceptance of ethnic diversity.

At the end of the twentieth century, neither realism nor a theoretically driven constructivist approach is adequate as a way of understanding Australia. The concept of Australia has been, and continues to be, created on the basis of traits and achievements which can only be explained for the most part by Australian agency. We are no longer, if we ever were, second-hand English men and women. We are not the suckling society derided by Humphrey McQueen, ever dependent on great and powerful allies, derivative and sterile (McQueen 1973). We are a people whose creativity has been stimulated and fostered by access to a rich variety of experiences and identities. Confidence in that creativity is still less widespread than it should be, and, in our view, historians have not done enough to promote it.

During the last half century Australia has renegotiated its international relationships. No longer merely a far-flung outpost of the British Empire, nor a spectator of the competition for supremacy in the Western Pacific between the United States and Japan, today Australia is entering upon new relationships with the rest of the world, and notably with the nations of Southeast and East Asia. Malaysia and Indonesia, to say nothing of China, sometimes proclaim concepts of nationalism which strike a little harshly on Australian ears. We are accustomed to accepting criticism from overseas, the most pointed coming often from our traditional partners, the British and the Americans. For the tigers of Southeast Asia, however, criticisms from foreigners may be deemed an impertinence. We are habituated to abusing our politicians robustly and to examining their conduct searchingly. The political leaders of Southeast Asia are less receptive to challenge. Since our strategic and commercial future is intertwined with the new nationalism of Southeast Asia, it behoves us not only to cultivate a sensitive understanding of our neighbours' national self-concepts, but also to foster a more confident awareness of our own. Old stereotypes of Australian identity will no longer serve. Australian history is more than simply a record of past events. It is also something which changes and has to change as we create Australia. Against this background, we argue that new perspectives on the Australian past are needed: perspectives which emphasise the originality, independence and activity of Australians in the context of creations of multiple Australian identities, most of them sites of contest and struggle.

Admitting multiple identities undermines monolithic notions of what we mean by 'Australia'. In recent years, Australians whose ancestors lived in the continent before 1788 have been reminding us of the inadequacy of lumping them together as 'Aborigines'. Most will accept the justice of distinguishing a Bibbulman of the Nyoongar from a Kalkadoon, though there may be some debate before the North American practice of describing pre-colonial indigenous communities as 'first nations' is accepted (Reynolds 1996). Regional variations also persist among those Australians whose ancestors arrived somewhat later. Seekers after an Australian identity have often tended to undervalue provincial diversity, but it would be impossible to grasp the fullness of the Australian experience without acknowledging equally the rural Tasmania of Christopher Koch and the Melbourne which is the background for Helen Garner's characters no less than Martin Boyd's. Australia is regionally an increasingly diverse society, and the statistics of the census confirm this.

Even the '98 percent British' Australia of the late nineteenth and early twentieth centuries was never close to monolithic. Categories of class and gender tended to shift and blur in that fluid colonial environment. The shearer who joined the Australian Workers' Union to fight the scabs and defy the squatters was often at the same time a cocky farmer working his wife and family hard and dreaming of yeoman self-sufficiency (Merritt 1986). Some of the pioneer telegraph operators employed by the West Australian postal service were young Aboriginal women from Bishop Salvado's New Norcia mission. Less obviously, that most subtle and creative of Australia's early prime ministers, Alfred Deakin, gave much of his thought and emotional energy to religious mysticism (Gabay 1992). But then many Australians had hidden or covert identities hard to guess from their public personas. Some were theosophists and spiritualists. Many men joined the Freemasons, a body whose pervasive influence in Australian society has been grossly neglected by historians, and it is fair to assume that Masons were attracted to the lodge, not merely through motives of careerism, but also because of the ideals and rituals which they found in it. Among the respectable working class, lodges, such as the Druids, the Rechabites, the Buffaloes and the Oddfellows, provided support systems of considerable strength and durability. Catholics had their own religious orders and lay sodalities, although their diversity and importance for the heterogeneous texture of Australian political and cultural life is little studied.

Nor should we uncritically assume that multiculturalism is entirely an invention of recent years. Consider the numerous Caledonian societies with their popular Burns nights, the German societies which flourished in South Australia until obliterated by the disgraceful jingoism of the 1914–18 war, the Russian Club which excited the Brisbane rioters of 1919, the organisations by which the Australian Chinese supported their members. But this ethnic richness has yet to inform adequately the general histories of our country. Politics, too, were perhaps less monolithic 60 or 70 years ago than they are today. Minority groups such as the Social Credit movement, the British Israelites, the Protestant Labor Party, and above all the communists, each commanded the allegiance of loyal minorities, not all of whom came to the public eye. Even before the ethnic diversification of the last 50 years, even before the communications revolution of the last 30, Australia as a settler society was always a mosaic rather than a monolith.

Historians have been slow to acknowledge and study this diversity. In colonial and post-colonial Australia, emphasis has understandably been given to identifying the characteristics which distinguish us from metropolitan Britain. This emphasis had its effect on Manning Clark's *History*. Originally planned around the theme of three great faiths, Catholicism, Protestantism and Enlightenment, endeavouring to adapt to the inhospitable Australian environment, Clark's *History* in its later volumes stressed the failure of Australians to cast off the social and cultural influences of Britain in favour of republican national authenticity. This failure, Clark implied, is an outward sign of spiritual mediocrity. A distinctive Australian nationalism could not be asserted in a society where 'No-one had anything to say' (Clark 1987, p. 500).

Clark is the best known but not the only historian in recent years to take a pessimistic view of Australian achievement. Several flourishing branches among the newer schools of Australian historiography have tended to paint in dark colours (Burgmann & Lee 1988). The ferment of activity by the new left social scientists during the 1970s found its summation in Connell and Irving's *Class Structure in Australian History* (1980), which portrayed an endless resourcefulness in the ability of capitalists to manipulate Australian workers through control of education, the media and the levers of governments. A little earlier Miriam Dixson, in a significant early contribution to feminist history, had argued that Australian history had resulted in a uniquely oppressive regime for women (Dixson 1976), and her findings have remained influential on many readers, although later queried by Patricia Grimshaw and others. The most comprehensive among Australian environmental histories, *Taming the Great South Land*, painted a sombre picture of the uncomprehendingly destructive impact of much rural capitalist development (Lines 1991). Fearing that history on the national scale might too easily become self-serving and triumphalist, a significant number of recent Australian historians have seemed to show a relish for gloom, provoking conservative sneers about 'black armband history'. We believe that other responses need to be taken into account. If instead of attempting nation-wide generalisations we look for instances of Australian agency, of capacity to respond originally to specific challenges and problems, we may find evidence which complicates some of the gloomier assessments, at least to some degree. We may also gain new insights into the processes by which Australian identities are created.

A model for this approach may be found in the work of Henry Reynolds. Before the publication of Charles Rowley's three-volume *The Destruction of Aboriginal Society*, the story of Aboriginal–white relations had been relegated to the margins of Australian history, if not ignored altogether. Historians of race in the 1970s were quick to rectify this neglect, but where Rowley's analysis was informed by a comparative perspective shaped by years of experience in Papua New Guinea some of his successors tended to portray indigenous Australians as hapless victims of European aggression, incapable of effective response to invasion. Through his studies of Queensland and Tasmania, Reynolds has shown that Aboriginal responses to white settlement were marked by considerable initiative and adaptability, whether in resistance or in negotiating terms with the newcomers. He does not minimise or palliate the extent of European aggression, but instead of relegating the Aborigines to the lowly status of victims, he shows them as capable of dynamic response to unprecedented pressures. He reminds us that, contrary to earlier myth, traditional Aboriginal societies were never static but responded intelligently to change. Aboriginal communities at the end of the twentieth century are still responding to change. They are not identical with what was once dubbed 'traditional society', although tradition, both inherited and invented, is an important ingredient in the self-definition of contemporary Aborigines. In like manner, we would argue that Australia as a settler society has not been static or unresponsive to change since 1788. The stereotypes of the past, whether the independent Australian Britons of W.K. Hancock's formulation in 1930, or the noble bushman depicted by Ward a generation later, came into being only at the moment of obsolescence, when Australia as a settler society had already evolved into something different and more complex. Such stereotypes are misleading as descriptions of contemporary Australians, though undeniably they have their part, both through attraction and repulsion, in defining the concepts which Australians have of themselves.

Australians, however, should not be reduced to their myths. Instead, they need to recognise their own creativity and originality, an originality often inflected by multiple identities. Consider the development of Australian cuisine. Fifty years ago the legacy of the British lower middle class sat heavily on Australian stomachs. Today as a result of venturesome experiment we are blending European and Asian traditions, native Australian ingredients and access to some of the world's finest vineyards, to produce a distinctive culinary tradition which is unlike any other in the world. And its outstanding merits are gaining both local and international recognition. As with food and drink, so in less homely aspects of national self-expression.

The British historian E.P. Thompson saw the English working class as coming into being through the purposeful activities of thousands of individuals and groups responding to the pressures of displacement and industrialisation. In a related way, we see Australian characteristics as coming into being through the agency of many groups and individuals. We do not see nationalism as something solely created through government initiatives. Nor do we believe that national characteristics magically arise from 'the land'. We think that groups and individuals act to create 'Australia', and that the time has now come for an increased acknowledgment of Australian creativity and originality as part of a greater and more self-confident national self-awareness.

In advancing these themes, we seek to promote a re-reading of the standard narratives of Australian history. As scholars working in Queensland and Western Australia we are unconvinced by accounts centred almost exclusively on the concerns of the Sydney–Canberra–Melbourne axis. We also believe that the work done on ethnic and gender history since 1970 has transformed Australian history in ways which establish new ground rules. Henceforth, Australian history must include Australians who are not mono-national, Australians of various sexual orientations and Australians who do not conform. A more inclusive Australian history can also be a more positive Australian history because the evidence for creativity and originality is strong over many different areas.

Attentive readers will note that this volume is not primarily theoretical, even though we believe that theoretical perspectives on Australian history are needed. No doubt we shall not be using the term 'Australian' in only one sense. Nor do we assume that Australian characteristics existed before they were created. In emphasising the need to create Australia, we acknowledge the influence of Richard White's *Inventing Australia*, which was arguably the first systematic analysis of the motives and processes behind the promotion of popular Australian national stereotypes. White's work did not mark the end of the older quest for a definition of Australian nationalism as an expression of independence from Britain. In the wake of the somewhat forced bicentennial celebrations of 1988, at least two major contributions were made based on the concept of a single Australian nationalism (McLachlan 1989; Alomes 1988). But the questions raised by White proved impossible to ignore, and in the intervening fifteen years since he raised them he has continued to reflect on them.

We also owe a debt to four feminist historians who not long ago achieved a major breakthrough in Australian historiography with the publication of *Creating a Nation* (Grimshaw, Lake, McGrath & Quartly 1994). Coming after twenty years of vigorous productivity in Australian feminist history, they rejected the marginalisation of feminist history and wrote instead a general social history of Australia consciously shaped by feminist perspectives, just as earlier general histories were (often less consciously) shaped by the unacknowledged gender bias of their authors. In doing so they have enlarged our readings of Australia's past.

This volume continues this quest for inclusion. Our contribution is to bring together essays by some of the most active practitioners currently in the field, emphasising the originality, independence and agency of Australians. Their essays, in areas as diverse as citizenship, political theory, popular culture, law, sexuality and ethnicity, support the view that Australians have been more active, creative, original and independent than the existing literature allows. They suggest a possible connection between a more positive view of what happened in Australian history and research into how multiple identities may have helped Australians to make original achievements in many different fields.

The essays divide themselves into two roughly equal sections. In the first half we look at multiple Australian identities. Following an important chapter by Richard White in which he reconsiders his views in *Inventing Australia* in response to our emphasis on multiple identities, Ann Curthoys reconsiders attempts to interpret Australian ethnic and national identities in terms of distinctiveness, and concludes that the fascination and drama of Australian history is still often lost in stereotypes. If we attempt to understand how present Australians of all ethnicities fit into world history then we may find that it is what we share with other societies rather than any alleged distinctiveness which matters most. In the next two chapters, Robert Reynolds and Ann McGrath write on Australian sexual identities. McGrath shows that an emphasis on agency and multiple identities brings out the rich complexity and diversity of Australian sexual identities while Reynolds imagines what a 'queer' history of Australia informed by a sense of multiple identities might look like. In chapters six and seven, Peter Read emphasises the insufficiently acknowledged record of active agency by Aboriginal groups in Australia, and Jan Ryan alerts us to the absence of Chinese in general histories of Australia and explores the need to take account of multiple Australian Chinese identities. Ryan suggests that separate ethnic histories of the Chinese are not enough. Next Joy Damousi argues the case for a radical rewriting of Australian labour history to take account of poststructuralism. None of these writers is working in an isolated field and all build on the research of colleagues. By bringing them together with an insistence on the role of agency, we hope to reframe the way much of this research is read.

The second half of the volume considers a variety of original Australian achievements. The tone is set by Janet McCalman who repudiates the tendency to write about ordinary Australians as if they were the passive recipients of agenda doled out by powerful impersonal forces. Instead she focuses on the creative activities of everyday life, rescuing suburban Australians from the enormous condescension of satirists from Patrick White onwards. Marilyn Lake looks at the political achievement of Australian women in creating new notions and practices of citizenship earlier than almost all other advanced political communities. Then Bruce Kercher shows how Australians, even in the nineteenth century, were creative and original in their use and interpretation of the legal traditions inherited from Britain. Very soon we developed a jurisprudence which was neither British nor American. Its practitioners were well aware of the potential for distortion in Privy Council appeals, and it is no coincidence that at the time of Federation this issue was the main bone of contention between the Australian delegates and the Home government. The themes of independence and orginality are also applicable to Australian political thought. In a wide-ranging discussion, Gregory Melleuish and Geoff Stokes explore the creativity and originality of Australian political thought and show how this thought arose from and impacted upon Australian public experience

Moving into less explored territory, William Metcalf stresses the underrated creativity of the Australian communalist movement and the often underestimated strength of alternative imaginations. The American frontier has long been recognised as a nursery of new faiths, and it is time to recognise that, although different in form, Australia also nursed dreamers and prophets, especially in parts of the country which are frequently overlooked by scholars working in Sydney or Melbourne. In the next chapter, David Walker looks outward at early Australian attempts to come to terms with Asia and to envisage a western Pacific region to which Australia could belong. In the following chapter Bruce Johnson challenges the established canon of Australian music and argues that whole domains of Australian musical experience need to be taken into account and celebrated in Australian music history. Then, in a characteristically lively chapter, McKenzie Wark pursues the question of originality in the secret history of Australian postmodernism. The volume concludes with a chapter by Wayne Hudson linking the exploration of originality in Australian intellectual history to both multiple identities and a better appreciation of our civic heritage.

Creating Australia draws on work in progress across a range of those disciplines in the social sciences and humanities which have seen some of the liveliest intellectual activity in recent years; it also draws readily on some of the latest and most original research. The point is worth making, not for self-advertisement, but because in the current adverse financial climate it is easy to underestimate the capacity of Australian scholarship for originality and self-renewal. Recently there has been a good deal of rather sterile debate about the alleged readiness of Australian academics to succumb unthinkingly to the doctrines of French intellectuals. Foucault, Althusser and Lyotard, though united in little else, figure among the suspects. Even creative artists such as David Williamson and Christopher Koch have given credence to the myth of a postmodernist (or is it poststructuralist?) domination of Australian academe. This debate illustrates our concerns nicely by failing to take account of either Australian multiple identities or the range and quality of Australian originality. This volume demonstrates that rumours of a foreign takeover of Australian scholarship are grossly exaggerated, just as it confirms that some Australian historians have benefited from the astonishingly rich contemporary literature on postmodernism and poststructuralism. Overall, it suggests that Australian historians are as eclectic as ever, borrowing unabashedly from any and every accessible source; but blending what they borrow into illuminating and distinctive patterns. This is no new development but draws directly on a pioneering tradition reaching far back into intellectual origins in the nineteenth century.

In so far as the essays in this volume emphasise the originality, independence and agency of Australians, they imply a distinctive response to the question of what Australian history should now be. Without retreating in any way from the need for subversive and socially critical history, they imply that Australian history can help to create Australia precisely by acknowledging the creativity and originality of Australians. They also defend a post-positivist history which acknowledges an obligation to contribute to a better social life. This civic emphasis is controversial, and our individual contributors would doubtless interpret it in different ways, but it gives, we believe, much of the best contemporary Australian history its energy and edge.

NOTE

1 There is now a considerable literature on the concept of 'identities', much of it critical of 'essentialist' approaches to identity and 'identification politics'. See Butler (1990) and Laclau (1994).

REFERENCES

Alomes, S. 1988, *A Nation at Last? The Changing Character of Australian Nationalism 1880–1988*, Angus & Robertson, Sydney.

Burgmann, V. & Lee, J. 1988, *A People's History of Australia Since 1788*, 4 vols, McPhee Gribble, Melbourne.

Blainey, G. 1994, *A Shorter History of Australia*, William Heinemann, Port Melbourne.

Butler, J. 1990, *Gender Trouble: Feminism and the Subversion of Identity*, Routledge, London.

Clark, C.M.H. 1987, *A History of Australia*, vol. 6, *The Old Dead Tree and the Young Tree Green, 1916–1935*, Melbourne University Press, Melbourne.

Connell, R.W. & Irving, T.H. 1980, *Class Structure in Australian History: Document, Narrative and Argument*, Longman Cheshire, Melbourne.

Dixson, M. 1976, *The Real Matilda: Women and Identity in Australia, 1788–1975*, Penguin, Ringwood.

Gabay, A. 1992, *The Mystic Life of Alfred Deakin*, Cambridge University Press, Melbourne.

Grimshaw, P., Lake, M., McGrath, A. & Quartly, M. 1994, *Creating a Nation*, McPhee Gribble, Melbourne.

Hudson, W. & Stokes, G. 1997, 'Australia and Asia: Place, Determinism and National Identities', in *The Politics of Identity in Australia*, ed. G. Stokes, Cambridge Universtiy Press, Melbourne, ch. 10.

Laclau, E. 1994, *The Making of Political Identities*, Verso, London.

Lines, W. J. 1991, *Taming the Great South Land: A History of the Conquest of Nature in Australia*, Allen & Unwin, Sydney.

McLachlan, N. 1989, *Waiting for the Revolution: A History of Australian Nationalism*, Penguin, Melbourne.

McQueen, H. 1973, 'The suckling society', in *Australian Politics: A Third Leader*, eds Henry Mayer & Helen Nelson, Cheshire, Melbourne, pp. 5–13.

Merritt, J. 1986, *The Making of the AWU*, Oxford University Press, Melbourne.

Reynolds (ed.) 1982, *The Other Side of the Frontier: Aboriginal Resistance to the European Invasion of Australia*, Penguin, Melbourne.

—— 1990, *With the White People: The Crucial Role of Aborigines in the Exploration and Development of Australia*, Penguin, Melbourne.

—— 1995, *Fate of a Free People: A Radical Re-examination of the Tasmanian Wars*, Penguin, Melbourne.

—— 1996, *Aboriginal Sovereignty. Race, State and Nation*, Allen & Unwin, Sydney.

Roe, J. 1986, *Beyond Belief: Theosophy in Australia 1879–1939*, NSW University Press, Sydney.

Rowley, C.D. 1970. *The Destruction of Aboriginal Society*, 3 vols, Australian National University Press, Canberra.

Ward, R. 1958, *The Australian Legend*, Oxford University Press, Melbourne.

White, R. 1981, *Inventing Australia: Images and Identity, 1688–1980*, Allen & Unwin, Sydney.

2 *Inventing Australia* revisited

Richard White

Richard White's Inventing Australia *was a turning point in history-making in Australia. White broke with the Australian tradition of social realist historiography, and under the influence of poststructuralism laid unprecedented emphasis on the idea that 'Australia' was 'invented' and in many different ways. At the time his views were widely attacked, although they proved attractive to many younger scholars. In recent years an American version of postmodernism which alleges that no coherent distinction can be drawn between reality and representation has enjoyed considerable popularity in Australia, especially among feminists. Nonetheless, as he makes clear in an essay specially written for this volume, White's own views were never as anti-realist as his critics were wont to suggest, and he was in fact sympathetic to an emphasis on multiple identities in Australian history, which is very different from a cult of endlessly differing interpretations.*

All books are the product of their time and place. Or places. *Inventing Australia* was written in many places—in a tent in a soggy camping ground near Heidelberg; in a pensione in Rome which overflowed into the owner's loungeroom when demand demanded; in converted stables opposite a frost-etched churchyard in a Norfolk market town. It was influenced by the intellectual traditions of Sydney, where I had studied, and Melbourne, where I had taught history, at a time when the rising interest in Australia's own past was meeting the declining power of the grand narratives of history—and when a carefree year overseas was still an easy option for young Australians.

Now, fifteen years on, it all seems a long time ago. Much has changed. Much hasn't. This is an opportunity to reconsider *Inventing Australia* in the light of some of the most persistent concerns of its critics, particularly regarding the 'reality' of nation. My intention is not to respond to critics specifically—a book ought to be left to fend for itself—but to consider how some of the criticisms reflect what I would see as misunderstandings, not just of the book, but of the meaning and significance of 'nation' itself. Then it will be possible to consider the principal concerns of this book: how recognition of multiple Australian identities and the agency of ordinary Australians contributes to and complicates the writing of Australian history. But before dealing with each of those concerns, it is worth clarifying what *Inventing Australia* was, as well as what it was not.

I

Inventing Australia began with a very simple and not particularly original proposition: 'Australia' exists pre-eminently as an idea. While it has a real existence as a geographical space with defined boundaries, and as a political entity, a nation-state organised for the pursuit of political power, 'Australia' for the most part is something we carry around in our heads. Benedict Anderson has put it another way: a nation is an imagined community. Whereas we experience most communities we relate to—a family, a school, a village—as accumulations of individuals we actually know, and are constantly negotiating community boundaries, the nation is something so large we can only ever imagine it (Anderson 1983).

Inventing Australia was a history of *an idea*, an attempt to look at the imagining of Australia historically, tracing some of the dominant images of Australianness, from those of European explorers to 1980s mining entrepreneurs, and to investigate how they functioned. It was not a history of Australia as a place or as a political entity or a society. Nor was it a history of Australian nationalism.

Had it been a history of Australia as a *geographical space* it would have begun with the Aboriginal experience. But *Inventing Australia* began, pointedly, with European exploration (already, in 1981, a very old-fashioned way of beginning a book on Australian history), because Australia as an idea was a European imposition. Before the European occupation of the land, Aborigines did not think of themselves as 'Australian', though they were defined as 'Australian' by their invaders (before the name was given to anyone else). For Europeans the term 'Australian' in 1800 still meant Aborigine; by 1900 they had successfully shifted the word to mean white residents in such a way as to exclude the original Australians (Attwood 1989). Only from the 1970s, as a strategy in the politics of race, did some Aborigines conceptualise themselves as a nation. Ironically it was the bicentenary that—through their resistance to the celebration of what they saw as invasion—gave stimulus to the process of unifying Aboriginal peoples into a single political entity.

Had it been a history of Australia as a *nation-state*, *Inventing Australia* would have focused more on the political creation of the nation, the struggles and compromises that federated six relatively independent colonies of Britain into the Commonwealth of Australia in 1901. It would have stressed the competition of loyalties to other powerful political entities, wider loyalties to the empire, narrower loyalties to the various states, and shown how all this was demonstrably not an expression of a popular will. Such a history would also have considered the ways in which people were turned into Australians, both before and after Federation, through education, through the creation of a national market, through language and sport and the organisation of culture into national institutions, through the ideas of nationalist intellectuals, through the ways in which Australia as a political entity incorporated people into itself and defined them as citizens.

Had it been a history of *Australian society*, it would have been 'doing a Manning Clark', which was hardly necessary, and in any case the possibilities of writing such a grand narrative, if one were not Manning Clark, were shrinking in 1980. In passing it might have noted how conventional history operates to conceptualise and perpetuate the idea of the nation. Nations, by definition, embroider the past into their fabric. Their imagined community consists not just of its present-day citizens but past lives as well (and above all others, those who died in the name of the nation). National histories, even when they don't invoke the nation as their subject, are critical in providing the nation with the historical dimension so essential to its operation, by giving a diverse contemporary society a common past, as well as by giving the geographical space a cultural unity.

Had *Inventing Australia* been a history of *Australian nationalism*, it would have been different again, a history of a self-conscious movement, or overlapping intellectual, political and cultural movements. It would have had to define nationalists clearly as a group within the Australian population with their own particular objectives, and not as heroic representatives of a wider nation—which is of course how nationalists would like to portray themselves. Since 1981, two very different books, by Stephen Alomes and Noel McLachlan, have attempted the history of Australian nationalism, but both from within a national history framework, and they have both found it hard to separate the social history of nationalism from a history of the nation.

So *Inventing Australia* was not quite any of these things, though all of them needed doing. It was instead a modest history of the idealised nation. Of course, the idea of nation is an enormously powerful one, powerful enough for people to die in its name. Its very imprecision is its power. But it is not the same as the nation-state, which clearly defines its boundaries, its members, its power. The idealised nation is in many ways an invention, an artificial construction, rather than an expression of an underlying essence that all members of a particular nation share.

In retrospect I should have made that distinction more explicit, because it is at this point that, it seems to me, a number of critics misunderstood my argument. They assumed that to question the 'reality' of the nation was to question the reality of everything; Noel McLachlan, for example, thought I must be a nihilist.

Now it is arguable that there were good historical reasons for this confusion. *Inventing Australia* coincided with an upsurge of interest in Australia as an object of study. Australian literature, history, social sciences, film were all enjoying an unprecedented popularity through the 1970s. A new cultural nationalism, which *Inventing Australia* reported on (White 1981, p. 169) at the same time as being part of it, sustained many intellectual workers—writers, artists, teachers, publishers, filmmakers, curators. Their primary subject was Australia, their arena of operations was Australia, their main audience were Australians. At the same time there was a new postmodern interest in the construction of meanings, in cultural studies and cultural history. For many the two strands were simply aligned: the study of culture meant the study of Australia. Culture could not be conceptualised outside a national framework (Frow 1995, pp. 7–13).

For others poststructuralist interest in meaning, emphasising its ambiguity, multiplicity and dependence on the reader's interpretation over the writer's intention, simply dissolved 'reality', and encouraged a drift to cultural relativism. I was stranded somewhere in the middle, because while I was quite happy to borrow poststructuralist notions in examining the construction of something as nebulous as conceptions of Australia, I did not imagine or argue that all other aspects of the past—culture, experience—were equally nebulous. Some things are more constructs than others. Here was my sin of omission, perhaps, in not making the distinction between the invented quality of ideas about Australia and the 'reality' of other aspects of life in Australia clear; though I would have thought my analysis did deal with realities of power and experience, that I did find materialist explanations for particular points of view, that I had proved my 'realist' credentials. But through this confusion by some critics of the cultural with the national, I could find myself in the actually quite comfortable position of being criticised as a Marxist by some (e.g. Thornhill 1992) and a non-Marxist by others (e.g. Frankel 1992).

Perhaps the most convoluted recent example of that confusion is found in Gregory Melleuish's *Cultural Liberalism in Australia* (1995), in which he argues that I 'cannot distinguish between true and false statements' (p. 7), that my 'argument simply lacks coherence' (p. 8), that I necessarily have an unflattering view of the average Australian (p. 11). Because Melleuish slides so conveniently between culture, national identity and ideas of nation, he ends up claiming that I see culture as 'a force imposing itself on people from without and which they accept for fundamentally irrational reasons' (p. 11), that in my view 'culture is merely an invention' (p. 10). Ironically he can even claim that 'Blinded by notions of "hegemony", writers like White . . . make national identity the dominant and basic element of culture' (p. 9), which is precisely my complaint about him. Clearly there can be multiple readings of the same text. However, the tendency of some critics to equate what I said about the invention of 'Australia' with the idea that all cultural activity in Australia must in some way be 'invented' is understandable, given that many Australian intellectuals view culture as being explicable only in national terms.

To argue that the idea of 'Australia' is an invention is not to say that there are not 'realities' connected with Australia. It is after all a geographical and political term; there are institutions that give shape and substance to the idea of Australia. History does deal with real people and real experiences even if it also deals with (and necessarily uses as evidence) the representations of experience. However, what I would want to emphasise is the contingency and arbitrariness of naming those institutional, political and even geographical realities 'Australian'. The fact that the physical boundaries of the Australian nation happen to coincide with a single landmass (tossing in Tasmania) can blind us to the arbitrariness of most national boundaries. (In fact, of course, the sovereignty of the nation-state has been a negotiable thing that extends past the coastline we know on the map to the continental shelf and beyond). That Federation produced 'a nation for a continent' made Australia quite exceptional. Few national boundaries are as neat, but even in the Australian case there were other possibilities. The new political entity could have included New Zealand, and excluded Western Australia, and later there was a possibility of incorporating Papua New Guinea. In all cases we might still have called the result Australia. And even the idea of that single landmass is a trick of the mind, the geographical unity more apparent than real.

Physically the land itself, and an 'Australian' sense of place, can range from temperate Tasmania to northern tropical rainforest, from snowy mountains to sandy desert. The problem geography poses for national symbolism can be seen in Australia's version of the War of the Roses: the great battle between the advocates of the waratah and the wattle to find a floral emblem that would stand for the whole of Australia. The waratah was attacked because it was not spread widely enough throughout the continent, whereas the wattle was criticised because it was native to other parts of the world as well. No flower was 'Australian' in the sense that it could satisfy both conditions, being found throughout Australia and only within Australia.

Hardly important perhaps, but enough to to get a lot of people very cranky a century ago. My point is that there are realities—social, cultural, geographical—but when it comes to naming even the simplest realities 'Australian' we get into difficulties because we are inevitably touching on questions of power and identity. And this brings us to the concerns of this book: how do questions of nationality and culture touch on the issues of multiple identities and the agency of ordinary Australians?

II

If the idea of 'Australia' is an invention, an active and creative process rather than something that has a prior existence and simply needs to be discovered, then it follows that it will be invented and embroidered in different ways by different people for different reasons. This could be taken to mean that there is no single Australian identity but only multiple identities. Even when *Inventing Australia* was being written, with multiculturalism being formally adopted as a national cultural policy, this idea was not all that new. Nevertheless, *Inventing Australia* probably contributed to the process by which the notion of a single monolithic national identity—as portrayed for example in Russel Ward's *The Australian Legend*—was increasingly discredited through the 1970s and 1980s. It was a battle that still had to be fought in the lead-up to the bicentennial celebrations, and while there was a strong backlash against the Bicentennary, and the Bicentennial Authority's commitment to pluralism might have been as much strategic as heartfelt, multiple identities were recognised in 'Celebration of the Nation' (Spearritt 1988; Cochrane & Goodman 1988).

In *Inventing Australia* my concern with multiple Australian identities was with their multiplicity over time. Despite Melleuish's comment that 'a cursory examination of White's national images demonstrates that they are all quite similar' (1995, p. 9), I would suggest a slightly less cursory examination might show that they changed considerably over time, ranging from hell to paradise (which raises concerns about Melleuish's eschatology), from an Australia based in the bush to one found in suburbia, and, important in Melleuish's own work, from 'free trade' notions of Australia to protectionist ones. In examining that series of conceptions of Australia, I only considered those I judged to be dominant at any one time. I regret that I was not able to give more attention to alternative conceptions of Australia competing with the dominant ones, nor to the actual processes of dissemination by which some conceptions came to dominate. However, I did establish that there was a contest for supremacy going on among the different conceptions of Australia, and that contest was part of the wider struggles for dominance within Australian society. One problem with the bicentennial gloss of multiple identities, and of much public commitment to multiculturalism, is its tendency to leave out of the equation the contest for dominance in the public discourse of nation. All multiple identities are seen as equal, when in fact some are more equal than others.

The other problem with the pluralism of the bicentenary and official multiculturalism is that multiple identities were still seen as all being in some way versions of a privileged national identity. While multiple identities were admitted, there remained an insistence that they were all still expressions of 'Australianness'. But 'Australianness' only accounts for a tiny proportion of cultural identity in Australia. True, there is one particularly powerful strand in Australian culture—the *Bulletin* writers, the Heidelberg painters, the radical nationalist intellectuals, the 1970s costume drama films, the Mojo advertisements of the 1980s—in which the question of 'Australianness' looms particularly large. It is a tradition that has produced many great cultural artefacts. Another strand has always stressed the ambiguities of 'Australianness', the competition between Australian identity and other national loyalties, and it too has produced great work. But most cultural identity in Australia simply doesn't bother with the question of whether or not it is Australian. It too produces great work, simply out of the cultural hybrid of borrowings, creativity, regionalism, local knowledge, and the many contests between individual and group identities.

It is worth distinguishing at least three ways in which we can think of multiple identities: that there are many versions of Australian identity or of ways of thinking about Australia—as the bicentennial celebrations recognised; that there are many group identities within Australia competing with each other, and national identity is only one of them; that each individual has multiple identities in that everyone identifies with a range of social groups. *Inventing Australia* only addressed the first, and then only scratched the surface. Even any one individual will conjure up different Australias depending on immediate needs. The Australia we think of nostalgically travelling overseas is different from the one we think of when we are casting a vote and is again different from the one we have in mind watching the Olympics, and again different from the one we think of—if we think of it at all—when lying on the beach at Bondi. These versions of Australian identity were the little bit of historical territory I had marked out for myself in *Inventing Australia*. The work was in fact originally commissioned by Allen & Unwin to connect with a (long since abandoned) New South Wales Higher School Certificate history unit entitled 'To be Australian'. But to focus on national identity is not to imply that that is the only identity of significance, or that the many other identities people construct for themselves are irrelevant. I was not writing a history of cultural identity in Australia. I assumed that was reasonably self-evident, but I underestimated the strength of the view in some circles that national identity is the only one that matters, that all cultural history ought to be interpreted from its perspective and hence that anyone attempting to write a history of the idea of Australia was in fact writing a history of culture.

It is at this point that we need to consider a second concern of this book—the agency of ordinary people in the development of cultural identity—and another point on which *Inventing Australia* was often misinterpreted. I would argue strongly that it is only a small though influential minority of people who confuse nation and culture, who consider that national identity accounts for all cultural expression in Australia. As I suggested, multiple identities are not simply versions of being Australian. Each individual can be thought of as having multiple identities. Being Australian is simply one way among many that we construct ourselves as social beings. Most of us don't think much about being Australian; we have no cause to in everyday life, and only occasionally—in international sport, when voting, travelling overseas, engaging in war—do we think much about our Australianness at all. For most people, other identities—being a woman, being a builder's labourer, being a teenager, being a Catholic, being a skinhead or a Liberal voter or an Italian speaker, being part of a family, an organisation, a local community, in an occupation—are far more immediate and far more important in day-to-day life than being an

Australian. Aspects of those identities are 'invented' too, but they emerge much more out of the experience of everyday life and day-to-day social dealings.

However there are some for whom Australia provides the arena for much more of what they do, who of necessity think more about being Australian than most people. It is not that they are more patriotic, or more broadminded or more insightful; just that they have more reason to imagine Australia as a community. Consider some examples: the manufacturer whose products are destined for an Australian market; the federal politician who must construct national policies to appeal to a national interest; the journalist, the writer, the historian, the intellectual, whose words reach out to a readership of Australians. What they have in common is a notion of a market for their products, ideas and persuasive powers that is Australia-wide, and the market is perhaps the most powerful imagined community of all. There are other markets for goods and politics and ideas—international markets, local markets, niche markets. But the national market is the most accessible because it is the most thoroughly institutionalised by the power of the state. To acknowledge that intellectuals, like politicians or manufacturers, might have an interest in the creation of a national market is not to belittle or dismiss their role (see Frow 1995, pp. 168–9). Indeed, as I suggested at the outset, it is important for such a history to be written.

The intimate relationship between the market and the imagined community of the nation can be seen in the way the best known expressions of an Australian identity were in a broad sense marketing exercises. The Heidelberg school's national paintings were produced at a time when artists needed to appeal to new publicly funded galleries more than private collectors. The *Bulletin*'s success was based on the recognition of the potential of a single national popular market, and so its nationalism was a means of identifying that market. Federation resulted from, above all else, the recognition of the emerging Australian manufacturing sector's need for a continent-wide market. Manufacturers at the time enthusiastically embraced national symbols in advertising to identify their products with the national market. Mojo's nationalist advertising in the 1980s was connected to the reorganisation of the television industry—and the beer industry too—around national markets.

This is not to say, as economic rationalists would say, that the market is everything, the only possible way of relating to other human beings, any more than national identity accounts for our whole cultural experience. Other identities—the rich mix of the many social and cultural identities that we all construct and reinvent for ourselves in all our many relationships every day—are ultimately far more important. So while I would certainly not deny the active agency of all people in constructing social relationships and cultural identities—all of which historians ought to and do explore—I would question the importance of 'ordinary' people in actively inventing Australia. All Australians are constantly engaged in the historical process, in building cultures, in forging social relationships, in developing senses of place (Carter 1987), but only a few name it 'Australia'. I would still argue, despite the break-up of Yugoslavia and the Soviet Union into competing nationalisms, that national identity is something that is imposed on people, even if it does not explain the behaviour of most people most of the time.

But this leaves Benedict Anderson's resounding question: if the nation is an invention or not much more than a marketing exercise, why do people die for it? I have touched on the question of why Australians joined up in the Great War elsewhere (White 1986), arguing that while notions of national duty and honour made sense to some, the majority did not frame their motives in national terms. Most soldiers, if they do die (which is usually not their intention on joining up), die not for nation but for more pressing notions: of family perhaps, or local community. It is others that name their death national, that raise them up as martyrs to the nation, and through the nation offer them the possibility of immortality.

And it is often historians who do it. The writing of Australian history, by historians with their own particular interests and an eye to a national market, whose professional status is confirmed within a national arena, is itself part of the process of privileging national identity over other identities. To admit this is not to dismiss the value of what Australian historians have to say. But we must be wary of the pressure of constantly being asked to declare ourselves. Are we positive or negative in our view of Australia? Is Australian history a history of violence and exploitation? Or is it a history of achievement and creativity and originality? It is all of these things. But if we are asked whether ultimately Australia's history is a good or a bad thing, we know someone is trying to co-opt the idea of Australia for a particular political project, often without clarifying whether a geographical or a political entity is meant. To write the richest and fullest Australian history, we need to write against the notion of national history, the sort of history that takes the nation as its subject and teleological dynamic. In a sense we need to write the nation out of the national history first; to write about the many other identities of the people we name as Australian, and the many other ways they actively express themselves as social beings and actively participate in history. Only then will we be able to give the nation its proper place in its history.

REFERENCES

Alomes, S. 1988, *A Nation at Last? The Changing Character of Australian Nationalism*, Angus & Robertson, Sydney.

Anderson, B. 1983, *Imagined Communities*, Verso, London.

Attwood, B. 1989, *The Making of the Aborigines*, Allen & Unwin, Sydney.

Carter, P. 1987, *The Road to Botany Bay: An Essay in Spatial History*, Faber & Faber, London.

Cochrane, P. & Goodman, D. 1988, 'The great Australian journey: Cultural logic and nationalism in the postmodern era', *Australian Historical Studies*, vol. 23, no. 91, October.

Frankel, B. 1992, *From the Prophets Deserts Come*, Arena, Melbourne.

Frow, J. 1995, *Cultural Studies and Cultural Value*, Oxford University Press, Oxford.

McLachlan, N. 1989, *Waiting for the Revolution: A History of Australian Nationalism*, Penguin, Melbourne.

Melleuish, G. 1995, *Cultural Liberalism in Australia: A Study in Intellectual and Cultural History*, Cambridge University Press, Cambridge.

Spearritt, P. 1988, 'Celebration of a nation: The triumph of spectacle', *Australian Historical Studies*, vol. 23, no. 91, October.

Thornhill, J. 1992, *Making Australia: Exploring our National Conversation*, Millenium, Sydney.

Ward, R. 1958, *The Australian Legend*, Oxford University Press, Melbourne.

White, R. 1981, *Inventing Australia: Images and Identity 1688–1980*, Allen & Unwin, Sydney.

—— 1986, 'Motives for joining up: Self-sacrifice, self-interest and social class 1914–1918', *Journal of the Australian War Memorial*, October.

3 History and identity

Ann Curthoys

In response to multiculturalism, and the pressure of the claims and protests of indigenous peoples in Australia, what it means to say one is 'Australian'—and thereby to express some sense of national identity—has shifted dramatically. The argument has emerged in recent years that Australian distinctiveness lies in the diverse, not the common, ancestry of its people. We are, it is said, Australian in our multiculturalism. In such a society, we now say, everyone is a member of a cultural community, each of us has an ethnicity which is more specific than the identity 'Australian'. Australians of British descent, like myself, can no longer simply describe themselves as 'Australian'. We are now said to be as much members of a cultural community—as 'ethnic'—as anyone else.[1]

Anglo-Celtic Australians?

Such people are now, consequently, called 'Anglo-Celtic' Australians. Yet has this group of Australians really found a language to express its sense of identity? I wonder how much we really mean it when we say Anglo-Celtic Australians are just one ethnic group or cultural group or community among others. If we do mean it, do we know what the implications are? While most agree that ethnicity is not something possessed only by non-British Australians, few have thought through, in a practical cultural sense, what it means to say 'Australians of British descent are "ethnic" too'.

My thinking about this issue has been prompted by several things. There is my work as a historian on questions of cultural diversity, national identity, racism and especially Aboriginal–white relations.

Writing about racism, where do I locate myself? Who am I that speaks and writes about racism, cultural diversity and Aboriginal politics? I cannot find words for myself, stumbling around with phrases like Anglo-Australian, or British Australian, or European Australian, or white Australian, or non-Aboriginal Australian, or Anglo-Celtic Australian, feeling ever more clumsily named and ever less clear about how to describe and situate myself and those like me in current debate.

Then there was my experience of participating in the Anglo-Celtic session at a conference on women and museums in Canberra about two years ago, the first and only time I have participated in a group or workshop defined in that particular way. For one of the conference sessions, we were asked to divide into three groups, one discussing multicultural issues, one indigenous issues, and one Anglo-Celtic issues. While we didn't have to go to the group we actually ethnically identified with, I felt odd, and possibly unwelcome, sitting in on either of the other groups, and so I went to the Anglo-Celtic one. I found it fascinating and yet also somewhat uncomfortable, for I did not feel Anglo-Celtic, and it occurred to me that we had participated in this workshop because we had political and ideological rather than cultural reasons for doing so. Many of us did not feel that 'Anglo-Celtic' in any way described our cultural identity; we wanted to construct such an identity because we thought we ought to, not because we had to, because it truly was a part of us. In that sense, 'Anglo-Celtic' is scarcely an identity at all. I have been thinking about my feelings of discomfort ever since, especially about Christine Choo's response when we all returned to report to the plenary conference session. Christine said:

> When Ann mentioned that she felt uncomfortable being labelled as an Anglo-Celtic woman in that group, I kind of smiled in a knowing way because that is what happens to anybody who is a migrant . . . We are bundled together as Asian for example . . . When you are forced into a group like that, in a very artificial way, something happens . . . it really does something to you personally (National Museum 1994).

And recently, the Demidenko affair has given us all pause for thought. Some of the outrage at the news that the supposedly Ukrainian Australian Helen Demidenko was actually Helen Darville, with English parents, was based not on her claiming the wrong ethnicity, but that she had claimed any ethnicity at all. The somewhat puzzling furore over Darville's use of an 'ethnic' name, apparently guaranteeing the veracity of her fiction, indicates a point of tension, a crisis perhaps, of ethnicity in contemporary Australia (Docker 1996, pp. 213–24).

MAKING AUSTRALIA

Such questions of ethnic and national identity have their grounding in Australian colonial history. Migration was integral to colonisation, settlement and, later, nation-building; the processes cannot be considered apart. The volume of migration, the growth of the settler population, and the determination to establish new forms of land use were so great that the indigenous Aboriginal peoples were significantly displaced, their numbers drastically reduced by violent conflict and disease, and their communities damaged and dispersed.

Until the second half of the nineteenth century, migration was predominantly from Britain and Ireland. British migration was itself regionally diverse, involving English, Scottish, Welsh and Cornish immigrants. The gold rushes of the 1850s and later were the first occasion, since colonisation, for a significant influx of non-British immigrants. People from Europe, North America and China came to seek their fortunes, many staying on after the rushes were over to enter other economic activities, from farming and the trades and professions to the arts and intellectual pursuits. While the British proportion of immigrants rose again after the gold rushes were over, Germans, Italians, Russian Jews and other groups continued to come as well. Melanesians and Chinese came in significant numbers until immigration laws prevented or restricted them. After the Second World War, the volume and diversity of immigration again rapidly increased to include people from many parts of Europe. Refugee immigration became an important part of the Australian migration experience. From the 1970s, migration increased from the countries of Asia, the Middle East, South America and other parts of an ever turbulent world.

Throughout this story of immigration, there have been high rates of intermarriage between people of different national origins. Immigration and intermarriage have combined to make the Australian population ethnically mixed; a great many Australians have their origins in a number of distinct nationalities and cultural groups. In addition, the very substantial levels of sexual interaction between Aboriginal and non-Aboriginal people have further mixed the population, partly culturally, partly biologically. Like so many other colonial and post-colonial societies, we have become a hybrid people, with many individuals able to relate to a number of different cultural traditions and diaspora histories within their own families.

MAKING 'AUSTRALIANS'

Considerations of identity in such a society have necessarily taken many forms and occurred; for example, in many sites in policy debates over immigration, the relation between indigenous and incoming peoples, and the 'protection' of 'Australian' culture from incursions (usually American) from outside; within cultural spheres, such as literature, journalism and the visual arts in the nineteenth century, joined by film, radio and television in the twentieth; with national celebrations and commemorations from Federation through to Anzac Day, Australia Day, and the bicentenary; and, circulating through and around all these, within professional and popular historical discourse.

A major site for questions of identity has most certainly been the troubling issue of migration itself. In the nineteenth century, a century of endless national, racial, and ethnic typing and classification, these policies were debated especially in relation to the significant numbers of Chinese immigrants. While the reasons given for opposing Chinese immigration were many—as potential or actual sources of cheap labour, or for racial purity and morality—one of the most important was the frequently expressed desire to 'maintain the British character of the community'. In New South Wales from the 1850s to the 1880s, when the movement for restriction of Chinese immigration arose, the colonists, or British settlers, said again and again that they wished to defend the 'British'—not the English, or Scottish, or Australian—character of the community against the effects of large scale Chinese immigration. In the specific context of opposition to Chinese immigration, other differences were suddenly minimised (Curthoys 1984).

Yet these 'other differences' kept resurging. Particularly important were debates throughout the nineteenth century over the proper proportions of English, Scottish, Welsh and Irish, in part a debate by Protestants over how to keep down the Irish Catholic population. The high Irish proportion always meant that the Australian population could not be the replica of Britain many wished it to be. Conflict between Catholics and Protestants, in particular, and so closely related to the ethnic origins of the population, continued to inform Australian society and culture throughout the nineteenth century and well into the twentieth, as demonstrated so clearly in Manning Clark's six-volume *History of Australia*.

In the latter part of the nineteenth century, the significant number of German immigrants in the country precipitated serious debate about the proper composition of the population. Germans had been generally considered close enough to the English—sometimes it was said that both were Teutonic peoples—to be acceptable. In New South Wales, Germans were regarded as almost ideal immigrants, with their family values and farming and other skills, though they were not to be included in schemes for assisted migration. In Queensland, where the desire for labour and immigration was even stronger, Germans were in fact assisted in large numbers. By the nineteenth century in Australia, the Germans had become a thriving prosperous community, integrated yet distinctive, constituting the largest group of non-British. By later in the century, public festivities to mark the German national holiday drew large crowds of participants, including official government representatives (Fischer 1989).

It was not only the presence of Chinese, Germans and other groups that made late nineteenth-century Australian colonies something other than perfectly transplanted British societies. Even within the population of British descent, the desire for Britishness was never complete. At that time, and afterwards, there was much interest in other European identities. Think of J.F. Archibald, the editor of the Sydney *Bulletin*, who changed his given names from John Feltham to Jules François, and in the 1880s and 1890s claimed French and Jewish ancestry through his mother, though in fact of solidly Irish stock. Before the First World War, there was a considerable degree of fascination with things French, Jewish, Italian and German in much of Australian cultural life, suggesting a dissatisfaction with inherited English identifications (Docker 1992, p. 7). Much later, Patrick White was both Judaeophile and Graecophile. Robert Dessaix wrote in 1994 in his autobiography, *A Mother's Disgrace*, of his longstanding fascination with Russian language and culture. I have already alluded to Helen Darville's robust adoption for some years of a Ukrainian identity.

Despite these fascinations with Europe, there was, however, a strong and specific sense of Britishness. The new Australian nation, though sovereign in its governance of domestic matters, was still subject to Britain in matters of defence and foreign policy until the Balfour Declaration of 1931. Taking up Benedict Anderson's theme, in his influential *Imagined Communities*, that the strength of nationalism is indicated by the willingness of millions to die in its name, we can see that in the First World War Australians died in the name of the British Empire. An indication of the resurgence of British allegiance and feeling in the wake of the First World War, was the near destruction of the German Australian communities as autonomous sociocultural entities within Australian society. Generally speaking, there seems to have been an increased emphasis on Britishness, assimilation and ethnic homogeneity, to the point of wiping out popular memory of an earlier multiculturality. Today, those speaking of non-British immigration and multiculturalism invoke, and reject, an Australian history which they, somewhat mistakenly, see as having been almost entirely British in its people and cultural allegiances until the late 1940s (Wallace-Crabbe 1991, p. 3).

There is also a long tradition of national sentiment in Australia which is neither British nor imperial, and which asserts a distinct Australian identity. An early attempt to discern a distinct Australian people and culture responding to living in a specific environment can be found in discussions of the currency lads and lasses. The first generation of white native born in the colonial towns and countryside, they were said to embody a new race, sharing not the old world class-ridden problems of the society of their parents, but responding to the new opportunities afforded in a new world. Visitors (British, continental European, American) continued to note this trait in their travel writings, frequently finding Australians to be a new and distinctive people who had developed different cultural habits from their British and Irish forebears.

By the last quarter of the nineteenth century, the search for what was uniquely Australian came to focus on the distinctively rural as the true source of the culture of the people. Journalist and writer Marcus Clarke argued in 1876 that every continent has its particular natural environment and so its distinctive cultural spirit; the Australian continent would similarly become the cradle of a unique consciousness. Later, A.D. Hope, whose famous 1939 poem 'Australia' found the Australian interior singularly depressing—'the last of lands, the emptiest'—nevertheless concluded that the desert would yield a new distinctive national spirit, in a way cities never could. The notion that it was in rural not urban Australia that the true creative spirit of a national culture would be nurtured also pervaded the popular poetry of A.B. Paterson and C.J. Dennis and the work of novelists like Katharine Susannah Prichard, Vance Palmer and Patrick White. On the other hand, some writers, at least in certain modes and moods, wanted to counter any idealisation of rural life, as can be seen in the work of Henry Lawson, Barbara Baynton, Miles Franklin, Joseph Furphy and Steele Rudd (Docker 1984, pp. 19–23).

There was also a frequent desire to look to Aboriginal society for inspiration. The Jindyworobaks in the late 1930s and 1940s saw Aboriginal society as expressing a nature–culture harmony, an idea and ideal that continued through writers like Vance Palmer, Katharine Susannah Prichard, Xavier Herbert, Judith Wright and Patrick White. In recent decades there has been, in literature, film and art, a widespread desire to find in Aboriginal culture a way of rediscovering true human values; a unifying and simplifying understanding of indigenous cultures, seen as exemplifying, without complication, values of sharing, harmony and spirituality.

In his 1958 book, *The Australian Tradition*, A.A. Phillips outlined the successive phases in the development of the Australian mind, seeing the 1890s as 'socially and politically adventurous', if 'jingoistically assertive'. The desire to see the 1890s as a golden age, as a foundation of Australian white-settler separate identity and culture, has continued unabated since, if in increasingly ambivalent and contradictory ways (Docker 1991, pp. xv–xxviii). For others, it is the experience of the First World War, when soldiers were engaged in battle for the first time as Australian rather than colonial troops which was formative of Australian identity. The Anzac legend, commemorating Gallipoli in particular and Australia's dead in war more generally, was expressive of Australians belonging to the British Empire; over the years, however, it also acquired quite an anti-British tinge, as exemplified in the idea of Australian troops being needlessly sent to their deaths by incompetent and unfeeling British military officials.

GENDER AND NATIONAL IDENTITY

From the nineteenth century onwards the search for an identity which was distinctively Australian, and not some kind of pale imitation of Britain, became a highly gendered concern. Russel Ward, in *The Australian Legend*, gave expression to longstanding ideas of Australians as independent, imbued with an ethic of mateship, laconic, irreverent, egalitarian, sharing, cooperative. These were, he thought, ideals developed in rural Australia but now thought of as identifying Australians more generally:

> According to the myth the typical Australian is a practical man, rough and ready in his manners and quick to decry any appearance of affectation in others. He is a great improviser, ever willing to have a go at anything, but willing to be content with a task done in a way that is near enough . . . he swears hard and consistently, gambles heavily and often, and drinks deeply on occasion . . . he is usually taciturn rather than talkative . . . he believes that Jack is not only as good as his master, but, at least in principle, probably a good deal better and so he is a great knocker of eminent people (1958, pp. 1–2).

Ward's typical Australian was represented and sustained in a number of important Australian films in the film industry revival of the 1970s and 1980s—Jack Thompson in *Sunday Too Far Away*, Bryan Brown in *A Town Like Alice*, Paul Hogan in *Crocodile Dundee*.

Despite the enduring popularity of this image of a distinctly Australian type, a great deal has changed since the 1950s when these ways of thinking about Australian identity were being formulated. There have been many critiques of the ethnocentric, racist and sexist nature of this image, at least in many of its manifestations. In the 1970s, new left critics and historians, such as Humphrey McQueen, saw the bush workers and labour movement heroised by radical nationalists like Ward as enclosed within an exclusionary racism towards Aboriginal and Chinese people (McQueen 1970). In the 1980s, feminist historians and critics, such as Marilyn Lake, perceived such ideals as dominated by masculinism, as an attempted imposition of a male ideal on an emerging Australian culture. Feminist critique of this kind has been directed towards the supposed symbols of Australianness—the legendary *Bulletin* of the 1890s, the Anzac legend and associated notions of the Australian digger, and attempts like Ward's to define an Australian national character. Feminists point to the turn-of-the-century slogan—'Australia for the White Man'—adopted by the *Bulletin*, noting not only its evident racism, but also its assumption of the true Australian as inevitably and only male (Magarey et al. 1993). In the twentieth century, they argue, ideas of Australianness, founded so strongly as they have been in war, in the celebration of the Anzacs especially, have become ideals of masculinity.

In their gendering of notions of national identity, Australian debates are similar to those elsewhere. Gender is never far from discussion of history, identity and nation (Anthias & Yuval-Davis 1989; *Gender and History* 1993). Nation is frequently figured as the motherland, the state as fatherland, the citizens its sons and daughters. Anti-colonial nationalism in particular rests on familial metaphors, claiming an 'inside' of family, culture and language, the abiding and authentic, against the outside imperial power, the colonial invader (Pettman 1992, p. 4). 'Australia' becomes either our place of birth or our adopted country, the idea of adoption maintaining the symbolism of family and kinship. The kinship and family motif is continued in public discussions of past and future relations with Britain, in a language of birth, growth and maturation. Thus the Australian film producer George Miller on the Australian film revival of the 1970s:

> In retrospect, of course, it was this brand-new nation; no longer a child, as it were, beholden to Mother England or Big Brother America after the Vietnam War and the social upheaval of the 60s. It was suddenly a kid going out into the backyard, and being able to shout and yell, and no

one was going to tell it to keep quiet (*Sydney Morning Herald*, 23 May 1995, Arts p. 10).

IDENTITY AND HISTORICAL CONSCIOUSNESS

The project of colonisation, and later nation-building, is inherently and self-consciously historical. History is, in consequence, an extraordinarily national and often nationalist discipline, nowhere more so that in settler societies with their double-edged histories, looking both at their country of origin and at their struggles with indigenous peoples. Franz Fanon expressed this idea in a passage in *The Wretched of the Earth* that has intrigued and fascinated me for some years now:

> The settler makes history and is conscious of making it. And because he constantly refers to the history of his mother country, he clearly indicates that he himself is the extension of that mother country. Thus the history which he writes is not the history of the country which he plunders but the history of his own nation in regard to all that she skims off, all that she violates and starves (1961, p. 40).

For Australian historians, there has been a continuing search over several decades for ways to escape this settler logic, to write histories which examine, rather than exemplify, processes of colonisation and nation-making. For historians and their readers alike, the question of indigenous rights and sovereignty has, in recent years, been particularly transformative, calling the very notion of a shared Australian history and identity into question. Amongst non-Aboriginal Australians the responses to indigenous issues have been mixed. The intense public debates of 1992 and 1993 around questions of native title (Mabo), the constitution, and the notion of reconciliation between Aboriginal and non-Aboriginal people marked something of a watershed in public understandings of Australian history. Aboriginal issues were brought into the centre of national public consciousness, and forced even those who, as non-Aboriginal people, had thought themselves sympathetic with Aboriginal causes, to reassess their understanding of Australian politics and culture.

To historians, these debates revealed the continuing strength of non-Aboriginal Australia's belief in stories of pioneering, settlement and rightful occupation of the land, with many still holding the nineteenth-century view that invasion and dispossession had been justified because Aboriginal people did not use the land productively. At the same time, the Mabo debate also revealed the growing strength of an alternative historical understanding emphasising the impossibility of justifying invasion in these or any terms, and valuing rather than condemning Aboriginal societies.

Among Aboriginal people, at the same time, there has developed a form of national feeling, which also rests on history. The emergence of indigenous people's moves towards distinct national claims has many of the features of national movements elsewhere—the stress on separate origins, the importance of the question of land, the awareness of cultural heritage and difference, and the critique of the history of racism and cultural imperialism of the dominant colonising power or group. Calls for Aboriginal sovereignty are growing, and with them arguments for new conceptions of the relationship between state and nation. Some non-Aboriginal Australians are starting to think that perhaps there are, after all, ways to recognise Aboriginal nationhood and self-determination within a single nation-state, though it would need to be one very different from that we have now.

Sometimes there is an attempt to bring these very different histories into some kind of relation to one another. George Miller recently reflected, in the same interview quoted earlier, on the making of a historical film documentary to be called *40,000 Years of Dreaming—A Century of Australian Cinema*. The film, he said, draws parallels between 'the Aborigines' singing of the world into existence' and the role of cinema 'in defining an Australian identity'. Miller went on to note that as aspirations change, so the kind of history audiences want to read, see and hear changes. The costume drama films of the 1970s were, he felt, an attempt to understand the new national identity through an understanding of the past. Miller himself has become a major figure in the exploration of much more recent Australian history, his historical mini-series of the 1980s—especially *The Dismissal*, *Bodyline* and *Vietnam*—becoming significant events themselves in Australian cultural history. By the mid-1990s he had produced *Babe*, which, with its mix of Australian, American and British accents and references, and its enormous worldwide popularity, indicates a new, more international, and highly successful kind of Australian cinema.

MULTIPLE IDENTITIES

Once so unconsciously and confidently speaking for all Australians, the 'Anglo-Celtic' majority, with its own histories of conflict and division between English and Irish, and English and Scottish, has now become somewhat divided and uncertain on the question of identity; identity is now being actively, anxiously sought rather than comfortably assumed. This is manifested in numerous ways. One indication of the quest for identity amongst this group of Australians is the development since the 1960s of an immense interest in genealogical research and family history (Curthoys 1987). Where once an interest in origins was seen as a form of class snobbery, as inegalitarian, of interest only to those from a British upper-class background, it has in recent years become quite the opposite, something anyone can pursue. The passion for genealogical research and knowledge expresses a desire to construct a sense of belonging and continuity that for Australians of British and/or Irish descent, especially amongst working-class people, is frequently extremely elusive. Anglo-Celtic men who marry outside their own particular group, as many do, are notoriously unable to pass on sustained cultural and kinship knowledge. The process of migration seems to have cut these men off from their families and kin, and specific cultural knowledge is very often not passed on. As Diane Bell showed in her book *Generations*, it is usually the women who have kept the family knowledge, passed on stories about grandparents, and who keep in touch with their wider family of sisters and brothers, aunts and uncles, grandparents. It is usually the women who have kept the photographs, and who do the amateur genealogies, who invade public archives and research libraries.

It is not only a question of identity at a personal or family level. Many British Australians wish to preserve the British character of the country as a whole and its connections with Britain via the monarchy. While not all monarchists in Australia are of British descent, a great many of them are, as evident in the campaign to preserve the traditional functions of Government House in Sydney. Another example of a desire to retain Australia's Britishness is the organisation of a group called Friends of the First Government House in Sydney, who opposed the development of the Museum of Sydney on the site of the first Government House, seeing the museum's change of title, and its emphasis on indigenous people's relations to that particular place, as appallingly 'politically correct'.

Many other Anglo-Celtic Australians, though, now wish to do away with older conceptions of Australian society as a kind of British museum, a theme park where the aspirations of the old world are to be preserved and realised, protected by the monarchy and inherited British institutions. They—we—are very attracted to the notion of Australian society as successfully multicultural, bringing together people from a vast range of origins into a new society that is not like any of those from which its people came. Our desires are increasingly multicultural, republican and post-colonial. Australia, both officially and in much unofficial discourse, is seen as having gone beyond its racist past and as having embraced values of cultural pluralism (Stratton & Ang 1994, pp. 124–53). Asians have rapidly been transformed from the feared and hated other to those we particularly wish to include, as advertisements for citizenship ceremonies so clearly attest to.

Yet these multicultural and post-colonial ambitions have their limits. This story of progress from racist exclusion to multicultural inclusion is too simple (Ang 1995, p. 57). The campaign for and adoption of racial vilification laws indicate both public aspirations, a desire to stamp out the racist past from the Australian make-up, and continuing realities that such racism remains an issue of concern. In the early 1990s, racial hostility and resentment often went underground, surviving vigorously in many local contexts, especially in those regions which have relatively high Aboriginal or Asian populations, but not openly in the public sphere, in the national media. The 1996 election campaign was notable for the re-emergence of racial discourse into public debate, the strong electoral support its rural exponents received, and the high levels of concern at these developments expressed by party leaders and many other politicians.

In recognition of the difficulties arising from the older search for a common Australian character and set of values, some commentators have argued that now, in a multicultural Australia, what we hold in common is not a specific culture, but a common set of political institutions. Donald Horne asks: 'What declarations of common purpose now purport to hold us together?' His answer is 'civic faith', defined by 'respect for the rule of law and the equal rights of Australians under the law and for the principles of tolerance and liberal democracy, along with a commitment to guardianship of the land we share'. For Horne, this common set of political values and institutions should be enshrined in public life, in ceremonies and oath-takings. It should also be preserved in a national 'civic memory'. In Australia, he says, we have 'never celebrated our civic victories . . . we now need some new stories of Australia as an active, relatively successful polity'. Warming to his theme, he urges that the story of the creation of Australia through Federation should be 'turned into instructive tales taught in all schools and made available to all citizens'. History in schools, then, becomes a means of encouraging attachment to our particular form of liberal democracy (1996, p. 27).

Horne's search for expressions of national unity in public ceremony and school-based history contains many of the same problems as the earlier ideas it seeks to replace. His belief in the virtual attainment of multicultural harmony can be seen as yet another example in the long quest for Australian uniqueness and distinctiveness, simply replacing earlier rural cultural ideals with particular urban political values. In the notion of civic successes, we have a surrogate 'Australian legend', reworked for a multicultural Australia, yet equally homogenising, and similarly desiring universal assent and agreement. Horne's argument has a surprisingly conservative ring to it, taking Australian political institutions as more or less fully formed, uncontested and uncontestable, and advocating that Australian history be taught in a celebratory way. Yet it seems that the highly moralistic tone of much history teaching, whether from the right or the left, together with a repetitive and compulsory curriculum in junior years, is turning many students at secondary level away from studying Australian history (*Sydney Morning Herald*, 29 March 1996, p. 1).

The attachment of Donald Horne and many other 'Anglo-Celtic' Australians to multicultural tolerance bears further examination. Tolerance, as has often been remarked, asserts the power of the tolerant, the dominant majority being the one to have the power to tolerate, while minorities are its well-behaved beneficiaries. As critics like Ghassan Hage and Ien Ang have argued, there emerges a power-laden division between the tolerating and the tolerated. Hage writes: 'For the Anglo-Celtic Australian . . . the discourse of enrichment still positions him or her in the centre of the Australian cultural map . . . While Anglo-Celtic culture merely and unquestionably exists, migrant cultures exist for the latter' (Hage 1994, pp. 31–2). Tolerance may be better than intolerance, but it does not guarantee equality. 'Anglo-Celtic' Australians, in their enthusiasm for multiculturalism and thereby a new inclusive Australian identity, are, then, still expressing power relations, still speaking from a self-confident centre, the Australian nation. They are doing the including, not being included. The politics of inclusion, based as it is on a notion of community and identity, absorbs difference within a pre-given and predefined space (Ang 1995, p. 57).

We can take these arguments one step further. Everyone in Australia who is non-indigenous, the 'tolerators' and 'tolerated' alike, still share in and are advantaged by a history of colonisation. We may grow to love the country, to develop a passionate attachment to place, as writers such as Cassandra Pybus have shown. Pybus commands our attention when she writes in *Community of Thieves*:

> It seems to me that the stories contained in this landscape I love so immoderately are critical to my self-definition; to my pride in being

> Australian and a fifth generation of white immigrants born into this benign and lovely place. (1991, pp. 15–16).

But as Pybus herself asks, can it ever be truly hers, or ours, to love in this way? If historically created and still salient differences—especially those to do with Aboriginal dispossession—are to be fully recognised and understood, we may have to learn, as Ang warns, to be satisfied with a notion of partial community, a limited and incomplete sense of home.

Let's hope, then, that the long-running debate over Australian national identity can finally stop looking for a completed, unique and distinguishing Australian character and set of values, whether these are conceived of as cultural or political. So too might it also avoid seeing ethnicities as being represented in sharply distinct groups of people. Perhaps the desire to define ourselves as different from the rest of the world, or from one another, has been leading us down some unrewarding paths. Too often, the fascination and drama of Australian history is lost and forgotten in stereotypes—whether the older stereotype of Australian mateship, or the more recent one of multicultural harmony and tolerance. Our sense of history could become one which recognises that non-indigenous claims to belonging must always remain limited and complex, and that what we need to understand now is how present-day Australians of all ethnicities fit into a larger world history. In our stories of creativity, survival and day-to-day heroism, alongside stories of invasion, migration, colonisation and conflict, we may find that it is what we share with other societies, in Europe, in Asia, in America and Africa, that matters to us most.

NOTES

1 This chapter is based on a paper delivered to the Fourth Summer School, Nationalism and National Identity, at the Humanities Research Centre, Australian National University, 12–16 February 1996. On 2 March 1996, the federal elections led to a change of government and the sudden disappearance of Paul Keating from the political scene. Surrounding that disappearance has been much talk of a resurgent racism, a rejection of Keating's concerns with national identity and the republic, and the end of 'political correctness'. The time of writing means that the chapter registers some of the concerns of the Keating era as well as those which are being debated in its aftermath.

REFERENCES

Anderson, B. 1983, *Imagined Communities*, Verso, London.

Ang, I. 1995, 'I'm a feminist but . . . "Other" women and postnational feminism', in *Transitions: New Australian Feminisms*, eds B. Caine & R. Pringle, Allen & Unwin, Sydney.

—— 1996, 'The Curse of the Smile', *Feminist Review*, no. 52, February.

Anthias, F. & Yuval-Davis, N. (eds) 1989, *Woman-Nation-State*, Macmillan, Houndmills.

Bell, D. 1987, *Generations: Grandmothers, Mothers and Daughters*, McPhee Gribble/Penguin, Melbourne.

Clark, C.M.H. 1962–87, *A History of Australia*, vols 1–6, Melbourne University Press, Melbourne.

Curthoys, A. 1984, 'Class and racism in nineteenth century Australia', in *Surrender Australia: Historians and Geoffrey Blainey*, eds A. Markus & M. Ricklefs, Allen & Unwin, Sydney.

—— 1987, 'Into history', in *Australians Since 1939*, eds A. Curthoys, A.W. Martin & T. Rowse, Fairfax, Syme & Weldon, Sydney.

Dessaix, R. 1994, *A Mother's Disgrace*, Angus & Robertson, Sydney.

Docker, J. 1984, *In a Critical Condition*, Penguin, Melbourne.

—— 1991, *The Nervous Nineties*, Oxford University Press, Melbourne.

—— 1992, 'Dilemmas of identity: The desire for the other in colonial and post colonial cultural history', *Working Papers in Australian Studies*, no. 74, Sir Robert Menzies Centre for Australian Studies, Institute of Commonwealth Studies, University of London.

—— 1996, 'Debating ethnicity and history: From Enzensberger to Darville/Demidenko', in *Debating Enzensberger: 'Great Migration' and 'Civil War'*, ed. G. Fischer, Stauffenburg Verlaf, Tubingen.

Fanon, F. 1973 [1961], *The Wretched of the Earth*, Penguin, Harmondsworth.

Fischer, G. 1989, *Enemy Aliens: Internment and the Homefront Experience in Australia 1914–1918*, University of Queensland Press, St Lucia.

Gender and History, special issue 1993, 'Gender, nationalisms and national identities', no. 2, summer.

Hage, G. 1994, 'Locating multiculturalism's other: A critique of practical tolerance', *New Formations*, 24, winter.

—— 1995, 'Anglo-Celtics today: Cosmo-multiculturalism and the phase of the fading phallus', in *An Inquiry into the State of Anglo-Saxonness within the Nation*, eds G. Hage, J. Lloyd and L. Johnson, special issue of *Communal/Plural*, no. 4.

Horne, D. 1996, 'Keating's unfinished business', *Weekend Australian*, 17–18 February.

Magarey, S., Rowley, S. & Sheridan, S. (eds) 1993, *Debutante Nation: Feminism Contests the 1890s*, Allen & Unwin, Sydney.

McQueen, H. 1970, *A New Britannia*, Penguin, Melbourne.

National Museum of Australia 1994, *Proceedings of 'Images of Women', Conference on Women in Museums, October 1993*, AGPS, Canberra.

Pettman, Jan Jindy 1992, 'Women, nationalism and the state: Towards an international feminist perspective', paper for Australian Women's Studies Association Conference, Canberra.

Pybus, C. 1991, *Community of Thieves*, Heinemann, Melbourne.

Stratton, J. & Ang I. 1994, 'Multicultural imagined communities: Cultural diversity and national identity in Australia and the USA', *Continuum*, vol. 19, no. 2.

Wallace-Crabbe, C. 1991, 'The ethnic red herring', in *Multicultural Australia: The Challenges of Change*, eds D. Goodman, D.J. O'Hearn & C. Wallace-Crabbe, Scribe, Newham.

Ward, R. 1966 [1958], *The Australian Legend*, Oxford University Press, Melbourne.

4 Sexuality and Australian identities

Ann McGrath

Stories of nation and national types grew from, reacted to and existed in opposition to Australia's lived sexual history. In their search for a singular, historically based identity, the legend-makers hunted archetypes which appealed to them as white men, and which reinforced hegemonic national ideals. But it was not just a convenient blindness which made sexuality, gender and race their most obvious omissions. Rather, these were the troublesome instruments which split the nation into multiple and plural identities.

The Case of Russel Ward

On his first trip to the northern frontier in the 1930s, Russel Ward, later the author of the classic tome on Australian identity, *The Australian Legend* (1958), was a youthful university student engaged to be married. He described his desire to visit central Australia as 'a kind of subliminal itch', part of his 'growing need to find himself and his identity as an Australian'. Looking for a masculine ideal, he found it in Harry the camel-driving dingo trapper, who worked hard for his earnings, then binged them away on alcohol and Aboriginal women. Ward admired this exotic lifestyle, which defied the values of thrift, restraint and suburban respectability. What could be further removed from his middle-class Adelaide upbringing, with his Wesleyan Methodist father who graduated in classics? In his own rite of passage, Ward announced that in Harry he had found the 'archetypal Australian man', the one upon which he could base his oft-repeated description of the 'typical Australian', a bachelor who shared male and animal company, and whose heterosexual needs were satisfied on a casual basis.

Ward also told a story of frontier women:

> In one cool home built of whitewashed stone, while I was talking to the 'missus' in the kitchen, a beautiful young Aboriginal woman, known then as a 'house lubra', wordlessly but smilingly ogled me as she passed—only to be ordered angrily out of the house by the manager's wife. Unlike English servants, she did not have any idea of 'her place' though her employer manifestly did. As much was true of nearly all Australians, black and white (1988, pp. 108–12, 109).

This was another tale of awakening and insight into the essence of imagined nation. Ward saw it as a story of egalitarianism and mateship rather than about gender, race and sexuality. It is also a tale of repression versus sensuality, a recognition of contrasting female archetypes. The story is swimming with metaphor. The 'cool' and 'white' house signified a place of purity and respectability, a place symbolising class, power and inequality. Cold as marble and death, but also housing anger, the sparks send the dark woman out into the glare and heat of the unwashed world outside the home. While one woman enforces the whitewashed boundaries, the Aboriginal woman brashly disregards them. In *The Australian Legend*, Ward describes Aboriginal women as helping to keep sodomy out of mateship (1958, p. 98), reflecting the desire of Australian men—even rebellious frontiersmen—to be recognised as heterosexual conformists, the manliest of men.

Another reading of the above story is of Ward putting women in their place—the white woman is God's police, the moral guardian, the Aboriginal woman the whore, occupying a sexualised space, whose 'unbridled' passions supposedly made the outback and colonisation more exciting. In her class consciousness, the white woman is judged as 'un-Australian' and it is the Aboriginal woman Ward considers a preferable female archetype, for she refuses to stay 'in her place'. The dualistic archetypes of damned whores and God's police (Summers 1975) categorise women according to differing sexual practices and sensibilities. Thus divided, no woman could fit the category of 'typical Australian' and the underlying sexual tensions between men, women and nation were exposed.

WOMEN AS AGENTS

Local Aboriginal women were perceived by First Fleet gentlemen of 1788 as potential sexual partners, though diplomacy warned against impatience. Embarrassed and fascinated by the women's nudity, such writers described their bodies in lurid detail, though in a language which resorted to coy allusion, the cover of French and Latin, comparisons with Greek statuary and Christian allusions to Eve and the Garden of Eden. Upper-class British attitudes to sexuality were in flux: an often conflicting smorgasbord of aesthetics, morality and social order. The British gentry saw New South Wales as part of an imperial continuum, one of many new lands of sexual adventure, but they had difficulty in understanding Aboriginal men and women's reactions to their sexual attentions. The British used European courtship rituals, such as dropping handkerchiefs, and gifts of shiny buttons and any other bits of clothing. The language of sexual communication was thus one of the first to be used between the parties. The women played sexual games, flirting, adopting coquettish manners and, from a safe distance, openly soliciting sex. Before long, they were spending nights aboard ship with sailors and returning with concealed gifts. While such liaisons provoked misunderstanding, disease, abuse and murder, they also brought coloniser and colonised together in the most total and intimate way, enabling moments of cultural insight, of physical sharing, of diplomacy and of the biological mingling of the peoples.

Convict women played an equally important role in setting the sexual tone of white Australian society. A significant number had experience in prostitution before arriving in New South Wales and their defiance was often expressed in sexual gestures. They used highly sexual language, spoke openly about sexual acts and refused to confine sex to private space. They engaged in sex in the segregated ships on the journey out, in jails with warders, outside on hills and in bushes. Ralph Clark, who was in charge of the women aboard one ship, was especially slanderous about their rapaciousness. The men, too, showed some ingenuity or at least brawn in breaking through the women's bulkhead at least twice so they could indulge in sex. Participating women were flogged and put in irons. Another woman who had drunk a lot of liquor said that the captain wanted to 'kiss her C—t'. She spoke abusively of the doctor, saying he wanted to fuck her and that she was not a whore (Clark, 18 July 1787, in McGrath 1995). For sexual language and for vilifying some influential men, she was tied up and gagged.

The disembarkation of the female convicts at Port Jackson in February 1788 resulted in a riotous, probably long-awaited, sex spree. Although historians debate whether it constituted a founding orgy or a mass rape, contemporaries described it as a scene of 'debauchery', 'whoredome', 'licentiousness'. Military men also took their choice of mistresses from the convict ranks (Hughes 1987; Kociumbas 1992). From Governor Phillip's time, couples were encouraged to marry in the hope of 'settling' the society. Christian monogamous marriage and repressive concepts of the body stood alongside scientific theories arguing the necessity and 'naturalness' of male heterosexuality and regular ejaculation. The availability of women as sexual partners and prostitutes was considered a means of keeping the men content and of discouraging homosexuality and bestiality, which were viewed by authorities as not only horrific and sinful but as a waste of imperial sperm. The male convicts outnumbered the women three to one; awful cases of pack rapes, child rape and bestiality were reported.

Nonetheless, convict women deployed sexual defiance humorously and theatrically. On a visit of Sir John and Lady Franklin and several ladies to the Cascades factory in Van Diemen's Land, a group of women started to cough down a boring preacher. When the warders demanded silence, the women raised their clothes in unison and smacked their bums loudly. The parson was horrified, the governor was shocked, but the aide-de-campe and the lady visitors could not control their laughter (Summers 1975, p. 284).

Convict women adapted to the demand for wives by participating in a sort of 'marriage mart' in the convict factories. Unwilling women were judged unnatural and a threat to social order. An 1837 report into the convict system explained that the women lined up like cattle in a fair. The potential husband, an emancipated convict or a free settler, inspected them and motioned to the one of his choice, who then stepped to the side. If the woman refused, the man tried another, whom he interviewed. But generally the girls were interested, adopting flirtatious poses, shy smiles and blushes (Damousi 1995, p. 41; and Summers 1975, p. 282). After all, marriage was a passport to freedom.

Convict women's sexual morality reflected their working-class origins, but this was so different from what the upper echelons condoned as British that the women were classed as uncivilised. The women were judged especially depraved by writers such as the love-struck Lieutenant Clark, who compared them with his pretty wife Betsey in England. Nonetheless, he found a convict mistress and fathered her child, whom he named after his wife. While men were not condemned for extra-marital sex, women living as de facto wives, sexually active, lesbian or drinking women were all included in the immoral whore category. The women had been exported from England because they were considered irredeemable, but also to serve men's sexual needs. Some historians estimate that one-fifth of the female convicts were previously prostitutes, but the label was applied very broadly. Some convict and ex-convict women casually cohabited with men and some did work as prostitutes, but others were in stable relationships, with no more desire to marry than they would have had back in Britain. Men of their own class did not condemn such sexual behaviour.

The ruling-class men, however, saw women's sexual assertiveness as threatening. They labelled it 'pollution', associating it with disease and dirt, which symbolically threatened to contaminate the empire. The image of 'drunken and abandoned prostitutes' also served good propaganda purposes for the colony's anti-transportationists, for it symbolised all that was bad in the convict system. The profligacy of convict women, homosexuality and other unmentionables, were seen as proof that convict society was abnormal (Aveling 1992, pp. 154–6).

Historical interpretations of female convict sexuality in Australia's formative years mirror changes in the national identity debate. The term 'whore' was adopted by later historians to assert the immorality and inferiority of the convict women compared with the men. They judged the women as mostly 'bad', or unrespectable, on the grounds of their sexual behaviour, whether it be use of sexual language or activities with men. Feminist historians of the 1970s used whore representations to prove the status of women as victims who were 'colonised' by imperial patriarchy for sexual purposes. Despite their own quest for sexual liberation and role models, seventies feminists saw greater utility in an oppressed past than a sexually expressive one. Other historians, like Portia Robinson, have attempted to rescue them as 'good women'. Approaching the 1988 bicentennary, the convict era came to be cherished as a heritage item, with descendants and historians then rescuing a wider spectrum of women from their evil reputation. Convict women were rediscovered as self-reformers, good wives and individual success stories. More recently, Oxley dubbed them convict maids or workers, pointing out that prostitution was never a transportable offence; the records proving that sex work was relatively unimportant amidst the range of past employment and skills (Damousi 1995; Oxley 1996).

On the frontier and in pioneer history, it was the respectable women who got into the national legends through an asexual or maternal image which emodied sexual control, restraint and policing the sexuality of others. In twentieth-century school texts, the squeaky clean Caroline Chisholm was revered for her efforts to marry off vulnerable girls in early New South Wales. Such respectable white women could tame male sexuality on the frontier. Not bloodied by the worst violence of frontier conflict, women became healers, practised nursing and medical techniques. Outback nurses ventured out of cities and into the 'male world', but their lives were modelled in part on the nursing tradition of the religious orders. Monogamy, celibacy or the widowhood of Mrs Aeneas Gunn enhanced their status. Respectable women were placed on a rather unsexy pedestal.

Against the sunny sexual freedom of the white man's frontier, married frontier women's sexuality has been portrayed as bleak conjugal obligation and a threat to their safety. Writers like Barbara Baynton and Henry Lawson still chill modern audiences with stories like 'The Chosen Vessel', 'Squeaker's Mate' and 'The Drover's Wife'. Set against a hostile wilderness, women are cast as captives of a sadistic biological game. Men far outnumbered women on frontiers, so while it was easier for them to find husbands, they were more likely to be alone, lacking female company and prone to male violence and rape. Additionally, married women often endured repeated and unwanted pregnancies, had to learn to make do in basic shelters with few facilities, cope with childbirth, miscarriage and infant death. But women also attempted to take some control of this, exemplified in the bravery of midwives who travelled all over the countryside and in the courage of outback nurses. While it is difficult to believe that there was no fun in outback sex, the evidence so far uncovered concerns unwanted sex and the wives' clever methods of avoiding their disliked husbands.

Although Australia had the highest male to female ratio in the world in 1860, its prostitution trade has been omitted from the bush legend. Yet Japanese and white prostitutes and pimps established brothels in northern towns and on goldfields to serve the large groups of men gathered. Aboriginal women set up a more informal trade. Prostitutes were automatically outsiders, but other white women engaged in gender bending in order to lead lives following their chosen paths. Novelists like 'Miles' Franklin and 'Henry' Handel Richardson had to eschew their sexuality as a precondition to being taken seriously. The heroines of Eve Langley's *The Pea Pickers* also dressed as boys to enjoy some excitement and travel. Aboriginal women wore male stockman's clothing to work as drovers and to accompany white men as lovers, as told in Ted Egan's song 'The Drover's Boy'.

THE SEXUAL ECONOMY OF COLONIALISM

The sexual economy of colonialism inevitably destabilised the categorisations of the old world and had a creative role in shaping the composition of the Australian colonies. The dispossession of Aboriginal Australians, the arrival of convicts and an immigrant labour force threw together people from diverse ethnic and religious backgrounds.

New sexual choices and amalgams took place, and in the case of Irish Catholics with English Protestants, defied old world hatreds. Intermarriage also took place in opposition to the racial beliefs of white Australia. White men and women married Chinese and Aboriginal people. Some Chinese workers, and Melanesian and Indian indentured labourers cohabited with or married Aboriginal women, creating dynasties and new cultural communities. White women's interest in Chinese men horrified white male nationalists, who said they had been lured by opium and vice. While ethnic mixing was the norm, women who married across colour boundaries were considered 'fallen' by moralisers, and so were the men who acknowledged their Aboriginal female partners. Various official policies to restrict cohabitation and interracial marriage were introduced, though the most powerful was the *Immigration Restriction Act* of 1901, known as the white Australia policy. But people of diverse origins remained in the country, and married outside their own religious and ethnic groups.

Australia's heterosexual unions between members of many groups engendered diversification of sexual attitudes and practices. Aboriginal women and frontier men developed a cross-cultural sexuality hushed by historical neglect. The women were vulnerable to extreme exploitation, and if they subsequently bore children, the fathers could easily avoid paternal responsibilities. Legislation constructed all Aboriginal women as prostitutes. Reacting to this, some Aboriginal historians describe all sex acts between coloniser and colonised as rape. Rapes of Aboriginal women commonly occurred, but alongside these there were negotiated sexual relationships, some of which led to stable family life. White men introduced rum, tobacco, food, horses and motor cars as courtship tools, but they had to tread a fine line as Aborigines in the remote areas had considerable power. On Wrotham Park cattle station in the 1920s, Aboriginal men used their knowledge of white men's sexual relations with their women to demand a better work deal. They revealed that the local policeman and the station accountant had allowed Aboriginal women and some men to take over the homestead, play the gramophone and teach them dancing. The Aboriginal women defined the spatial parameters of sexuality, shielding their husbands from open displays of their other sexual relationships by ensuring these occurred at a particular place which was a respectable distance from their community centre. The few Aboriginal men remaining at the homestead also prevented younger women from going with the men

Aboriginal men and women had different sexual styles from the British Australians, and these styles shaped the nature of the sexual interactions which took place. Mainly between white men and Aboriginal women, these led to the creation of a unique, largely unexplored language and culture of frontier sexuality. White men blew their earnings on a 'gin-spree' or orgy of alcohol and Aboriginal women. When association between black women and white men was banned in the Northern Territory, the liaisons were carried out more discreetly. From the 1900s, it was not unusual for young Australian men in country towns or on pastoral properties, working-class or gentry, to have their first sexual encounters with Aboriginal girls. Cases of white women's interest in Aboriginal men were usually hushed up altogether by all concerned, while the famous case of the Governor brothers, which led to murder, was sustained in Australian folklore with Tom Keneally's book, *The Chant of Jimmy Blacksmith*.

Class was another factor leading to multiple Australian sexual identities. During the nineteenth century, working-class women spoke of sex openly and descriptively, without an assumption of privacy. By the 1910s, their knowledge was breaking down, influenced perhaps by middle-class sexual mores. The women of the nineteenth-century gentry established their moral authority by working at an image both sexually constrained, cultivated and ornamental. Yet the need for restraint in posture, dress and expression implied an only partially covered sexuality. They knew more than they let on about sex and genitalia and were adept at creating an evasive, but encoded language referring to sexual matters. When the complex demands on their sexual and maternal selves became too stressful, women could express this in unexplained illness (Russell 1994, pp. 92–4). Young women were often sent to England for finishing school and when they returned home, were expected to be exemplars of civilised society. On the other hand, they had some liberties their English sisters lacked, as the warm climate favoured more outings, including longer organised trips in mixed groups with less chaperonage.

It was middle-class women who were most active in sexual and social reform. In 1916, Jessie Street's Social Hygiene Association started to educate the working classes about contraception and sexuality. Australia's emergent social and political climate promised greater opportunities to implement their ideas than Britain's. Feminist reformers saw the women's vote and greater female political influence as promising less sexual violence and abuse in the home, less prostitution and less alcohol consumption. Constructing lower-class women as potential victims of male sexual debauchery, they lobbied to increase the age of consent for girls; to rescue the unmarried mothers and prostitutes. Suffrage women, in their emphasis upon male sexual control and alcohol, have often been portrayed as dreadful wowsers or kill-joys, but their sisters certainly bore the brunt of sexual exploitation, having to cope with unwanted pregnancies, abortions, the slur of bearing illegitimate babies and the violence associated with alcohol abuse. Furthermore, their intertwining of voting with moral crusading worked, as they achieved the vote ahead of their English and American sisters.

Leading feminists, like Jessie Street, Rose Scott and Mary Bennett, believed women were moral guardians with the potential to change society's prevailing sexual codes. Drawing upon her knowledge of Australian manhood, Rose Scott saw men as untamed animals. The uncontrolled lusts of white frontiersmen were of special concern, with Aboriginal women, their most vulnerable prey, desperately requiring rescue, preferably by female protectors. In the 1920s and 1930s, feminist rhetoric linked primitivist images of Aboriginal women as sex slaves with white women's slave status in marriage.

White men's lust for Aboriginal women represented a reversion to primitive pasts; the 'combo' was a sign of degeneracy, threatening the future purity of the nation. Black or coloured men's sexuality was considered even more untamed than white men's. If a girl disappeared, it was believed she had fallen prey to the 'white slave trade'. The worst degredation for a white woman was to be held captive by a horde of savages. Captivity stories like the white woman of Gippsland, the Eliza Fraser story and the white woman of Arnhem Land horrified and enthralled the colonial imagination.

So too did the threat of the fecund 'Asian hordes'. After Federation in 1901, the first royal commission examined the problem of Australia's decreasing birthrate. While conforming with patterns in other developed countries, Australia's geographic situation and partial colonisation gave cause to panic. The Birthrate Commission (NSW) focused the public eye on private sexual practices, inextricably linking women's 'duty' to reproduce with the national good. Its moralistic messages, targeted at women in the middle and working classes, opposed family limitation. Ruling beliefs promoted the ethic of racially exclusive sexual selection as part of creating a vigorous nation. Now that immigration restrictions were in place to keep out Asians, the eugenics movement exaggerated the need for a large pool of healthy babies of 'superior' race and class to ensure a 'virile nation', which meant a potent military force.

Alongside the open talk about sexuality in the post-Freudian era, sex talk relating to the body became constrained to a medicalised discourse privileging the 'natural' (Finch 1995, p. 52). However, Australia produced some outstanding figures in popular education and sexual science. Marion Piddington authored parental advice manuals, such as *Tell Them!* (1925), to provide sex education for children, though often her approach contained more birds and bees than humans. Sexologist William Chidley became notorious for challenging the boundaries of masculine dress and preaching a passive male sexual role. Composer-pianist Percy Grainger was innovative with his towelling clothing, and as a collector not only of musical instruments but also sado-masochistic bondage paraphernalia.

Unmarried Australian women sometimes travelled overseas for premarital sexual adventures, especially in the 1950s and 1960s, when far more women travelled than men. Australian men travelled in large numbers during war, with their sexual adventuring only curbed by regular venereal disease and high rates of syphilis. The Second World War created an unusual situation with many local Australian men fighting overseas and large numbers of American soldiers resident in Australia. Women had to face greater physical dangers, but in the charged atmosphere of war, they embraced dating opportunities. Australian women enjoyed the more lavish courtship rituals and conversation skills of the smartly dressed American soldiers, with their gifts of chocolates, flowers and reminders of Hollywood glamour and wealth. Despite repressive organisation to prevent such associations, Queensland women dared to fraternise with black Americans. Australian soldiers lampooned their American competition as effeminate or childlike because of their liking for icecreams and aftershave. This was unsuccessful as between 12 000 and 15 000 Australian women migrated to the United States as brides and some American men immigrated to marry Australians. The American presence served to challenge many Australian assumptions about race and also narrowly defined sexual behaviours and roles (Campbell 1989).

Well into the 1970s Australian men remained awkward with women, harbouring immature attitudes to sex, referring to it as having 'a naughty', and jokingly denigrating women as 'dirty' or 'cheap' if they consented. Men seemed exclusively interested in football, cars and booze. Jokes followed about Australian men's incompetence as lovers, especially regarding their speedy ejaculation. 'Lesbian separatists', the radical feminist contingent, gave up on men altogether, celebrating the joys of sex between women as a political act. Australian men said they were ugly and couldn't get a bloke.

Stereotypes of Australian males were as sexually dualistic as damned whores versus God's police, but instead they divided 'blokes' from 'pooftahs'. The cherished mateship was exclusively homosocial rather than sexual. The ocker image thus functioned as a paranoid over-assertion of mateship's non-pooftah status. Australia has long had the reputation of being a homophobic society; its all-encompassing derogatory term 'pooftah' being satirised by the Monty Python group. Australian gays found it all too easy to transgress the straight boundaries of Australian masculinity, which in the 1960s and 1970s included distaste for theatre, wine, poetry, literature and the arts. Yet by the 1980s, the Australian gay lobby had been highly successful, with Australia leading the world in its widely advertised 'safe sex' campaigns to tackle the AIDS virus. Australians created the internationally successful *Priscilla*, an Oscar-winning movie celebrating drag queens, or transvestites. Sydney now boasts the annual Gay and Lesbian Mardi Gras, probably the largest and most widely attended gay festival in the world.

MULTIPLE IDENTITIES AND FURTHER RESEARCH

Much of Australia's sexual history demands further research and analysis. We know more about contraceptive history than about the changing story of courtship, sexual foreplay, positions and other practice. The most sexually charged times of puberty and adolescence have rarely been analysed, though Lesley Johnson's *The Modern Girl* and Kathy Lette's *Puberty Blues* are a great start. In search of a unified national identity for women, Miriam Dixson presented a bleak picture which she blamed partly on convict origins, upon moral guilt and Irish culture; she does not believe much has changed. Summers contends there has been dramatic progress: assertive girls are now not seen as 'bad' and the dichotomies reflective of damned whores and God's police are no longer relevant. According to a 'global sex survey' by the glossy magazine *Cosmopolitan*, Australian women in the 1990s are more sexually adventurous than elsewhere, and while still worried about being branded a 'slut', these days the boys also feared the label. More Anglo-Australians are marrying Asians and others with different coloured skins and cultural backgrounds.

Rather than trying to trace the history of a unilinear identity, we might ask instead how sexual experience varied between people: how did they understand it, how did they visualise or verbalise it, if at all? And what were the social, economic and political effects of sexual unions? Many questions about multiple identities still wait to be addressed. How did the sexual practices of Irish couples vary from the English, the Welsh and the Scottish, or what were the regional variations of all these groups? What about the Afghans, Greeks,

Maltese, Italians, Chinese, Japanese, Jews, Javanese, Indians, Turks and the many other cultural groups who comprised Australian history? How will Australia's growing Asian and Middle Eastern populations affect the agenda of sexual debate and practice? Debates about clitorectomy and circumcision have already taken place, but Anglo-Irish Australia needs to critique its own sexual codes. Investigations into paedophilia revealed how the practice has been virtually condoned by the Catholic church, welfare authorities, the diplomatic service, schools, police, the law. Are the parameters of public and private in the process of being shifted? To what extent can or should an emergent multicultural society define and enforce its sexual codes?

Just as there were multiple identities throughout the history of Australian culture, so too are there many sexualities and the scope for many histories of them. Sexuality varied between individuals, classes and cultures, and became part of the creative process of change, of the conflict and mergence which became Australian history. Sexuality was not just how one copulated, it was how one thought about it, what social rituals led up to it; it involved the parameters of suitable and unsuitable partners, which in turn were defined by religion, class, ethnicity, colour, culture and other shared beliefs. It was the mish-mash of physicality which defined gendered experiences like motherhood and fatherhood. Sexuality was affected by everything around it: changing geography and climate, changing ethnic, social and class composition, demographic trends of gender ratios, marriage ages, numbers of children, diet, work, dress, region, available contraceptive technology.

The history of Australian sexuality largely remains a hidden world, a forbidden place, containing the potential to either further disguise or further reveal the nature of things. In Australia today, there remains a mixture of shared public views, state edicts, private and revealed secrets. While it is true that the old sexual categories and dualities are breaking down for both women and men, they still haunt Australia's historical understandings and our present identities. Australian-style institutions of marriage, cohabitation and the family, premised on race, heterosexuality, and gender conformism, promised order. But with its continuing ability to dissolve boundaries, sexual desire also redefined cultures and multiplied identities; sex remains the itch which is able to throw the nation into a creative, if not a romping, chaos.

REFERENCES

Allen, J. 1990, *Sex and Secrets*, Oxford University Press, Melbourne

Aveling, M. 1992, 'Bending the bars: Convict women and the State', in *Gender Relations in Australia*, eds K. Saunders & R. Evans, Harcourt Brace Jovanovich, Sydney.

Campbell, R. 1989, *Heroes and Lovers*, Allen & Unwin, Sydney.

Damousi, J. 1995, '"Depravity and disorder": The sexuality of convict women', *Labour History*, no. 68, May.

Dixson, M. 1994 [1976], *The Real Matilda: Women and Identity in Australia, 1788–1975*, Penguin, Melbourne.

Finch, L. 1993, *The Classing Gaze*, Allen & Unwin, Sydney.

Grimshaw, P., Lake, M., McGrath, A. & Quartly, M. 1994, *Creating a Nation*, McPhee Gribble, Melbourne.

Hughes, R. 1987, *The Fatal Shore*, Collins Harvill, London.

Kingston, B. 1976, *My Wife, My Daughter and Poor Mary Ann*, Nelson, Melbourne.

—— 1988, *Glad, Confident, Morning*, Oxford University Press, Melbourne.

Kociumbas, J. 1992, *Possessions: Oxford History of Australia*, vol. 2, Oxford University Press, Melbourne.

Lake, M. 1990, 'Female desires: The meaning of World War II', *Australian Historical Studies*, vol. 24, no. 95, October.

McGrath, A. 1990, 'White man's looking glass', *Australian Historical Studies*, vol. 24, no. 95, October.

—— 1995, *Contested Ground: Aborigines under the British Crown*, Allen & Unwin, Sydney.

Oxley, D. 1996, *Convict Maids: The Forced Migration of Women to Australia*, Cambridge University Press, Melbourne.

Pesman, R. 1996, *Duty Free: Australian Women Abroad*, Oxford University Press, Melbourne.

Quartly, M., Janson, S. & Grimshaw, P. (eds) 1995, *Freedom Bound 1*, Allen & Unwin, Sydney.

Robinson, P. 1993 [1988], *The Women of Botany Bay*, Penguin, Melbourne.

Russell, P. 1994, *A Wish of Distinction*, Melbourne University Press, Melbourne.

Saunders, K. & Taylor, H. 1988, 'To combat the plague: The construction of moral alarm and State intervention in Queensland during World War II', *Hecate* 14.

Spearritt, K. 1994, 'The sexual economics of colonial marriage' in *On the Edge*, ed. G. Reekie, University of Queensland, St Lucia.

Summers, A. 1975 [1994], *Damned Whores and God's Police*, Penguin, Melbourne.

Ward, R. 1958, *The Australian Legend*, Oxford University Press, Melbourne.

—— 1988, *A Radical Life*, Macmillan, Melbourne.

5 Queer histories

Robert Reynolds

In his landmark text, *Homosexual*, Dennis Altman reflected upon his interest in the questions of identity and definition. Calling his final chapter 'The end of the homosexual', Altman wondered if the gay liberation impulse to transcend the division between homosexual and heterosexual would lead to a loss of identity. In responding to his own question Altman wrote, 'One hopes that the answer lies in the creation of a new human for whom such distinctions no longer are necessary for the establishment of identity' (1972, p. 226).

From a historical point of view *Homosexual* was an important text. Although its focus was primarily North American, its Australian publication in 1972 represented a significant moment in Australian cultural history. Like Germaine Greer's *The Female Eunuch*, Altman's *Homosexual* embodied the spirit of change that swept the West during the late 1960s and early 1970s. His book was an innovative and creative analysis of homosexuality as a modern identity and category.

Beyond this historical importance, it seems to me that Altman's 1972 book raised questions and dilemmas that remain relevant today in surveying what place, if any, 'the homosexual' could take in an analysis of the Australian cultural landscape. Picking up on Altman's concern with questions of identity and definition, I want to ponder how histories of homosexuality might illuminate the multiplicity of identities which create an individual's sense of self. I suggest that in investigating multiple Australian identities we need to go beyond simply reclaiming a place in the pantheon of cultural history for the heroic homosexual who has withstood a distinctly Australian form of oppression. Rather, I want to imagine what a 'queer' history of Australia might look like. How could sexuality as one category of analysis among many, rework singular stories about Australian history and identity? In these new accounts, how might queer perspectives enable us to historicise the individuals and the circumstances which have created Australia?

I shall begin by reviewing a number of books and articles that have investigated Australian gay and lesbian history and identity. I shall suggest that some of these texts have better represented the complex and multiple nature of sexual identity than others. I shall then look to the emerging international field of queer theory and consider how these new theoretical insights might fill out our local accounts of multiple identities and the stories we tell ourselves about these identities.

GAY AND LESBIAN HISTORY

To what degree has the writing of local gay and lesbian history engaged with the issue of multiple identities? In considering this question I will draw upon the work of Garry Wotherspoon, Robert French and Sheila Jeffreys. They represent, in different ways, 'the establishment' of gay and lesbian historians in this country.

Their histories, I would argue, have lost touch with the early gay liberationist impulse to dismantle sexual identities, whether homosexual or heterosexual. Rather, their project has become charting, celebrating and reinforcing certain contemporary ways of being gay or lesbian. Whilst this project is of value, it can result in somewhat insular histories that are easily marginalised. Furthermore, these gay and lesbian histories do not rigorously grapple with the postmodern idea that individuals are made up of multiple identities which are in a constant state of production and movement. In the work of Wotherspoon and French, 'the homosexual' is presented as a discrete but as yet unacknowledged player in Australian history. For these historians the project is to reclaim the homosexual. There are similarities here between this approach to gay history and the first phase of the writing of women's history. Predictably, it is the homosexual who becomes the missing ingredient in this recipe for a more representative account of Australian culture.

Garry Wotherspoon's two studies, *Being Different* (1986) and *City of the Plain* (1991), have been pivotal in establishing gay history in this country. *Being Different* brings together the experiences of nine men 'growing up gay in Australia'. *City of the Plain* shifts focus to look specifically at the emergence of a gay subculture in Sydney. Although both of these books are valuable, the key themes of identity and definition remain somewhat opaque. In *Being Different*, for example, the notion of experience is untheorised. The essays tend to chart a fairly straightforward progression to some point in the individual's life where a homosexual identity is achieved and resolved. This is the reassuring story of 'coming out'. Its overall effect, however, is to dull the richness and complexity of gay men's lives and to deplete the stories we tell ourselves about gay identity. As the feminist historian Joan Scott suggests in her influential article 'The evidence of experience', individuals do not unproblematically own experience. Instead, it is individuals who are created through experience. Scott writes: 'Experience in this definition becomes not the origin of our explanation but rather that which we seek to explain, that about which knowledge is produced. To think about experience in this way is to historicise the identities it produces' (1991, p. 780).

To take seriously the creation of experience, rather than taking the individual's experience as a given, would be to make problematic the attainment and resolution of gay identity. Indeed, it would make problematic the 'coming out' story of a stable and singular gay identity which simply awaits discovery. If the researcher views identity as a complex product of discourse, as Scott recommends, then identity becomes not a linear progression but a relatively fragile illusion, shot with discontinuity and change. In terms of Wotherspoon's *Being Different*, this would have required some engagement with issues of memory and nostalgia. To reminisce is to engage in the discursive construction of a self-history. How might this illuminate the multiplicity of discourses at work in recalling the past? A discursive analysis of identity may have also filled out Wotherspoon's *City of the Plain*. Here Wotherspoon gives an incisive account of the material transformations which provided the conditions in which a gay subculture in Sydney emerged and changed over time. But again, just as *Being Different* traces the lives of men who against adversity live as homosexual and resolve the contradictions of living outside the centre, so too in his second book is there a sense of pre-existing homosexual identities building a gay subculture. *City of the Plain* thus becomes, to mix biblical references, the chronicle of a journey to the promised land, a place that gays can call 'our' home.

If Garry Wotherspoon represents the established face of academic gay history, then Robert French could claim to be Australia's foremost gay community historian. His short and accessible articles have appeared in numerous gay newspapers and magazines throughout the country. As a community historian, however, French has been unwilling to critically deconstruct dominant notions of gay identity and community. Despite a nod in the direction of the French philosopher Michel Foucault, Robert French's work slides perilously close to a model of homosexuality which takes identity as somehow given. In the introduction to his recently published collection of essays, French describes his aim in writing gay history as 'a simple one'. 'It is', he continues, 'to bring to light the lives and experiences of the ancestors of our tribe' (1993, p. 2).

French is at pains to distinguish his work from the ' "famous fags" of history' approach to gay history, which aimed to reclaim famous past homosexuals in order to legitimise the contemporary gay movement. Yet in some important aspects French's work does not substantially reshape the borders of gay history. Sexuality as a category of analysis is not rigorously contextualised, other categories of analysis are largely ignored. Homosexual acts are viewed primarily through a contemporary lens. For French, ultimately, it is the story, or pre-history, of a singular gay identity and community that he wishes to tell. Events and characters of the past are moulded into a history of coherence and progression, leading up to what it means to be gay or lesbian today. This is the smooth history of continuity rather than disruption. It is a history which, in fact, produces the coherent gay identity it claims to have discovered.

Sheila Jeffreys' work is a recent addition to local histories of sexuality. At first glance, as a radical feminist, her work should hold more promise in disrupting hegemonic readings of Australian history. Rather than simply adding lesbians to the narrative, her aim is indeed to overturn the centre. From such a challenge might have emerged a history which was attuned to a multiplicity of gendered and sexual identities. However, as I have argued at some length elsewhere, her work is disappointing in its failure to interrogate the makings of multiple sexual identities and definitions sensitively (Reynolds 1994). As demonstrated in her most recent book, *The Lesbian Heresy* (1993), Jeffreys is more interested in privileging a particular strand of revolutionary feminism than engaging in nuanced readings of cultural history. Lesbian history, in Jeffreys' hands, has become a tool to defend the identity and project of a late 1970s revolutionary lesbian feminism. Accordingly, competing ways of being lesbian are expelled. This does not auger well for sophisticated readings of multiple identities or individual creativity.

ANALYSING GAY AND LESBIAN SUBJECTIVITIES

To this point I have covered histories that chart gays and lesbians in a 'pure' sense. By this I mean that homosexuality and lesbianism are perceived as a pure form of subjectivity, relatively untouched by other variables. While this is an advance on histories which ignored homosexuality, it nevertheless still presents gay and lesbian identities as singular and coherent identities. One way of moving beyond these forms of pure gay and lesbian history is to turn our attention again to those key themes of identity and definition.

A useful starter for queer history would be to rigorously contextualise homosexuality and make it relational to other elements of subjectivity such as gender, race, class, location and chance. In terms of individual histories, sexuality thus becomes only one element of subjectivity. This allows the historian of sexuality to analyse how a sexual subjectivity is itself structured and experienced through a range of discourses and variables. Sexuality emerges as something complex and contingent. This takes us well beyond a 'tribal' history. Moreover, such accounts of homosexual subjectivities could prove antithetical to the project of making authentic contemporary gay and lesbian identities.

Two recent works point toward ways in which such studies of gay subjectivities could be written. Although not strictly historical, a 1992 article by Dowsett et al., 'Gay lifestyles of the not-so-rich and quite unfamous', gives a sophisticated reading of how class moulds working-class men's homosexual identity and sexuality. This article contextualises homosexuality to reveal the multiple identities that lie within the category. The authors argue that for working-class gay men, 'life is profoundly shaped by their experience of training, work and the labour market' (1992, p. 156). By making the concept of gay identity relational, the authors also destabilise the idea of a homogenous gay community. Indeed, their working-class subjects experience themselves as marginal to dominant definitions of gay identity and community.

Dino Hodge's collection of oral histories from the Northern Territory, *Did You Meet Any Malangas? A Homosexual History of Australia's Tropical Capital* (1993), is another example of how sensitive accounts of gay subjectivities can be written. Hodge does far more than reclaim a pure gay history of the Northern Territory. His questioning of white gay men reveals the way in which class and race intersect to create a commercial subculture dominated by relatively affluent white men. Yet Hodge also leaves some space open for creative contact across divides of class and race, though that contact is always structured through power. Darwin beats, public meeting places for gay sex, are represented as sites where different cultures and different ways of experiencing homosexuality converge.

The contextual and relational nature of homosexuality becomes clear in Dino Hodge's interviews with Aboriginal and Asian gays, and two white gay men in close contact with Aboriginal communities. These interviews reveal a knowledge of sexuality that cannot be reduced to a Western model of sexual identity. This is not to construct Aboriginal sexuality as monolithic and static, or as an exotic 'other' to the West, but rather to contextualise dominant understandings of homosexuality and sexual identity. Perhaps it will be through such cross-cultural readings that we will come to appreciate better the existence of multiple sexualities.

TOWARD A QUEER HISTORY

During the late 1970s and well into the 1980s, it was historical research that set the pace in North American and British gay and lesbian studies. The leading figures in gay and lesbian academic studies were often historians. Today it is queer cultural theorists, particularly in North America, who are rewriting gay and lesbian studies. I want to consider now how some of these queer insights might add to readings of gay and lesbian subjectivities.

The term 'queer', even for the theoretically initiated, is a tricky one to define. This difficulty in definition is itself consistent with much of queer theory. Picking up on recent literary and social theory, queer theorists have set about destabilising dominant definitions of sexuality and sexual identity. One of the most influential texts for queer theorists and historians would have to be Eve Kosofsky Sedgwick's 1990 book, *Epistemology of the Closet*. Sedgwick claims that 'an understanding of virtually any aspect of modern Western culture must be not merely incomplete, but damaged in its central substance to the degree that it does not incorporate a critical analysis of modern homo/heterosexual definition' (1990, p. 1).

Sedgwick's dictum is a startling and innovative claim, holding within it the promise of radically reconceptualising gay and lesbian history. This is not simply the project of adding homosexuals to already written historical narratives, though it may bring to the fore sexual subjectivities of past subjects. A Sedgwickian history does not shore up existing gay and lesbian identities, though the queer reader may well find her work empowering. Nor does Sedgwick collapse a sexual subjectivity into a gendered one. Indeed, building on the work of Gayle

Rubin, Sedgwick argues that 'the question of gender and the question of sexuality, inextricable from one another though they are in that each can be expressed only in terms of the other, are nonetheless not the same question' (1990, p. 30).

Where then does Sedgwick take gay and lesbian history? This is a question that Sedgwick prefers to keep open as she writes, 'no one can know in advance where the limits of a gay-centred inquiry are to be drawn' (1990, p. 53). Sedgwick herself conceives of homophobic oppression having 'special centrality' in the twentieth century because of its 'inextricability from the question of knowledge and the process of knowing in modern Western culture at large' (1990, pp. 33–4).

In this model of history, ways of knowing and not knowing sexuality, and in particular the homosexual/heterosexual division, inform and mould 'many of the major nodes of thought and knowledge in twentieth-century Western culture as a whole' (Sedgwick 1990, p. 1). In terms of white Australian history, this would mean that sexuality would become one of the primary tools of analysis. This is not adding homosexuals as a discrete group of historical actors to the tapestry of white invasion and settlement, but rather throwing open the categories of mainstream historical narratives.

In terms of histories of subjectivity, Sedgwick's insights can be used to prise open unitary categories of identity. Difference, ambiguity and discontinuity thus replace linear histories of the acculturated self. As another theorist of queer, Diana Fuss, has written (and here again there are shades of Altman and the early liberationist program): 'To the extent that identity always contains the specter of non-identity within it, the subject is always divided and identity is always purchased at the price of the exclusion of the Other, the repression or repudiation of non-identity' (Fuss 1989, pp. 102–3). Queer identities, made other to hegemonic heterosexuality, can thus write not only their own histories, but also in the process, histories that add to our understanding of how Australia has been created.

What might one future queer history look like? Perhaps a queer history could break down identity as a category around which queer histories are structured. Another queer theorist, Douglas Crimp, has proposed studying the shifting and incomplete identifications that exist within and between identities. Such a formulation insists on a further engagement with the multiple and relational nature of identity. For, as Crimp points out, 'Identification . . . means that identity is never identical to itself' (1993, p. 313).

Alternatively, perhaps histories of desire might prove more disruptive than histories of identity. Desire as a concept is fluid and unpredictable, with its object and practice indeterminate. It does not sit easily within strictly defined categories. Desire can also threaten to surpass the objects of our investigation. Moreover, desire is an area of investigation where psychoanalytic and discursive analyses may be able to play creatively off each other. Perhaps these histories of desire and of identification might better represent the delicate creation of multiple identities than histories which claim to reveal the truth of sexual identity.

Finally, we might ponder whether we even need this new concept of queer when writing histories of sexuality. Is it not, as its critics complain, simply another regulatory identity? This is not the space to replay the arguments for and against queer. Suffice to say that what I find exciting about queer theory is its critical, potentially creative and constantly inquisitive impulse. It seems to me quite conceivable that any historian, no matter what their sexuality, could write quite queerly. Indeed there are, as I have suggested with the quote from Altman's *Homosexual*, some historical continuities between queer and early gay liberation. These continuities are sometimes forgotten in this exciting present moment of queer theory.

CONCLUSION

In this country, representing the past and understanding the present is often laced with a desire to discover an authentic 'Australianness' that exists out there for the describing. We might see traces of this desire in gay history's search for 'the Australian homosexual' and perhaps even gay liberation's millennial visions of a 'new human'. Yet such expeditions, though often creative and useful, can end up marking their own lack. Under the cover of historical authenticity, an identity which has not been found is instead covertly produced.

Queer history attempts to avert this melancholic search. Rather than remain haunted by lack, queer history attempts to investigate the ongoing production of complex and multiple identities. Though often playful in its dismantling of these identities and categories, it remains attuned to conflict and ambiguity. In its better moments, queer history might assist us to historicise the contingent creation of Australia.

REFERENCES

Altman, D. 1972, *Homosexual*, Angus & Robertson, Sydney.

Crimp, D. 1993, 'Right on, girlfriend', in *Fear of a Queer Planet*, ed. M. Warner, University of Minnesota Press, Minneapolis.

Dowsett, G. Davis, M. & Connell, R.W. 1992, 'Gay lifestyles of the not-so-rich and quite unfamous', in *Gay Perspectives*, ed. G. Wotherspoon and R. Aldrich, Department of Economic History, University of Sydney, Sydney.

French, R. 1993, *Camping by a Billabong*, Blackwattle Press, Sydney.

Fuss, D. 1989, *Essentially Speaking*, Routledge, New York.

Hodge, D. 1993, *Did You Meet Any Malangas? A Homosexual History of Australia's Tropical History*, Little Gem Publications, Nightcliff.

Jeffreys, S. 1993, *The Lesbian Heresy*, Spinifex, Melbourne.

Reynolds, R. 1994, 'Review article: *Anti-climax* and *the lesbian heresy*', *Melbourne Journal of Politics: Sexuality*, vol. 22.

Sedgwick, E.K. 1990, *Epistemology of the Closet*, University of California Press, Berkeley.

Scott, J. 1991, 'The evidence of experience', *Critical Inquiry*, summer.

Wotherspoon, G. 1986, *Being Different*, Hale & Iremonger, Sydney.

—— 1991, *City of the Plain*, Hale & Iremonger, Sydney.

6 Aborigines making history

Peter Read

Within the limits allowed by the legal and political systems, Aborigines today govern their destinies locally rather than nationally. Cultural and history committees, housing co-ops, land councils, municipal councils, and medical, welfare, women's and legal centres are some of the ways in which Aboriginal people find active roles. The Commonwealth government funds some 1200 Aboriginal corporations which provide a great deal of the employment opportunities, and almost all the managerial experience, for Aboriginal men and women. Expanding their agency from local government through self-management to self-determination seems to be what Aborigines want for the present and for the future. Interpreting the agency of Aborigines in the past, though, is more problematic.

Acting—or being acted upon?

In 1987 a memorial entitled 'Jew scrubbing the pavements of Vienna' was commissioned by the authorities of that city, marking the annexation of Austria by the Nazis 50 years earlier. The sculptor, Albert Hrdlicka, created the life-size figure of a kneeling, bearded Jew scrubbing the pavement. At first no one objected. The memorial seemed to present the historical fact of the subjection of Austrian Jews during the Nazi period and in particular the time when they were forced to scrub the streets. Objections began when it occurred to some of the Jewish community that the monument implied that Jews had done nothing else during the war. They argued that while they had escaped from, organised and fought against the Nazis, the monument implied that they had done nothing more than submit to their own destruction.

When stylised barbed wire was placed on the back of the kneeling figure to stop tourists from sitting on it, accusations were made that the sculpture was recreating the death camps. 'First you force the Jew down on his knees, then you place him behind wire'.[1] A serious and passionate discussion began about the meaning of the sculpture. Were the Jews no more than the helpless victims of barbarity? To what extent could their role in recent history have been different? Could the future be changed and directed by the former victims?

No less than the Jews, Aborigines, whose lives have been traumatised by seemingly inexplicable or malevolent actions directed against themselves, have come to understand that the past is *understandable*. Those who have endured the emotional process of understanding their own role in history seem best able to manage the present and to take responsibility for the future.

For 200 years Aboriginal children were removed from their own parents and raised by non-Aborigines. One purpose of these cruel actions was to break up the communities and separate Aborigines from each other. Naturally the officials who carried out separations or cared for the children did not explain that their actions were the result of certain inspectors travelling in the region, nor of Acts of parliaments, nor of regulations contained in a station manager's handbook of instructions, still less that the state policies which allowed children to be removed echoed certain intellectual currents current in eighteenth-century Britain. The officials either blamed their victims or made no explanation at all, and the separated children were left to formulate their own accounts that separation was beneficial or was simply a fact of life to which all Aboriginal children were subjected.

Hagar Roberts, for example, was removed from her parents and placed in the Roper River (Northern Territory) church mission in about 1910. She regarded her separation from her parents as simply a fact of life requiring no further explanation. To the question whether her parents were sad, she replied:

> Yeah they always bin sad, but they never bin sad much, you see. They was forgive [forgave] because they bin know missionary bin care us, look after us very well.
>
> And the Christmas, every Christmas, they was coming visit us, and go away again . . .
>
> I never bin think for my mother and father. Because I . . . had very nice teacher for us, to look afterem, care us (Roberts in Read & Read 1993).

Another removed child was Herbie Laughton who, far from blaming the officials who removed him from his parents, recalled 'The Old Bungalow' at Alice Springs with nostalgia:

> I can picture the old Home so clearly
> As it was many years so long ago
> And I'll cherish the memories so dearly
> Of the days at the old Bungalow.

Thus some of the first Aborigines of recent times to speak about the experience of separation denied themselves or their parents any historical agency. Each seemed, in their own mind, to be no more than the pawn of unstoppable forces acting for their own good. But by the 1990s many Aborigines had become very angry about their removal. They saw it as a consequence of actual government or church policy: collective not individual, cruel not kind, painful not nostalgic.

What began this process of reassessing the past? One turning point occurred in 1980 when Coral Edwards, herself a removed person, made a film called *It's A Long Road Back*. Though the film was about her own journey of self-awareness, for the first time several women were shown talking together about their experiences of removal and their time together in an institution. History was being understood here as something collective as well as personal, the consequence of actions taken by certain known individuals from a number of policy options. It followed that if separation had occurred because of certain policies, then the present and the future could be determined in the same way—this time by Aboriginal individuals and policies.

So, in the early 1980s, the first Link-Up agency was established. The workers' task, at one level, was to find the missing relatives and reunite them. At another, it was to convince their clients that neither the past nor the present was caused by chance. They wrote:

> The removal of Aboriginal children from their families was systematically carried out, in an attempt to break down the social structure of Aboriginal culture (Link-Up [Qld] n.d., p. 6)

The present was understandable:

> Most importantly it is comforting to realise that what is happening to you [feeling nervous or emotional at the prospect of meeting one's real family] is quite normal and in fact necessary when dealing with situations of loss and grief (Link-Up [Qld] n.d., p. 6).

and the future was in the hands of the Link-Up clients themselves:

> If we can work through our grief then we have a good chance of healing the wounds of separation and beginning on the road to recovery (Link-Up [NSW] n.d., introduction)

Since the 1970s Aborigines have been confronting the implications of new historical analyses. Seven years before Hrdlicka created his controversial sculpture, Aboriginal historians began consultations with the editors of a massive series of histories marking the two-hundredth anniversary of British civilisation in Australia entitled *Australians: A Historical Library*. The past was to be divided into slices 50 years apart so that individual volumes would spotlight pre-1788, 1788, 1838, 1888 and so on. In 1981 discussions were turning on the content of the 1938 volume. It was the first volume in the series in which oral history was to have a place. Among the critical questions were: who should write the Aboriginal sections? How much space should they occupy in the total volume? How much history should be based on oral history? Should one or many Aboriginal voices be represented? And what sort of history should it be? Did Aborigines see themselves as helpless victims, or courageous but unsuccessful resisters, or as people who had never been defeated? Or all three?

As part of the negotiations, four leading Aboriginal historians—Wayne Atkinson, Michael Williams, Doreen Wanganeen and Marcia Langton—met in Canberra, framed a forceful resolution and took it to a public meeting. Their manifesto read in part:

> Just as colonised peoples and oppressed indigenous peoples have insisted that their histories and cultures are their own to be portrayed and represented by their own people, Aboriginal people are reclaiming their history and culture. We are the guardians and custodians of our history and culture, and it is our responsibility to pass on to future generations our set of truths.
>
> Justifiably, Aboriginal people regard the white version of history since colonisation as colonialist propaganda, as a denial of our set of truths. We have never conceded defeat: our resistance must therefore continue in the realm of history as well as in the political forums.[2]

Such were the parameters of Aboriginal historical writing in the 1980s, and the 1838 volume of *Australians: A Historical Library* presented accounts both of victims and resisters (Gammage & Spearritt 1987). Nevertheless writing real history was much more difficult than the manifesto suggested. The past was peopled by individuals exercising choices whether to fight, resist, go along with what others did, or interpret the scenario in quite different terms. Self-portrayal as helpless victim—which seemed at times necessary to demonstrate the crushing inevitability of the invasion—was not far from leaving the dispossessed people in the unwelcome state of passivity.

The tension was particularly apparent in accounts by Aboriginal people of massacres. Many Aboriginal historians tackled the subject, with results sometimes at variance with the working party's pronouncements that Aborigines had never conceded defeat and that resistance must continue in the realm of history. The Nyungar playwright Jack Davis, in his play *Kullark*, narrated the attempted extermination of the indigenous population of the Swan River Valley, Western Australia in the 1840s, in which the passivity of the victims parallels the passivity of the first self-analyses of the separated children:

> ACTRESS: As white settlement spread south, similar incidents occurred. In eighteen forty-one at Vasse, seven Aborigines were shot by Mr Bussell. In eighteen forty-two Bussell shot an Aboriginal caught stealing flour. The verdict was self defence. In the same year he shot a seven year old girl at point blank range. The verdict: accidental death. In eighteen forty-two Captain Molloy rounded up an entire tribe at Vasse and according to reports exterminated them and burnt their bodies. In eighteen twenty-nine the Aboriginal population of the South West was estimated at around thirteen thousand. By nineteen hundred and one there were less than eight hundred full bloods left (Davis 1982, p. 38).

The Nyungar, in Davis's interpretation, were helpless victims who had done almost nothing to offend the invaders. The whites' motivations were taken to be no more complex than mindless cruelty and greed.

Some years later Mary Coe, a Wiradjuri woman of New South Wales, wrote the much more politically aware *Windradyne A Wiradjuri Koori*. She described her people resisting the arrival of the squatters in the Bathurst district:

> The elders called Windradyne and the young warriors forward and together they worked out the best way to hurt the white man. The elders told Windradyne to hit the white man at the economic source of his existence—his livestock and herds. Windradyne and his warriors attacked a property on the Cudgegong river, drove away the stockmen and the sheep and cattle . . . They continued their attacks . . . (Coe 1986, p. 24).

Here were no helpless victims, but warriors whose battles continued, in Coe's depictions, to the present.

The explosion of Aboriginal oral histories in the later 1980s showed traditional Aborigines relating the past in different terms. Tommy Thompson, a Katetye man of the Northern Territory, told the story of the massacre of his people of the Barrow Creek region in 1874. To Thompson the killings by the whites were not purposeless but in fact precipitated by an older Katetye man sending a woman to the white men in the Telegraph Station.

> And they took her inside and made her camp overnight with them. The next morning they sent her back to her father and her promised husband. They gave her some salt meat and tobacco, and a little bit of tea and sugar to take back to that old man, her father. And her promised husband said, 'Hey, that young girl, my father-in-law, has given her to me. That's my promised [intended] wife! My father-in-law sent her to the whitefellas. They might take her away from me!'
>
> Well, that's true. Those whitefellers used to take women away from them. Well that's why they got worked up.
>
> 'Those white men are robbing us of our women. Ah, we'll have to fight with them now.'
>
> That's what happened. They fought then. They speared the whites who had rifles. They only had their spears, plus backup spears and boomerangs. Some of them didn't have a chance against the shells. Some of the old people got shot and some got away, and still they killed two [white] men. That's what happened. (Thompson in Koch & Koch 1993, pp. 15–16).

A fourth example of massacre narration was that of Little Mick Inginma, a Bilignara of the Victoria River district of the Northern Territory. In his account, certain Aborigines were not resisters but collaborators. The massacre occurred because two women from another tribe lured the Bilignara into an ambush by promising them work (building a yard) in exchange for tobacco:

> [The two women said to the Bilignara] All right, well we bin findem good boss.
>
> Here's the tobacco, here's the tobacco, here's the tobacco.
>
> Here's a good boss. We're going to go down up there. Him [the boss] wantem for work. That's why him bin sendem me two-feller [us].
>
> That man, him like Aborigin. Him wantem for work . . . Want to makem yard. He got to man to help him. Him got nothing. Him only got three tracker (Inginma in Read & Read 1993).

So the Bilignara, trusting the reassurances of their fellow Aborigines, came in to get their work and tobacco—and were murdered.

Nobody knows exactly what happened at any of these sites in Bathurst, Swan River, Barrow Creek and Victoria River Downs. Indeed, a non-Aboriginal historian writing about the massacre of Windradyne's Wiradjuri people argued that there was no way of knowing whether any massacres actually occurred at the places they were supposed to have happened. In fact it is quite likely that the four events followed a similar pattern at each place: the Aborigines initially welcomed, or at least tolerated the whites until they realised the extent of the newcomers' exploitation of the land and their attitude towards themselves. Spasmodic, sometimes planned, guerilla attacks on whites began in each region within a few years, which were answered by massive reprisals by the whites, who called out large numbers of armed men to put down the Aborigines. These narratives illustrate that the tensions between acting in approved ways, acting in unapproved ways, and not acting at all are no easier for black historians to resolve than for anyone else. And in the 1990s, Aboriginal historical analyses are taken seriously. The Oxford history of Australia uses Mary Coe's book as a source for its account of martial law. Jack Davis's play has been performed hundreds of times to Aboriginal and non-Aboriginal audiences. If history has a political purpose, which the working party asserted that it did, then the interpretation of 'agency' is debatable and in part contingent upon contemporary politics. Taking some responsibility for the past, then, releases the victim from powerlessness and helplessness, but causes new problems within contemporary ideology.

The apparently crucial question has thus begun to emerge from the discussion: does the concession that Aborigines contributed to their own destruction by assisting the white settlers weaken their claim to prior or continuing sovereignty? Aboriginal intellectuals have only recently begun to face this dilemma.

The historian Ysola Best, writing of the settlement of her own country southwest of Brisbane, objected to non-Aboriginal historians making too little of Aboriginal assistance towards European settlement, as if conflict were the only possible result of the European intrusion (Best 1994, pp. 87–94). Kevin Gilbert's book *Living Black* concluded with the words of 'Grandfather Koori':

> It is not possible for anyone to love you unless you do something or are something worth loving. You can't find happiness without first making rules to stamp out the things that make unhappiness. You can't find value in yourself until you build it by respecting yourself through living right. If you tolerate crumminess, gutlessness, meanness, wife bashing, kid bashing and neglect then you'll never get the strength to climb out of hell (Gilbert 1977, p. 305).

Charles Perkins maintained that Aborigines must rid themselves of dependence upon non-Aborigines and sieze the initiative:

> Aboriginal people must remove the concept of welfare from their politcal and economic affairs . . . the false economy of the welfare lifeline, they must build viable community economies that do not rely on politicians' discretion. Such economies would provide a more secure and independent base for their survival (Perkins 1994, p. 882).

Such opinions have not been accepted with much enthusiasm by other Aborigines.

Non-Aboriginal historians, however, have embarked on the subject of Aboriginal agency with more willingness. Bob Reece has been amongst several who have castigated other non-Aboriginal historians for exaggerating or distorting frontier violence (Reece 1996). To Roger Milliss, the Aborigines killed in the Myall Ceek massacre, New South Wales, were 'weeping blacks stumbling and pitching to the yankings of the rope, half-dragged, half-borne along by utter resignation', but the sceptical Gordon Reid, writing of the Northern Territory, found that 'in the absence of better evidence than oral history, the claims made for large-scale black resistance and white retaliation in Arnhem Land are unconvincing'. The most thoughtful discussion of Aboriginal historical agency is Henry Reynolds' *With The White People*. He argued that in northern and central Australia the Aborigines were the mainstay of the European economy. Their labour was of crucial importance to the sheep farmers of Western Australia and central Queensland, to pearl and trepang producers in the north; their domestic labour important in towns and mining camps; and women provided the sexual pleasure and companionship which made harsh frontier life bearable. Perhaps 10 000 Aborigines were working for Europeans in 1900. In southern Australia they assisted the pioneers. In the north, they were the pioneers. There have been more troublesome complications. Reynolds estimated that perhaps one in four of all Aborigines killed in frontier skirmishing was killed by other Aborigines of the Black Police, or by assisting the whites in other ways. Perhaps the invaders could not have been repulsed, but Aborigines certainly did not need to have helped the Europeans quite so much!

AGENCY AND THE FUTURE

The implications run further than Reynolds' discussion. While it is true that many Aboriginal families, as Paul Coe once put it, are the result of 'gin jockeying', it is also true that contemporary part-Aboriginal families began as a result of a relationship of love, or casual but unforced sex. It is possible that in southern Australia many, perhaps most, modern Aboriginal families are descended from those who co-operated with the whites, since those who actively resisted the invaders died lonely or violent deaths in the bush and perhaps left fewer descendants than those who learned English, or worked in the paddocks or the mission stations. Many more Aborigines are descended from Chinese, Afghan and African Americans than is currently allowed for. It is possible that successive waves of people from the north invaded Australia over many millenia, to muddy the claimed clear connection between time immemorial and the present. Tim Flannery argues that the ancestors of Aborigines destroyed the megafauna of Australia many thousands of years before the whites continued and magnified the process of environmental wastage.

Are Aborigines, then, the national and international actors that they wish to be? It remains true that Aborigines continue to suffer great discrimination. The Aboriginal and Torres Strait Islander Commission remains at the mercy of the nonindigenous accountant, lawyer and politician. Michael Dodson, the Aboriginal and Torres Strait Islander Social Justice Commissioner, rightly pointed out that the Mabo decision should not be seen as an end point but a catalyst for a further, deeper act of recognition. Clearly Aborigines lack agency in important respects.

Yet the very complexity of Aboriginal identities accounts for the richness of the contribution which Aborigines have made and are making. Aboriginal businesses thrive because certain Aborigines believe that being an entrepreneur does not compromise one's Aboriginality. The same argument can be made about Aborigines who, in the teeth of Aboriginal criticism, publicly discuss child abuse in Aboriginal communities, sing American country and western, allow mining in traditional lands, vote conservative or teach Chinese history. Aborigines are not, and never have been, united in their views on anything.

NOTES

1 I am grateful to Dr Adi Wimmer, of the University of Klagenfurt, for this information and comment.

2 'Resolution passed at meeting of Aboriginal historians and others interested in Aboriginal History, 9 February 1981', in *Australia 1939–1988: A Bicentennial History Bulletin*, 3 (May 1981), p. 22.

REFERENCES

Best, Y. 1994, 'An uneasy coexistence: An Aboriginal perspective of "contact history" in Southeast Queensland', *Aboriginal History* 18.

Coe, M. 1986, *Windradyne—A Wiradjuri Koori*, Blackbook.

Davis, J. 1982, *Kullark, The Dreamers*, Currency Press, Sydney.

Gammage, B. & Spearritt, P. (eds), 1987, *Australians 1938*, Fairfax, Syme & Weldon, Sydney.

Gilbert, K. (ed.) 1977, *Living Black*, Penguin, Melbourne.

Koch, G. and Koch, H. (eds) 1993, *Katetye Country*, IAD, Alice Springs.

Link-Up (NSW) Aboriginal Corporation, 'Link-Up', n.d., Sydney [1995].

Link-Up (Qld) Aboriginal Corporation, 'Link-Up', n.d., Brisbane [1991].

Perkins, C. 1994, 'Politics', in D. Horton (general ed.), *The Encyclopaedia of Aboriginal Australia*, Aboriginal Studies Press, Canberra, II.

Read, P. & Read, J. 1993, *Long Time Olden Time. Aboriginal Accounts of Northern Territory History*, CD ROM, Firmware, Penrith.

Reece, B. 1996, 'Inventing Aborigines', in *Terrible Hard Biscuits*, eds V. Chapman and P. Read, Allen & Unwin, Sydney, ch. 3.

Reid, G. 1990, *A Picnic with the Natives*, Melbourne University Press, Melbourne.

Reynolds, H. 1990, *With the White People*, Penguin, Melbourne.

7 Chinese Australian history

Jan Ryan

Where are Chinese in the history books of Australia? There is a proliferation of ethnic histories of Chinese, Japanese, Irish, Hungarian, Italians *in* Australia. There are local studies on Chinese *in* Australia (or Chinese *in* Victoria or *in* New South Wales), but the Chinese are not there in our grand national histories and the token fragments that are included retain familiar stereotypes of Chinese as a homogenous 'race', a detached entity, with a separate and alien identity. By such inclusion they remain excluded.

An investigation of the 'national' histories published during our 'multicultural' era is revealing. John Rickard's *Cultural History of Australia* (1988) rarely mentions Chinese, although he fleetingly recognises them as a source of conflict in the goldfields of Ballarat. He sees Chinese as a problem—or as novelty. The *Oxford History of Australia* is no better. In volume three, 1860–1900 (Kingston 1988), a significant era for Chinese in Australia, Beverley Kingston merely sees Chinese as victims of escalating racist sentiments, and the reason for the implementation of restrictive legislation. Volume four, *1901–1942*, has not a single Chinese indexed. Volume five, *1942—1988*, (Bolton 1990) talks of multiculturalism, but there is nothing about Chinese, or for that matter Italians, Greeks, Japanese or other ethnic groups in this text. Aboriginals and women, previously marginalised identities, have made their mark, but the new-wave Asian immigrants remain invisible, and people of Chinese descent are not mentioned. Perhaps one of the more surprising omissions is the failure to include Chinese in the book *Australians from 1939* (ed. A. Curthoys et al. 1987), even though the book does discuss Asian immigration, and furthermore includes vignettes of European migrants.

Creating a Nation (Grimshaw et al. 1994), an inspirational text, setting new standards for reappraising Australian history, draws on women and Aboriginal histories, yet fails to mention Chinese women or women from other Asian ethnic backgrounds. There are a host of other national histories which also ignore the contributions of those loosely dubbed 'Chinese'. Why are historians not considering Chinese within discussions of Australia's identities? It may well be, as Sneja Gunew suggests, that 'consideration of one kind of history produces an even greater amnesia regarding other histories, including postwar migration histories', and that 'Australians continue to seek national unities, coherent narratives of the nation' (Gunew 1993).

Clearly there is a profound ignorance about the variety of roles that peoples of Chinese extraction have played in Australia's history, and also of the ways in which these people have been suppressed and prevented from moving outside those roles, both in their life experiences and in the historical discourse that has marginalised and 'coloured' these experiences. Both the agency and the multiple identities of Chinese have been repressed.

The 'token fragments' of Chinese experiences in Australian histories reveal stereotypes of Chinese coolies, Chinese gold-diggers, Chinese market gardeners, and Chinese cooks, frequently portrayed in a mysterious and clearly alien Chinatown. The dominant society of the nineteenth century conferred an identity on these people, and, moulded by governments, these identities have been mythologised by virtue of consent by 'mainstream' society. As Kay Anderson has warned, 'we end up unable to see people as they are, because of the seductive convenience of types that rob people of their particularity' (Anderson 1991).

The stereotype images of 'John Chinaman' need to be reassessed. The immigrants came from different cultural backgrounds, and faced very different conditions and circumstances to which they responded in very different ways. It was not so much a story of group solidarity against oppression and ostracism as one of individual struggle against hardship and loneliness in the harsh virgin bush and the hostile frontier townships, against discrimination and the lack of communication with Europeans, as well as the hostility and inter-clan rivalry in their relationships with Chinese from other dialectal groups. From the colonial period on, Chinese were among the frontier men and women who helped forge Australia's history.

In order to avoid constructing a misleading single Chinese identity it is important to consider the sharp contrasts in the life experiences of individual Chinese. It is easy to become submerged in the black and white of archival records and to ignore the multidimensional histories obscured in the layers of these records. Chinese laughed, they cried, they felt elated or depressed just like 'white' Europeans. There were successes and failures, there were tragic incidents and amusing stories. But all this has often been repressed by myths of Chinese and Australian single identities. As oral historian Norma King Koi recalls:

> my grandparents did not practise many Chinese customs or teach them to their children. My parents were brought up as 'white Australians' practising the customs and etiquette of well-mannered white children so that they would not appear inferior in any way. They had to prove that they were as good as if not better than white Australians (King Koi in Ryan 1995, p. 47).

The coming of multiculturalism did not change this entirely because multiculturalism often legitimated the notion that Australia was a culturally homogeneous nation before post-Second World War immigration.

There is also truth in the charge that Australian governments have embraced multiculturalism, encouraging cultural diversity and expression, without accommodating the complexity of ethnic diversity in Australian institutional structures, such as education, health services, policing, court procedures and so forth—which remain Anglocentric. Thus Susan Wang, a popularly acclaimed Chinese dancer, received government monetary grants for her Chinese dance performances and choreography. However, when she sought to pursue her newly acquired 'Australian' choreographic goals she was refused funds to do so. While she pursues a separate, exotic and distinctive 'Chinese' style, support is hers; when she encroaches on 'Australian' territory, 'Australian' dance, this is not the case (Fisher in Ryan 1995b, pp. 57–8).

The censure of different ethnic voices began with early settlement, and exploring new paths to the present means redefining familiar territory or exploring unfamiliar territories. There is a wealth of written material about the 'Australian frontier'. The bush and bush pioneers have generated a genre of ballads, reminiscences and local histories, celebrating a view of this frontier as the outward fringe of an agreeable European civilisation (Jebb & Haebich 1992, p. 20). Revisionist writers have explored Aboriginal frontiers and women's frontiers, serving to increase their visibility and experiences. But there are also frontiers for Chinese, for Japanese, for Italians and for Greeks. Each culture has a presence, trying both to maintain their cultural uniqueness and to come to working relationships with other cultures and to make cultural accommodations. Paul Macgregor points out that 'more than one community inhabits the same space we call Australia . . . Chinese people in Australia, like others, have a need for a shared zone and that area need not be contiguous . . . it can be a string of sites scattered across a city, across a continent, across the globe; the physical places which are the sites of communal activity—a series of homes of the extended family, the shops they frequent, our temples, churches, clan halls' (Macgregor 1995a, pp. 7–11).

Macgregor postulates that there are degrees in which Chinese and European Australians ventured into the other's territory, and that those Chinese Australians who did make journeys into European culture absorbed the frontier within themselves, sometimes being Chinese, sometimes being European. This captures multiple identities but does not clearly signal that 'European' and 'Chinese' are also multiple identities. Of course, for the Chinese themselves singular identities were important in their experience. For example, while undertaking Chinese oral history research, Norma King Koi was caught in a time warp as she relived the interviewee's experiences:

> I saw all their faces and felt all their emotions. Instead of being a 'lost soul', I became a part of all of their worlds and all of them became a part of me . . . they are speaking through me. Non Chinese generally consider me to be Chinese but Chinese consider me to be a westerner . . . I am no longer a 'lost soul' . . . I have been reborn and am beginning to understand ancient Chinese culture. I think that I think like an Australian, I feel that my heart is Chinese, my soul is a blend of both, but often my heart rules my head' (King Koi in Ryan 1995, p. 51).

Perhaps it is only to be expected that singular constructions of Chineseness are qualified in stages. K.H. Chin in his article 'Chinese in modern Australia' (1988, pp. 317–18) explains the complexities of the term 'Chinese' when it is applied to those who consider themselves *huaqiao* (Chinese living overseas) or *huaren* (generally Chinese who are born in Australia and/or who have acquired foreign citizenship). The term *huaren* is applied to Chinese who call themselves Malaysian, Singaporean, Indonesian, American, Canadian or Australian. Yet Chin explains that in Australia such 'Chinese' continue to apply terms such as *aohua*—Chinese Australians—to themselves. Noting the multiplicity of terms available to 'Chinese' in Australia is only a first step towards taking account of the heterogeneous identities of peoples of Chinese descent, and the complexity and diversity of cultural experiences. 'Chinese' views of both their Chineseness and Australianness (and divided loyalties associated with being Malayasian, Indonesian etc.) cannot be simply reduced to single identities.

Once the point about multiple identities is taken, there need be no dichotomy between being 'Chinese' and being 'Australian'. However, more needs to be made of the Chinese input into Australian multiple identities, including both the original contributions of 'upgraded migrants', professionals and business people, and Chinese intercultural impacts on education, the arts, literature and sport. Today there is a danger that the old myths of 'John Chinaman' will be supplanted by new stereotypes of 'Chinese' gaining too many tertiary placements and usurping professional appointments whereas the significant contributions of men and women of Chinese descent to business, education, medicine and the sciences should all be included in Australia's changing profile.

The deficiencies of broad-stroke 'Australian histories' have been counterbalanced to some extent by the proliferation of 'ethnic' studies that have emerged. The publication of studies of 'Chinese' in Australia during the last decade has provided a significant research base from which to analyse and trace a broad range of 'Chinese' perspectives. On the other hand, a single identity 'ethnic' view of the 'Chinese' has too often prevailed.

In 1984, Jenny Cushman, in her perceptive article 'The Chinese community in Australian historiography', made a passionate plea for historians to move away from studies of Australian attitudes to Chinese and to 'relocate the Chinese experience within the Chinese community itself'. She further urged researchers to investigate the way Chinese customs, legal notions and kinship relations were adapted to the Australian physical and social environment. It is tempting to credit many of the succeeding changes to Cushman's appeal. However, the new approaches must be viewed within the context of the changing tide of historiography and the impact of 'multiculturalism'. There has been a shift from the expansive works of writers such as Migra, Willard, P. Crawford Campbell, C. Price and C.F. Yong to the narrow focus of state and place of scholars such as C. May, K. Cronin, A. Atkinson and J. Ryan. There have also been efforts to re-analyse localities such as Chinatown, and the workplace and homes of people of Chinese heritage.

The earlier studies over-focused upon Chinese in Victoria and New South Wales and ignored regional and cultural disparities. These historians largely assumed the homogeneity of the Cantonese population in Australia in the nineteenth-century (findings that have been challenged in studies outside the eastern colonies), and a view of a collective Chinese community emerged which portrayed Chinese as victims. In recent multidisciplinary studies, however, historians, anthropologists, archaeologists, geographers, sociologists, economists, oral historians, genealogists and museum curators have joined together to search for the variety and diversity of experiences of peoples of Chinese descent in Australia.

The complexity of 'Chinese' experience is slowly gaining adequate attention. In her recent publication, *Beyond Chinatown* (1995, p. 48), Diana Giese argues that:

> the reworking of the stories of Chinese Australians is part of a redefinition of what it is to be Australian. In chronicling the first and second generation of Chinese Australians, local and community history opens up areas that have been of little interest to the great national histories.

'Chinese voices' are now being heard in their diversity through oral histories. Both Morag and Wendy Lowestein have been pathfinders in their immigrant interviews. Loh's *Dinky-Di: The Contributions of Chinese Immigrants and Australians of Chinese Descent to Australia's Defence Forces and War Efforts, 1899–1988* (1989), in particular, reveals an innovative and sensitive approach to interviews of people of Chinese descent. While Loh, Gibes, Jan Wilton and Norma King Koi lead a small band of oral historians, there is much more work to be done in this area to explicate the diverse experiences of people of Chinese extraction. Recently a wide range of topics has been explored, with a clever use of sources. For example, the 1993 international public conference on Chinese in Australasia and the South Pacific held at the Chinese Museum in Melbourne, heralded the growing popularity of the area. Some 40 papers were presented to a large audience of academics and community participants, resulting in the publication *Histories of the Chinese in Australasia and the South Pacific* (1995). This volume testifies to the extensive interest in varied aspects of 'Chinese' experiences; it includes for example studies of gold mining and running market gardens and laundries marking work practices of the colonial period, along with those of contemporary business migrants and their contributions. It covers changing patterns of migration, migration processes and implications; herbalists, patients, morbidity and mortality; burial practices and burial sites; family ties and histories; participation in government agencies, such as the armed forces and the police forces; dance, literature, art and culture; archaeological sites and heritage; crime and the criminal and civil law procedures.

Such local studies have yet to be placed in the broader perspectives of global issues. An exception is the 1992 publication *Asians in Australia: The Dynamics of Migration and Settlement* (C. Inglis et al. (eds)). Stephen Castles and Rogelia Pe-Pua have examined the effects on wives and families of the sojourning migrational habits of professional and business migrants from Hong Kong. Such studies show that unified discussion of 'Chinese' as those with 'Chinese' ancestry need to be replaced by accounts which factor in the country of birth, be it Hong Kong, China, Taiwan, Singapore, Malaysia or elsewhere. These birthplaces have a significant impact on the cultural heritage of Chinese peoples and radically broaden the multidimensional features of Australia's intercultural identities.

To sum up, there is no cohesive 'Chineseness' organising the heterogenous identities of peoples of Chinese descent in Australia. Today no Australian history can ignore the breadth and depth of the experiences of the Chinese who came to Australia and the complexities of the ever shifting cultural dialogues in which they engaged. On the contrary, these cultural intersections are powerful indices towards a reinventing of multiple Australian identities.

But to say this is to point to wider implications for history-making in Australia. The Eurocentric histories of the past cannot simply be corrected by including the 'Chinese', especially if clear ethnic separations based on assumed single identities are maintained. It is necessary to go beyond Orientalist contrasts between us and them, Australian and Chinese, and to engage in a re-examination of sites of difference and dialogue. These sites will show the need to envisage multiple identities. They may also sometimes point to shared experiences of a shared world. Separate histories of ethnic peoples are not enough, especially if they serve to contain and exclude these peoples. Instead there is a need for a new synthesis in Australian history. The crucial shift for historians is to personally engage with the contemporary politics of difference, to question the received notion of racially neutral histories, and to contest the social and political constructs of race. The personal worlds of peoples of ethnic ancestry have not been erased. They are locked in our historical cellars, dormant in the historical field of vision, waiting for historians to seek the appropriate alternative and multiple cultural connections.

REFERENCES

Anderson, K.J. 1991, *Vancouver's Chinatown: Racial Discourse in Canada, 1875–1980*, McGill-Queens University Press, Montreal.

Bolton, G.C. 1990, *Oxford History of Australia 1942–1988*, vol. 5, Oxford University Press, Melbourne.

Broinowski, A. 1992, *The Yellow Lady: Australian Impressions of Asia*, Oxford University Press, Melbourne.

Chin, K.H. 1988, 'Chinese in modern Australia' in *The Australian People*, ed. J. Jupp, Angus & Robertson, Sydney.

Curthoys, A., Martin, A.W., & Rowse, T. (eds) 1987, *Australians Since 1939*, Fairfax, Syme & Weldon, Sydney.

Cushman, J.W. 1984, 'A "colonial casualty": The Chinese community in Australian Historiography', *Asian Studies of Australia*, vol. 7, no. 3.

Giese, D. 1991, 'The ancestral village: The top end Chinese, ourselves and others', *Voices*, vol. 1, no. 3, spring.

——1995, *Beyond Chinatown*, National Library of Australia, Canberra.

Grimshaw, P., Lake, M., McGrath, A. & Quartly M. 1994, *Creating a Nation*, Penguin, Melbourne.

Gunew, S. 1993, 'Multiple Multiplicities, US, Canada, Australia', *Meanjin*, no. 3.

Inglis, C., Gunasekaran, S., Sullivan, G., & Wu C-T 1992, *Asians in Australia: The Dynamics of Migration and Settlement*, Institute of Southeast Asian Studies, Singapore.

Inglis, C. & Wu Tong 1994, 'The Hong Kong Chinese in Sydney' in *Reluctant Exiles? Migration from Hong Kong and the New Overseas Chinese*, ed. R. Skeldon, University of Hong Kong, Hong Kong.

Jebb, M.A. & Haebich, A. 1992, 'Across the Great Divide: Gender relations on Australian Frontiers' in *Gender Relations in Australian: Domination and Negotiation*, eds K. Saunders & R. Evans, Harcourt Brace Jovanovich, Sydney.

Kee Pookong & Skeldon, R. 1994, 'The migration and settlement of Hong Kong Chinese in Australia', in *Reluctant Exiles? Migration from Hong Kong and the New Overseas Chinese*, ed. R. Skeldon, University of Hong Kong, Hong Kong.

Kingston, B. 1988, *Oxford History of Australia 1860–1900*, vol. 3, Oxford University Press, Melbourne.

Loh, M. 1989, *Dinky-Di: The Contributions of Chinese Immigrants and Australians of Chinese Descent to Australia's Defence Forces and War Efforts 1899–1988*, AGPS, Canberra.

Macgregor, P. 1995a, 'Chinese? Australian? The limits of geography and ethnicity as determinants of cultural diversity', in *Chinese in Australia and New Zealand: A Multidisciplinary Approach*, ed. J. Ryan, New Age International Ltd, New Delhi.

—— (ed.) 1995b, *Histories of the Chinese in Australasia and the South Pacific: Proceedings of an International Public Conference held at the Museum of Chinese Australian History*, Chinese Museum, Melbourne.

Marcus, A. 1979, *Fear and Hatred: Purifying Australian and California 1850–1901*, Hale & Ironmonger, Sydney.

Miles, R. 1993, *Racism after 'Race Relations'*, Routledge, New York.

Rickard, J. 1988, *Cultural History of Australia*, Longman Cheshire, Melbourne.

Ryan, J. 1995a, *Ancestors: Chinese in Colonial Australia*, Fremantle Arts Centre Press, Fremantle.

—— (ed.) 1995b, *Chinese in Australia and New Zealand: A Multidisciplinary Approach*, New Age International Ltd, New Delhi.

Wang Gungwu 1994, 'Upgrading the migrant: Neither huaqiao nor huaren', keynote address, 'The last half century of Chinese overseas' conference, University of Hong Kong, Hong Kong.

8 Multiple political identities

Joy Damousi

Students of labour history in Australia have long been concerned with Australian political identities, but they have failed to address the problem of multiple identities. In this chapter I argue that current understandings of the nature of Australian political identities need to be reformulated in the light of insights from poststructuralist theory, and that when this is done the problem of multiple identities emerges clearly. The existing approaches have largely taken our understandings of political subjectivity, language and experience, and the role of these in the complex process of cultural production and identity, as unproblematic. Marilyn Lake (1994) and Peter Beilharz (1994) have alerted us to the potential value and importance of exploring the challenges of poststructuralist concepts such as subjectivity. A sustained analysis of this critique has emerged from a number of feminist historians, many of whom have adopted its main tenets, while sounding a caution about its method.

In this chapter, I wish to point to several categories that have emerged from these discussions which can enhance our understanding of issues at the heart of labour and social history: work, gender, class, ethnicity and, centrally for our preoccupations here, the construction of multiple political identities. Many contemporary feminist historians, however, stress the need for a shift from the base/superstructure model promoted by Marxism to that of analysing symbolisation and representation.

A shift to discussions of subjectivity, discourse and language allows us both to understand the specificity of 'Australianness' and to highlight the competing and contradictory discourses which construct it and its multilayered dimensions. Moving beyond the earlier focus on radical nationalist traditions which celebrated masculinist and white icons, the challenge is to explore the plurality, diversity and fragility of the meaning of 'Australianness'—to recognise that the construction of 'Australianness' is a process, formed and defined in relation to a range of discourses and related to constructions of subjectivity. Doing so allows us to identify the specificities and distinctiveness of the competing discourses which comprise 'Australianness'. What is at stake is our understanding of 'Australian' identity and the forces which come to shape and construct this identity.

From the outset, it is important to recall how and why the conventional orthodoxies come to be contested. It was precisely because of a dissatisfaction with the explanatory power of Marxist and socialist theories of difference—in terms of gender, sexuality and race, which could not be accommodated within its unitary framework—that historians, social theorists and political scientists began to critique existing labour history methodologies and expose the deficiencies of their theoretical apparatus. But the challenge of poststructuralist theory goes futher, especially in its feminist versions. For good reasons feminist historians more than most have appreciated the political significance of the death of the metanarrative, a shift to considering how language constructs rather than just reflects meaning, and the need to formulate more adequate accounts of agency and subjectivity. They have also questioned universalist explanations couched in terms of false consciousness and class hegemony. Such challenges to a gender- and ethnicity-blind Marxism have unsettled the complacency of labour historians and are changing the ways in which they understand 'culture', 'class', 'politics' and 'agency'.

HISTORICISING SUBJECTIVITY

'Subjectivity'—the way we make sense of ourselves and our understanding of ourselves in relation to the world around us—has been left untheorised in histories of Australian political culture. The ways in which political subjectivity within a specific time and place have come to be shaped are often characterised as static and fixed. In positing the question of *how* the political identities of men and women are constituted, and by looking at a *range* of categories, including ethnicity, masculinity, femininity and sexuality, we can then create a space where identities and categories are open to change. To ask these questions is to consider how and why historical actors have come to construct their Australian identity around a particular discourse, what it offers them, how it helps them make sense of their world and how this undergoes shifts and changes. The underlying assumption of this perspective is that language, which contains a range of discourses, shapes our subjectivity, our self, our identities. This perspective also assumes that subjectivity is unstable, never fixed but in process. It is always historically produced in specific discourses, and is never one single fixed structure. Masculine, feminine, ethnic and racial identities are constructed in this way: their meanings are historically constructed through particular discourses at particular times.

Part of the impetus to consider the ways in which Australian identity is historically constructed is to provide a different understanding of power and of the different ways men and women have negotiated power within society. A notion of the multiplicity of power, where power is situated in a range of 'sites', can liberate us from viewing power relations within a top-down model. Thus, considering the various sites of the power of patriarchy and capitalism allows us to re-conceptualise the ways in which men and women have negotiated and undermined asymmetrical power relations. Such an understanding can focus our attention on the range of sites for resistance—such as the body—and redefines the 'political' to include a range of ways in which 'the poor/oppressed/privileged' have negotiated and subverted power relations. This is not to say that the tools of former theories should be jettisoned entirely. Indeed, materialist frameworks and theories of the psyche remain central and inform the work of historians who have adopted some of the insights of poststructuralist theory (Walkowitz 1992; Roper 1994).

A focus on subjectivity can allow for change and transformation and a consideration of the multifaceted processes which construct our identity. Subjectivity is not an ahistorical, unchanging entity, and it demands that we consider how negotiations change over time, how categories which are used and the meanings attached to them are historically contingent. Discourses on communism, fascism, eugenics, motherhood, war, paid and unpaid work, crime, citizenship and nationhood can been analysed to come to some understanding of how such discourses gave meaning to men and women and inspired their practices.

This issue is important if we are to understand why it is that women, for instance, remain in political parties which relegate them secondary status, or how and why they adopt a particular political discourse which they perceive as empowering, such as citizenship and motherhood. In what ways have parties of the left and right appealed to women, and how have women negotiated this discourse to empower themselves? What different terms have been used by men to empower *themselves* and construct *their* masculine identity? In what ways have women's organisations such as the conservative Australian Women's National League appealed to women's political subjectivity?

LANGUAGE AND DISCOURSE

Discourse is central to the construction of political identities. Attention to language has long preoccupied historians of political culture, but the shift in recent theory has been from language *conveying* meaning to *constructing* meaning. This emphasis has profound implications for analysing language and speech. Judith Brett's study of Menzies' use of particular language is a brilliant example of such an analysis (Brett 1992). Within feminist history debates, this insight has been particularly salient. In labour history, feminist historians have highlighted the ways in which notions of 'worker', 'skill', 'work' and 'labour' have assumed a masculinist dimension which has served to exclude women's work, a feminist voice from the labour force, and devalued their contribution to political movements. Attention to the construction of meaning through language can suggest how particular terms and slogans have shaped the dynamics of gender, race and class relations (Frances 1993).

Language is also central to gendered identity. Ernie Lane, the Queensland socialist, recalled in his memoirs that the advent of the Industrial Workers of the World (IWW) organisation in Australia provided a 'badly needed energy in the direction of militant industrialism, which under the combined . . . influence of arbitration courts and labor politicians, had lost its . . . virility' (Lane 1939). The IWW was the most vocal about this. For them, arbitration and Labor parliamentarians emasculated the working class. Arbitration caused the loss of working-class initiative, self-reliance, industrial solidarity, and was synonymous with acquiescence and dependence. Under parliamentary socialism, the revolutionary spirit would be smothered in reforms and palliatives because Labor politicians were of 'wishy washy' character and 'timid'. An attention to language can reveal not only the way in which masculinity found its expression within the labour movement, but also how the ways in which masculinity was defined served to repress women.

EXPERIENCE

In many studies of activists in Australian politics, 'political' experience is often locked in a determinist and static model of how material conditions define and shape political consciousness. Experience is presented as neutral, giving one access to a 'truth'. But 'experience' can be interpreted in a variety of ways, and is open to a multitude of interpretations, just as the meaning of one's 'experience' changes over time.

Today we need to question unified and linear accounts of experience, identity and politics. A concern with how identities and experiences are variable over time can suggest ways in which they can be historicised. In studies of Australian labour history, and in feminist history, men and women in the public political arena have long been portrayed as without aggression, frustration, desire, pleasure, anger, envy or anxiety, despite the fact that we do not suddenly shed these layers of our selves in the forum of public politics (Lake 1994, p. 80). Yet it is crucial to explore these impulses—not in order to somehow discover people's true 'motives'—but to move towards a more adequate understanding of how thought, action and self are shaped within a particular historical and cultural context. Raymond Evans, for example, in considering one explanation for the public violence displayed by conservative women towards women anti-conscriptionists during the First World War, suggests that these women had lost sons in the war, and that these violent, brutal outbursts were the only legitimate way in which they could express their loss and grief in public (Evans 1995).

A consideration of language offers another strategy for analysis. We can examine, for example, the ways in which it constructs various identities. Thus, the sexual anxiety experienced by ruling-class men, including their fear of and fascination with convict women can be explored by unpacking the *meaning* of the terms they used to describe them—such as 'pollution' and 'abandonment' (Damousi 1995). Similarly, Rose Scott's use of language to describe male sexuality—the 'animal in man' (Allen 1988)—offers us a tantalising portrait of her sense of violation.

Australian labour historians have been slow to theorise 'experience'. The proliferation of biographical and autobiographical texts and oral testimonies are witness to the importance of these genres for extending our understanding of the 'experience' of political activists and how these actors interpret and conceptualise their involvement in political life. The ways in which memory constructs experience and meaning is an area not addressed in the histories which make use of these texts. While there is now an international literature which considers the processes by which political activists have remembered their past experiences—through categories of myth, fantasy, dream and the imaginary and how these categories serve to empower themselves—in much labour history political 'experience' remains a value-free and uncontested terrain. Moreover, the ways in which the narratives and meanings of political experience are constructed and shaped by a range of internal and external variables *over time* is often not considered by those attempting to make sense of how men and women have reconstructed their political participation.

Clearly, an attention to language, experience and subjectivity can help us to think about how political identities are comprised, and how they are specific to time and place. Once the foundations of labour history are challenged by these methodological shifts it will be impossible simply to retell the old stories. Poststructuralism reasserts the 'difference' of subjectivities and makes the monologue of old-style labour history impossible. But it goes further than this and questions any notion of a single political identity. It insists that we look for multiple Australian political identities and the contestation between them. In doing so, poststructuralism challenges legitimising one version of political identity over others. Today, we confront a new and challenging radical pluralism—and we do not know as yet what it will teach us. We can be certain that poststructural labour history will help us to create new definitions of Australianness, and so Australias which will be more reflexive and sensitive to difference than the prematurely unified, even hegemonic Australias of the past.

ACKNOWLEDGMENT

I wish to thank Georgine Clarsen, Katie Holmes, Stuart Macintyre and Robert Reynolds for their important and very useful comments on earlier versions of this chapter.

REFERENCES

Allen, J. 1988, '"Our deeply degraded sex" and the "Animal in man"': Rose Scott, feminism and sexuality 1890–1925', *Australian Feminist Studies*, 7 & 8.

Beilharz, P. 1994, 'Labour history and social history', in *Challenges to Labour History*, ed. T. Irving, New South Wales University Press, Sydney.

Brett, J. 1992, *Robert Menzies' Forgotten People*, Macmillan, Melbourne.

Damousi, J. 1995, ' "Depraved and disorderly": The sexuality of convict women', *Labour History*, no. 68, May.

Evans, R. 1995, '"All the passion of our womanhood": Margaret Thorp and the battle of the Brisbane School of Arts, July 1917', in *Gender and War*, eds J. Damousi & M. Lake, Cambridge University Press, Melbourne.

Frances, R. 1993, *The Politics of Work*, Cambridge University Press, Cambridge.

Lake, M. 1994, 'The construction of political subjectivity and the writing of labour history', in *Challenges to Labour History*, ed. T. Irving, NSW University Press, Sydney.

Lane, E. 1939, *Reminiscences of a Rebel*, William Brooks, Brisbane.

Roper, L. 1994, *Oedipus and the Devil: Witchcraft, Sexuality and Religion in Early Modern Europe*, Routledge, London.

Walkowitz, J. 1992, *City of Dreadful Delight: Sexual Narrative in Victorian England*, Virago, London.

9 The originality of ordinary lives

Janet McCalman

Australia is a nation of ordinary people. Yet colonised Australia had a tragic birth in genocide, and European 'civilisation' was installed on this continent by a collection of gaolers, adventurers and thieves. It was a dreadful beginning, but it was redeemed in part by the waves of controlled immigration which re-peopled the continent from the middle of the nineteenth century. The gold rush immigrants of the 1850s were notable for their literacy, their enterprise and their greed; the government-assisted immigrants who followed were 'ordinary people' who longed for the chance to live out their lives as respectable and respected ordinary people. They wanted a regular income, a home of their own, education for their children, the vote and to call no man master. In nineteenth-century Britain and Ireland that was a tall order.

Australia was shaped by the aspirations of the poor but honest, the unacknowledged respectables, the people of talent but no capital. All the nations which built on immigration between the 1850s and 1914 were privileged to receive hundreds of thousands of people desperate to better themselves. Many were clever, and they had powerful reasons for getting out of their homelands. Quite a few were exceptionally gifted but stricken with tuberculosis, and emigrated primarily for their health. It was a fearful decision to make, because few were ever to see their families again and many could not maintain relationships by correspondence (Fitzpatrick 1995; Serle 1963; Richards et al. 1989 and 1991). Others wanted to get away from the surveillance of the extended family, the village, the church and the street community. Such immigrant societies were therefore full of new citizens who needed to repress the past with its griefs and frustrations. Why else, apart from hiding the convict stain, did so many families not pass down family history? And the answer has to be because they did not want to talk about it. This denial, this deliberate forgetting of the past was possible because, for many, life was better in Australia than it had been in England, Scotland or Ireland.

Australia was thus colonised by people distrustful of sentiment and preoccupied with the business of making good now and in the future. Of course many immigrants did nowhere near as well as they had hoped, and some failed utterly, finishing their days as indigents, existing in boarding houses, huts and benevolent asylums. As for the success stories, while some became genuinely rich, most ended their days living off the rental income of small properties they had either built or purchased as an investment. As the cities and country towns expanded in the years between the 1870s and the mid-1930s, it was easier than in Britain for people of modest means to become property owners and landlords. The houses were more often than not dark, damp and cramped, and their owners almost as poor as their tenants, but it was a society where ordinary people had a realistic hope of home ownership and personal equity. With the help of government in the 1950s and 1960s, Australians became a nation of home-owners almost without parallel. Working-class people moved out of the decaying inner city and built homes of their own in unmade streets and with septic tanks. There was space for children to play and the washing to dry. There were bathrooms inside, there were no rats and fleas, the stove turned on at a switch and there was hot water on tap (McCalman 1984 & 1988).

Of course, it is now possible to remember the slums fondly—the intimacy and caring, the fun and unpretentiousness—but we do the past and posterity a disservice if we overdo it. Poverty has always been awful—anxious, painful, relentless. Poor people die earlier than rich people, they lose more of their children to disease, they get sicker and for longer, they even enjoy less opportunity for carefree and private sex. If the neighbourliness is hankered after, people have forgotten what it is like listening to the neighbours' love life and rows and childbirth through thin party walls. And they have forgotten how oppressive it is to have everyone know everything about you and poking their noses into everything you do. Yet there is very little to do when you are poor: you cannot afford to go out (many poor Australians before the 1940s were deprived even of basic pleasures such as listening to music). You necessarily find your entertainment and interest in life in the activities and fortunes of others, sometimes at their expense. Melbourne District Nursing Society midwives rarely had difficulty finding the homes of women in labour on even the darkest night, because of the knot of neighbours 'listening in' out on the street, while inside the house not only close relatives, but also the self-appointed lay midwives and assistants were installed in the kitchen. The 'slum' nostalgia, the fantasy that life was somehow more human and socially virtuous back then in the 'Struggletowns', speaks more of the present need to alleviate class stigma than it does of past realities. Poverty brings crime, violence, drunkenness and waste. It is grim, cold, grubby and smelly and, even though one day the poor may inherit the earth, we must not allow nostalgia to blind us to its evils.

The escape to the suburbs in the 1950s, to a home of your own on a quarter-acre block, was in truth like entering heaven before your time. A space of one's own made private life and individual pursuits possible on a new scale: it provided the space to be original. And it was then that the dreams of all those poor but respectable immigrants of the past hundred years were realised across the nation. This was an immense national achievement, yet Australian intellectuals have had considerable difficulty coming to terms with our suburban national identities, in recognising their long history and their quality and significance. And at present these identities have become a postmodernist plaything.

The problem with the postmodernist project on Australian culture and identities is that it is intertwined with the baby boom legend. And since the baby boom legend has been created by the baby boomers themselves, it is inevitably psychologically regressive. The 'suburbia' of the baby boomers sprang to life in the 1950s, *sans* history, *sans* class, *sans* chic. Picture it: it is a place of safety and predictability, and its tropes are 'backyards' (Melbourne), 'the beach' (Sydney), 'Hill's hoists', 'Mum's in the kitchen', 'Dad's in the toolshed', Grandma's still in the inner suburbs (where real life goes on). Mr Menzies is in Canberra, the Reds have been chased out from under the beds, and all's well etc.

This is, of course, a child's view—the remembered world as seen from the sandpit, of legs and car wheels and vegetables and wood shavings, all impressed with the sameness imposed on the perceptions of an innocent. For one of the pleasures of living in the suburbs after growing up in the 'slums' was that parents and children had the space for privacy, and the grown-ups could keep the serious things from the kids—there would be 'time enough later' for 'problems' and dissonance. Meanwhile they were to get on with childish things, work hard at school and bathe in the love and security that difficult times, war and emotional repression had denied the children of generations before. Lurline Keck came from a loving home, but she can never remember sitting on her mother's knee 'having a cuddle': 'my mother wasn't at all demonstrative'. And so when Lurline came to have her own babies in the 1950s she gave them all the open affection she had once craved as a child. This is the stuff of suburban life, the affective universe of the individual and the communal context of private life. And it is here that we come to appreciate the 'originality' of ordinary people.

But it seems that some Australian intellectuals still have problems comprehending this. Part of the trouble is that much of the agenda was set in the 1950s by disaffected left-wing intellectuals who had much to fear. I know of this because I am a child of the middle-class left and there were books on my parents' shelves which were not to be found on those of our neighbours in upper working-class and lower middle-class, 'wowserish, Bible-bashing' Box Hill of the 1950s. I was sufficiently innocent to welcome the new Baptist minister's wife by announcing that she and her husband must come in for a beer some time. My parents laughed over that for years, but my mother was angry when I wanted to take the first grown-up book that I'd read to show my teacher: it was A.S. Makarenko's *The Road to Life*, and it had beautiful sepia photographs of Soviet orphans of the revolution with shaven heads. It was just a year after the Soviet invasion of Hungary, but I was too young to understand that my parents were both frightened and ashamed. I remember very clearly the first time that I saw Edna Everage and Sandy Stone. It was at the New Theatre in Melbourne, where my parents had met just after the war. Humphries' monologues became an obsession in my family, and when the records came out, we learnt them off by heart—at ten I could do it all: 'Dear Beryl, by the time this letter reaches you, you will be in the Old Country. I went to the RSL the other night and had a very nice night's entertainment . . . ' We savoured every swipe at sand-blasted doors, duck-egg blue and Royal Purple Para. As Humphries became more vicious and misogynist, right-wing and rich, we went off him a bit, but it was impossible to deny his comic genius. Our passion for him, we Labor-voting, wine-drinking, smelly-cheese-eating and bush-ballad-singing suburbanites, living in houses with low-pitched roofs and Stegbar windows, was born of frustration. We were radicals and democrats, yet we shrieked with laughter at what Robin Boyd dubbed 'featurism', the 'originality of ordinary Australians'. We did so because they had ignored us.

The middle-class left was a product of the Depression and the Second World War. Its members were very different from their fathers, who had returned from the 'war to end all wars' drained of all idealism, anxious only to slip into hearth and home and hard work, hoping the nightmares might recede in time. The brave young men and women who had visions of a better and safer world by 1945 wanted to do it differently from their fathers and mothers. Many were 'youthful hearts in life delighting', who 'learned to face life's battles' in church schools inspired by a vigorous, sometimes radical Christianity where they were enjoined to lead serious lives of service to mankind. Others were high-school scholars, made proud of their sense of service by teachers who resented any imputation that a secular state education produced a morally inferior citizen. Many of the returning youth became secular Christians, drawn to the missionary life—and they could be missionaries at home, bringing enlightenment, rational planning, good books, classical music, kindergartens, personal cleanliness, birth control, order and social justice to a refashioned Australia. Except that the people had turned on them by 1949 and succumbed to the charm of Mr Menzies' nice speaking voice. (We remain very much in their debt, nonetheless, for their ideals were right, but it was not until the Whitlam Government that they were able to place their stamp on the institutions and practices of Australian society.)

In the early 1950s members of the left were frightened, and with good reason, because if the Communist Party Dissolution Bill had passed many innocent people would have been ruined, even gaoled. They were thus culturally and politically marginalised. Yet they burned with a passion to lead and change the world, and so they became—inevitably and understandably—cultural snobs while the subjects of their mission wallowed in false consciousness. This argument is scarcely original. Alan Gilbert has written brilliantly of the middle-class left's alienation in the suburbs and the impulses in their anti-suburbanism (Gilbert 1988). Hugh Stretton also has been one of the few intellectuals to defend the suburbs as legitimate places of personal freedom and expression (Stretton 1970).

The world of our neighbours in Box Hill of the 1950s and 1960s, if it appeared ordinary, was far from trivial. They lived a rich life, mostly centred around their churches, but there were choirs and singing groups, a horticultural society, the Country Women's Association and the Friendly Circle. There were the Masons, the Scouts and the Guides, even political party branches. And I know that when they prayed in the Church of Christ or the Salvation Army halls or the Baptist, Methodist, or Presbyterian churches (it was a very Protestant place), God was there and real for them. Home improvements and gardening were a passion, and they could be very kind and neighbourly. Yet they were often intolerant and fearful of sin and difference, and difference above all was defined by religion and ethnicity. If Australia as a nation of immigrants was built on multiple identities, it is important to acknowledge the inevitable conflicts. In suburbs like mine in the 1950s, Catholics were a race apart from Protestants. The local department store and first supermarket would employ no convent girls, no matter how ladylike they might have been. Catholics had big families, ate fish on Fridays, drank, gambled, slavishly obeyed their ranting priests, went to different schools, wore scruffy blue uniforms and suffocated in classes of 70 where many could not speak English. Protestants, on the other hand, to a Catholic, were 'full of sin', and if they were in the Labor Party or in a union, were probably secret communists. If the communists ever took over, the nuns would be marched naked down the main street and raped in public. Few families had friends of 'the other faith' and the many who had unfortunate relatives in 'mixed marriages' either pursed their lips or covered it up. Judith Brett, growing up in the outer eastern suburbs of Melbourne, can remember the church denomination of every child in her state school class, because 'your church' was almost as important a signifier as your name.

The discourse about 'suburbia' goes back at least to the 1860s in England and to the 1870s in Australia, and it has always been complicated by distaste for the 'bourgeoisie', whatever that may be. The word itself has become a term of abuse, and no matter what the bourgeoisie do, they get it wrong. And when the working class move out of their 'slums' and into houses in the garden suburbs, they are despaired of for having become bourgeois also. But what is wrong with that? Must they remain in poverty to provide a life purpose for the missionaries of the middle-class left? Can they not too have warm, dry and roomy homes with gardens and cars in the carport? Cannot they and their children make more money and rise in the world? What the critics forget is that the labour movement and its political wing both here and in Britain were the work of men and women who were both working class and respectable. They wanted the financial security to be able to become more respectable and they wanted that because it made their private lives healthier and happier. And it liberated them from class stigma. Respectability in the suburbs betokened full citizenship and dignity. Oscar Comettant, while unable to resist some Gallic irony as he surveyed the 'suburbia' of Marvellous Melbourne a century ago, did also sense its satisfactions:

> It is a pleasure to see the railway trains leaving at short intervals every evening, all filled with husbands returning to stay with their wives and children until the next morning when their work in the city recalls them. In their pretty, well-furnished houses, each with its flower garden, large or small, the heads of families enjoy their rest (so beneficial to mind and body) in an atmosphere of sincere and sweet affection. They forget their

> disappointments and renew their strength for the morrow's struggles. The out-of-town family house is a sanctuary of pure joy, a respite from all the troubles, preoccupations, worries and sadnesses of which life is woven (Comettant 1890).

If art depends on conflict, problems and tragedy, good health and private happiness thrive on order, security and warmth. Do we truly want people to lead difficult lives in order that we may find them more interesting?

In fact the quiet suburban life has been the stem culture in Australia for almost a century and a half, and in thinking and writing about it we should concentrate on its virtues as much as its vices. Until the late 1960s middle Australia was a society of active sunday school attenders, and nominal Protestant church members and obedient Catholic practitioners. A great deal of daily life in families and even in workplaces centred around trying to be good. Goodness was different from prudishness. Goodness did not need to be puritanical or intolerant; goodness meant kindness and consideration for others. It meant probity and truthfulness, but it did not preclude 'white lies' to protect the feelings of someone who was vulnerable. It was not rigid and judgmental; on the contrary, its flexible humaneness gave it far greater force in the life of the individual than did any carping wowserism. It was secular Christianity in practice or common decency, and it held society together. People believed they should avoid conflict, dissent and all such unpleasantness, some to a pathological degree. There were unhappy families where a voice was never raised in anger, but there were even fewer explosive ones. In fact it was 'foreigners' who shamelessly expressed their feelings 'outside the home' or who screamed in childbirth while their Australian-born middle-class sisters demanded chloroform and their working-class sisters swore.

If suburbia was a world of lowered voices, the stress of poverty sometimes made the inner suburbs a world of raised ones: medical students from the Women's Hospital conducting home births in the 1920s and 1930s were shocked not just by the extremity of Melbourne poverty, but also by the affective harshness of some rougher families. T.L. Tyrer was called to the Burnley home of a mother of eight in the early 1920s:

> Was met by a woman carrying two poodles—Sister had not arrived so I was escorted into room with large double bed and a cot in which a small infant alternately slept and woke to cry 'Mummy'—to this remark 'mummy' would cleverly reply 'Shut up you little devil' (Royal Women's Hospital Archives).

This became the litany of the birth which all too rapidly followed.

If the lowered voices of the suburbs sometimes concealed hypocrisy, we should still not deny their originality. (People took very seriously the duty to be kind, to speak well of others and to avoid causing pain by word or deed.) But daily life was also different from today in the constancy of human company. One of the most important transformations of private life this century has been the rise of solitariness. More people of all classes and ages live alone than ever before. This has not necessarily been thrust upon individuals. In fact most have deliberately chosen to live alone. As people have become better off, they have sought more privacy and solitude. They may still be lonely, but they prefer that loneliness to living with someone who is not right for them—just anyone will not do. But until the 1960s most unattached working-class adults had a friend, relative or boarder living with them. In employment also people worked all the time in groups and they found their greatest entertainment in the company of others—family, friends, workmates and neighbours. It was a world of talk before television and universal electric light. If some had the space and lighting to retreat into the private realm of reading, many others had conversation and cards as their home pastimes, and the pub, the theatre, the cinema and dancing for their outside ones. Life was easier if families and friends could be nice to each other. The most loved and respected in a community were the kindly ones, who did things for others unasked, who were brave and uncomplaining, who were straight and true.

And if we look closely at that world of private social virtue among ordinary Australians we find it was rich and complex. This was a world full of variety and to depict it as a monoculture, to focus on its alleged conformism, is to get it quite wrong.

It is also to fail to recognise its true originality. Ordinary life everywhere is dominated by the great universals of human existence, but people have to cope with challenges and difficulties thrust upon them by the particularities of history. By the outbreak of the Second World War, white Australia, from a multicultural new society, had become outwardly a xenophobic and sectarian one. Race thinking was every man and woman's anthropology until the Holocaust revealed racism to be the evil it really is. After the war, urban Australians, especially the poorest ones, found their local worlds overrun by strange people speaking strange languages. What is utterly remarkable is how smoothly this country has again become a multicultural one. Yes, we are still racist, especially towards indigenous people, but we are better than we were. As frightening as the 1996 federal election was in

Queensland and Western Australia, both major parties distanced themselves from the white backlash. And in other parts of Australia, there have been signs of hope and progress. In working-class Melbourne, in the electorates where old Australians have Vietnamese neighbours and their children Vietnamese school mates and their teenagers Vietnamese friends in the dole queues, the racist immigration reform candidates lost their deposits. Millions of ordinary Australians have learnt to change their ideas and feelings, to tolerate difference, to recognise their common humanity with people from other cultures. For all our present faults, we are still doing better than anyone would have predicted in 1950.

And that change has come from ordinary Australians thinking for themselves, permitting their kindness and neighbourliness to overcome fear and ignorance. In Struggletown there were many who said: 'Oh I don't like all the Greeks coming here, but the lady next door, she's lovely.' People make terrible jokes about 'ethnics', but they do so to their faces and they are mates. Intolerance has crumbled under the deep kindness, the humour and the egalitarianism of ordinary Australians. This is not something taught them by the educated, their moral instructors, because for a long time these instructors—priests and parsons, teachers, politicians, bosses, doctors, and intellectuals—taught them religious intolerance, the white man's burden, the moral mission of superior womanhood, the glory of war, the right to authority of the already rich and powerful. To quietly reject these lessons has been in fact the originality of ordinary Australians.

REFERENCES

Comettant, O. 1980 [1890], *In the Land of Kangaroos and Goldmines*, trans. J. Armstrong, Wakefield Press, Adelaide (Paris).

Fitzpatrick, D. 1995, *Oceans of Consolation, Personal Accounts of Irish Migration to Australia*, Melbourne University Press, Melbourne.

Gilbert, A. 1988, 'The roots of Australian anti-suburbanism' in *Australian Cultural History*, eds S.L. Goldberg & F.B. Smith, Cambridge University Press, Melbourne.

McCalman, J. 1984 & 1988, *Struggletown: Public and Private Life in Richmond, 1900–1965*, Melbourne University Press, Melbourne.

—— 1993, *Journeyings: the Biography of a Middle-class Generation, 1920–1930*, Melbourne University Press, Melbourne.

Richards, E., Reid, R. & Fitzpatrick, D. 1989 & 1991, *Visible Immigrants*, vv. II, Department of History and Centre for Immigration and Multicultural Studies, Research School of Social Sciences, Australian National University, Canberra.

Royal Women's Hospital Archives, Melbourne Extern Delivery Books, 1920–1935, (closed collection).

Serle, G. 1963, *The Golden Age*, Melbourne University Press, Melbourne.
Stretton, H. 1970, *Ideas for Australian Cities*, Georgian House, Melbourne.

10 Feminists creating citizens

Marilyn Lake

Feminists today are among the most creative interpreters of citizenship, often unaware, however, that they are but the most recent voices in a tradition of political engagement that goes back to the early years of the Commonwealth. It is not surprising that in the first decades of the twentieth century, in the masculine, homo-social world that was Australia, feminists embarked on a grand affair with the state. In the new world that Australian feminists intended to make their own, the state's power and resources would be harnessed to provide for the security and independence of women citizens: that was the vision. The idea was that the state would provide a buffer between men and women, its agency invoked to protect and empower otherwise defenceless women against tyrannical, too powerful men. Feminism drew on liberal and socialist ideas as well as distinctive feminist traditions. In this little-known chapter in the history of women's political thought, feminists were able to effect a radical intervention in the public discourse on citizenship in a bid to make it work specifically for women.

Attention to the history of women's political thought highlights the multiplicity of citizenship traditions in this country. Feminists were innovative in drawing attention to the implications of the citizen being both a relational and individual self, and revolutionary in their equation of individuality with sexual inviolability. Masculine engagements with citizenship have, by contrast, tended to focus on ways to substantiate their rights as public men—the right to a basic wage, the right to trade union representation, the right to work, the right to unemployment benefits. In his recent discussion of Australian traditions of citizenship, Peter Beilharz refers only to those versions associated with T.H. Marshall, Walter Murdoch and the labour movement in Australia, where 'industrial citizenship came to be substituted for social citizenship . . . Workers were identified as citizens, citizens as workers' (Beilharz 1993, p. 113).

For modern Western men, citizenship has been a status pertaining to the rights and obligations of the public domain: it was a condition that rested on, indeed only made sense in terms of, a distinction between the public and private spheres, between the worlds of civil society and domestic, familial relations. As feminist scholars have noted, public man or the active citizen was freed from the demands of the private sphere because slaves or women have attended to his domestic affairs. Furthermore, in directing our attention to specifically political or civil equalities, a concentration on 'citizenship' has helped obscure the political nature of relations in the home. In using citizenship precisely to *highlight* what went on in the home, the first Australian women citizens proved a disruptive force in the polity. In using the public status of citizenship to challenge the personal tyrannies of men, their intervention marks a radical departure in the history of Australian political thought, anticipating by several decades the discovery by later generations of feminists that the personal was also political.

In world terms, Australian feminists had a head start in exploring the implications of citizenship for women. From 1902, the newly enfranchised women of Australia announced the arrival of the 'woman citizen' onto the social and political stage. Granted full political rights some twenty years before women in Britain and the United States, Australian activists spent those decades formulating a multifaceted program to achieve the moral, economic and physical independence associated with the status of citizenship. Their energies no longer required in campaigns for basic political rights, Australian feminists mobilised in the Australian Federation of Women Voters, the Women's Service Guild, the United Associations of Women, for example, to achieve a more secure and thus free nation-state for women—in the words of leading campaigner Bessie Rischbieth, 'the sort of civilisation women of all countries dream about' (Lake 1994).

Carole Pateman has pointed to the ways in which the fraternal social contract of Western democracies has rested on a sexual contract that secured men's power over and access to women in the private sphere—the 'law of male sex right' (Pateman 1988). Thus, the articulation of men's 'rights' was often accompanied by an explicit opposition to any state interference in the 'private' domain. Men have jealously guarded the privacy of the private sphere, a response that has worked to protect from scrutiny the major sites for the oppression of women: home and family. Thus did New South Wales Labor men in the 1940s object to feminist campaigns to award wives ownership of household savings on the grounds that the government should 'keep out of the domestic life of citizens'.[1]

Australian feminists invoked their status as citizens to promote a different understanding of rights and obligations, an understanding that centred on citizens' simultaneous rights to personal liberty and the duty of care. They were innovative in attempting to address the seeming tension in citizenship between the right to independence and the obligations of human interdependence, and in devising an original political program that spoke to this tension. Their interpretation of citizenship rights departed in significant ways from the masculine conceptions of rights, whether political, civil or social that prevailed in the West. Unlike women, Western men have rarely been moved to articulate rights to be free from bodily violation, from sexual degradation and harassment or personal dependence and tyranny. Nor have they demanded an end to the double moral standard. Men have rather demanded the rights which would enable them to participate in the public world—the right to work, a basic wage and unemployment benefits, the right to free speech and public assembly, the right to form trade unions and political parties. As feminist scholars have noted, the primacy traditionally given to civil and political rights by Western international lawyers and philosophers is directed toward protection for men within their public life in the context of their relationship with government (Charlesworth 1994, p. 60). Rights have been defined by the criterion of what men fear will happen to them, especially by public man's dread of exile from public life (Benton 1991, p. 156). In this framework, the distinction often drawn by masculine theorists between 'first generation' civil and political rights and 'second generation' social rights is not such a significant distinction, for both sets of rights were considered necessary to facilitate the engagements of public man. Feminists have, of course, shared with men an interest in the rights to work and to public office, but they have also been moved by different dreams, as Bessie Rischbieth suggested to veteran American suffragist Carrie Chapman Catt in 1924.

Challenging the public/private distinction by bringing 'rights discourse' into the private sphere was precisely the project pioneered by Australian feminists in the first decades of this century. Australian feminists deployed their citizenship status to bring about a revolutionary transformation of personal relations between men and women in the private sphere of home and family. In proposals for motherhood endowment as a state income to secure women's independence from men, Australian activists went much further than their overseas counterparts in pursuing the radical logic of their claim. Arguing for a minimum income as the 'individual right' of all women and men, Labor activist Muriel Heagney, writing in *Labor Call* in 1923, argued that state provision of motherhood and childhood endowment would bring about a 'revolutionary change in the relations of husband and wife' (Lake 1992, p. 11). Faced with the same ideas from a wide range of women at the 1927 royal commission appointed to enquire into the feasibility of motherhood and childhood endowment for women, astonished commissioners were moved to ask witness Irene Longman, of the Queensland branch of the National Council of Women—who had urged that women be treated as 'independent economic units'—whether she really meant that wives should be enabled 'to live apart from their husbands'. That, they observed, would mean 'an alteration to existing conditions'. 'Yes', replied Longman triumphantly, 'absolutely, it is revolutionary and that is what we wish' (Lake 1992, p. 19).

Needing to conceptualise the meaning of citizenship for women, Australian feminists imagined it as a condition of personal inviolability and self-determination. In appropriating citizenship as their own, they politicised the personal in new ways, challenging their contemporaries to see marriage as a relationship akin to feudal bondage. The 'bond of marriage', advised Mrs R.R. Doyle, in a radio broadcast on behalf of the United Associations of Women in 1943, was the only 'legal bondage' still in existence.[2] Feminist citizens formulated new demands on the state so that they might better be able to refuse the insistent demands of men. Women, they held, should be mistresses of themselves.

In particular women citizens demanded, first, that the state pass legislation to protect women and girls from men's 'seduction' (by raising the age of consent, for example) and provide for the appointment of women to public offices so that women need never fall into men's hands. During the first two decades of the century, feminists counted among their best achievements the appointment of women to a range of public positions as doctors, factory or hygiene inspectors, gaol warders and police officers. Appointments to such positions were not conceptualised as a matter of equal opportunity, but rather as an extension of care and protection to the vulnerable.

Most feminist citizenship organisations included the attainment of an 'equal moral standard' as a leading goal, meaning that men should be encouraged to become as sexually restrained as women needed to be. For men to impose themselves on women, in marriage or outside, made a mockery of women's status as inviolable citizens. Feminists also demanded that all women be provided with an independent income so that they they would not be forced into a degrading dependence on men, whether as prostitutes or as wives. Without an independent income, women lacked the capacity for self-determination: women who depended on men, observed Labor activist Jean Daley, 'moulded themselves to his desire' (Lake 1992, p. 14). If they entered the labour market women should be awarded equal pay, and if at home caring for children, their work should be recognised with the payment of motherhood endowment by the state. Without an independent income women were forced into 'sex slavery' of one kind or another. Women felt their lack of freedom most keenly at the personal level.

Thus was the state called upon to make good women's citizenship status, to fulfil the promise that women would henceforth enjoy the condition of self-governing, self-possessing individuals. As their campaign unfolded, it soon became clear, however, that such a status for women was incompatible with men's conjugal rights—their assumed citizen rights to the sexual and domestic services of women. So, for example, E.H. Barker, general secretary of the West Australian branch of the Labor party, was moved to insist in evidence to the 1927 royal commission that it was unacceptable to grant mothers an independent income from the state, 'for the simple reason that the wife is necessary to keep the husband working . . . a man cannot work if he has not someone to look after him' (Lake 1992, pp. 19–20). It often seems to be the case, as Sarah Benton has written, that because of the different ways in which men and women have defined freedom, 'men and women constitute continuous threats against each other's freedoms' (Benton 1991, p. 160).

As the new feminist citizens continued to argue their case for an independent income before the 1927 royal commission, the incompatibility between men's and women's claims on citizenship emerged as a major theme of the proceedings. Women citizens had rights as 'individuals'. Speaking in favour of the proposal for motherhood and childhood endowment, Lena Lynch, secretary of the Women's Central Organising Committee of the Labor Party in New South Wales, pointed out that the institution of the family wage, paid to the man, did not recognise women 'as individuals at all, they are just appendages to men. This endowment recognises the women citizens and the child.' But the right of the woman citizen to an individual income and the principle of equal pay seemed to strike at men's right to be cared for by women. Royal commissioner and Labor man (and future prime minister) John Curtin defended the higher wage paid to men because it included 'a sort of payment for her domestic services'. Married or not, men needed these services, 'that is to say the mending of his apparel, the cleaning of his room, and the housekeeping services'. A man also had to pay for his 'recreation and his leisure'.[3]

In this Australian debate on the rights and obligations of citizens, men's entitlement to leisure and recreation was represented as an important civil right: the right, as H.E. Boote, editor of the *Australian Worker*, put it, to a certain standard of enjoyment. Forms of amusement such as drinking, smoking, going to theatres and picture shows were posited as every Australian man's right. But an active engagement in leisure pursuits could even/also be conceptualised as a citizen's duty. Thus, 'the single man who sets the standard of enjoyment in this country is rendering a valuable service to the State'. There was therefore no justification for reducing his income to provide a living wage for women. Yet Jessie Street, member of the Sydney Feminist Club, made precisely that argument. Impressed by 'the enormous amount spent on amusements, liquor and drink' in Australia, she suggested to the royal commissioners that this spending was directly at the expense of women and children, who were refused an income of their own. Street's position was that the basic wage had to be fixed for the individual, 'irrespective of sex and irrespective of social responsibilities' (Lake 1992, p. 21).

While feminists called for the intervention of an Act of Parliament to redistribute the national income so that women would no longer be dependent on men, to transfer money from the wallet to the purse, male witnesses and the royal commissioners themselves constantly voiced misgivings and resentment at the 'interference' with men's freedom which was implied. Recognition of women's citizen rights to economic independence and equality was read as a diminishment of men. Labor women sought to assuage men's anxieties. Lena Lynch put the case for women's economic independence. 'Does that mean that husband and wife are at opposite ends of a board', asked one royal commissioner, 'so that if one goes up the other comes down?'.

'Not necessarily', she replied, 'under this system they would be equal, they would be partners'.

Non-party feminists, feeling no obligation to attend to masculine insecurities, were less conciliatory. Asked if the family group would be divided by the payment of motherhood endowment, Irene Longman agreed it might, but it would be 'better and fairer'—and in any case if there were friction between husband and wife it would be better for them to live apart. Asked if motherhood endowment would render the wife better off and the husband worse off, Longman replied without hesitation, 'Yes'.

To feminists such as Irene Longman and Jessie Street the situation was straightforward. Single women and married women without dependent children could join the paid workforce where they should receive equal pay. Mothers were in a more difficult position, but as citizens they performed a 'service to the state' and as citizens they were owed proper remuneration. The implications of these ideas proved deeply disturbing to male authorities and, not surprisingly, they were rejected by the royal commissioners and never adopted by either political party or any government. As the Majority Report of the royal commission put it, if such proposals were implemented 'a very powerful solvent' would be introduced into 'family life as we know it'. Women's admission to the status of citizenship was never intended to disrupt the foundational sexual contract between man and woman by setting in its place a new contract between woman and the state, whereby woman could feel 'justified in looking [to the state] for sustenance and reward while she is doing the state's work'. The institution of the family wage maintained the majority of women in a state of economic and personal dependence on men.

The contradiction between this condition of personal dependence and citizenship's promise of individual liberty was feminism's abiding preoccupation during the post-suffrage decades in Australia, a preoccupation that focused on the anomalous position of the wife in a modern polity. It generated an original and far-reaching political program, expressed in the three interrelated goals of equal pay, motherhood endowment and child endowment (Lake 1993b). Current feminist concern with the position of women in the home has focused on the prevalence of domestic violence and the unfair distribution of child care and domestic work. Women are considered to be oppressed by the persistence of the sexual division of labour and their vulnerability to sexual violence. In earlier decades, feminist activism focused on women's economic independence and sexual subjection and the two were assumed to be interrelated: lack of an independent income reduced women to the condition of 'sex slaves', 'mere outlets for the sexual impulses and alleged needs of men' (Lake 1993a, p. 381). 'Degradation' was thus the term commonly applied to women's condition, not 'oppression' or even 'exploitation'. Women's experience of personal debasement, especially in marriage, was at odds with their elevated status as citizens. That women citizens were forced to be suppliants of their husbands was thought to be especially demeaning. Men could refuse even the smallest request. 'To know that the average housewife', said Muriel Cheyne in a radio broadcast in 1938, 'has such a sword of Damocles hanging over her lessens the effect of those who preach so fervently of the "Liberty of the Individual" '.[4] The extent of women's humiliating personal dependence was emphasised again and again. Jessie Street, later as president of the United Association of Women (UAW) again speaking in a radio broadcast, hammered home their state of legal and practical subjection:

> She is not entitiled to any money, for housekeeping or any other purpose. The husband may order all the supplies for the house himself. Indeed he may even order and buy his wife's clothes and she has no legal cause for complaint. So long as he houses, clothes and feeds her at a standard in keeping with his income he need not give her a penny piece and she can do nothing whatever about it . . . She is not entitled to any money whatsoever for any purpose whatsoever.[5]

Throughout the 1930s and 1940s feminist citizen organisations proposed numerous schemes to povide women, especially married women at home, with an income. The UAW issued a series of pamphlets, the first of which was called 'Income for Wives: How It Can Be Managed or the Economic Independence of the Married Woman'.

Feminists also campaigned for citizenship rights for Aboriginal women in these years on precisely the same understanding—that it was their lack of economic independence that rendered them especially vulnerable to sexual abuse and systematic degradation. Rejecting the popular stereotype that portrayed Aboriginal women as naturally lascivious and promiscuous, reformers such as Mary Bennett and Edith Jones insisted that they, like white women, had an 'instinctive passion for purity'. 'The women intrinsically are fine', said Bennett 'and ready for a position of respect and independence'. They were, she further asserted, 'the most magnificent citizens that any country could desire' (Lake 1993a, p. 382; Paisley 1995). When Aboriginal women themselves petitioned in the 1930s for citizen rights, they asked for their personal freedom and in particular for the 'chance to marry a man of our choice' (Lake 1993a, p. 384).

What distinguished Australian feminist interpretations of the meaning and implications of citizenship was precisely that the specificity of women's experience—their experience as sexed embodied citizens—was its starting point. From the beginning post-suffrage activists insisted that a true equality of citizenship necessitated state intervention in the private sphere to address and redress the power relations between men and women. Rejecting the offer to be wives of men, they chose instead to be consorts of the state, or 'femocrats', as they would come to be known. In the early post-suffrage decades, feminist activists redefined the citizen's right of individuality as a condition of inviolability, bodily integrity and the right not only to self-government but also to personal respect. Feminists sought to enlist the power and the resources of the state to enable women to stand up to the power of men. To claim that this alliance with the state simply exchanged one form of dependence for another was to miss the point: citizen women could not be required to sleep with the state, nor trade in their bodily integrity, their personality or their self-respect.

The feminist strategy conceptualised citizens' individual rights in radical new ways, but without neglecting citizens' collective responsibilities. The figure of 'the mother' in the discourse on maternal citizenship was of key strategic importance in linking the assertion of rights to the assumption of responsibility. Central to their project was the insistence on the duty of citizens to protect and care for the more vulnerable, helpless members of the community—hence the campaigns for temperance, censorship of films and books, raising the age of consent, and the state provision of infant and maternal welfare. The policy of motherhood endowment had such a powerful appeal to women across classes and political parties because it seemed to combine the promise of personal independence with recognition of the importance of relationships and responsibilities to others. It was an interpretation of citizenship rights and responsibilities that spoke to women's desire for self-determination, but at the same time addressed the importance of women's connections with others.

Motherhood endowment as a citizen entitlement was supported by women of otherwise opposed party and class allegiances. Under the headline 'Labor women join hands with feminists', the Sydney *Labor Daily* acclaimed that this 'co-operation of women . . . in praiseworthy terms is the work of the Feminist Club spoken of by Labor women, who express their readiness to co-operate and assist in bringing about the reality of motherhood endowment'.[6] This unity of women in politics was matched, however, by the more powerful solidarity of men who ensured that this scheme for women's economic independence would never be introduced.

The campaign for motherhood endowment reinforced the sexual division of labour and a sexually differentiated conception of citizenship which is no longer an appropriate strategy to secure women equality as citizens. Nonetheless it expressed a yearning to reconcile activities and aspects of the self that citizenship has traditionally set apart. This yearning has also been voiced by Aboriginal women thinking about what citizenship might mean to them. Defining some of the ways that Aboriginal values can contribute to a rethinking of citizenship, Linda Burney points to the importance of belonging to the land, having a local identity and the Aboriginal sense of community and interdependence: 'Citizenship must be about belonging' (Burney 1994, p. 22). In thinking about the possible meanings of citizenship for Australians today, about ways of reconciling rights with responsibilites, individuality with belonging, contemporary debates must be enriched by drawing on the multiplicity of ways in which citizenship has been imagined so far.

NOTES

1 Newsclipping, *Sun* 1947, 9 Oct., ML MS 2160/Y791, United Association of Women papers, Mitchell Library, State Library of NSW.
2 Doyle, R.R. 1943, radio broadcast, April, MS ML 2160/Y791, United Association of Women papers, Mitchell Library, State Library of NSW.
3 Royal Commission into Childhood and Family Allowances Minutes of Evidence 1929, *Australian Parliamentary Papers*, p. 915.
4 Cheyne, M. c.1938, 'The fruit of her hands' radio broadcast, ML MS 2160/Y791, United Association of Women papers, Mitchell Library, State Library of NSW.
5 Street, J. 1936, radio broadcast, 1 November, MS 2683/3/641–3, National Library of Australia.
6 *Labor Daily* 25 January 1924, p. 9.

REFERENCES

Beilharz, P. 1993, 'Republicanism and citizenship', in *The Republicanism Debate*, eds W. Hudson & D. Carter, NSW University Press, Sydney.
Benton, S. 1991, 'Gender, sexuality and citizenship', in *Citizenship*, ed. G. Andrews, Lawrence & Wishart, London.
Burney, L. 1994, 'An Aboriginal way of being Australian', *Australian Feminist Studies*, no. 19.
Charlesworth, H. 1994, 'What are "Women's international human rights"?', in *Human Rights of Women National and International Perspectives*, ed. R.J. Cook, University of Pennsylvania Press, Philadelphia.
Lake, M. 1992, 'The independence of women and the brotherhood of man', *Labour History*, vol. 63, November.
Lake, M. 1993a, 'Colonised and colonising: The white Australian feminist subject', *Women's History Review*, vol. 2, no. 3.
—— 1993b, "A revolution in the family: The challenge and contradiction of maternal citizenship', in *Mothers of a New World: Maternalist Politics and the Origins of Welfare States*, eds S. Koven & S. Michel, Routledge, New York.
—— 1994, 'Personality, individuality, nationality: Feminist conceptions of citizenship 1902–1940', *Australian Feminist Studies*, no. 19, Autumn.
—— 1997, 'Marriage as bonding', *Australian Historical Studies*, forthcoming.
Paisley, F. 1995, Ideas have wings, PhD thesis, Women's Studies, La Trobe University.
Pateman, C. 1988, *The Sexual Contract*, Polity, Cambridge.

11 Creating Australian law

Bruce Kercher

The idea that Australian law was to a degree original even in the nineteenth century is still controversial, but it should not be. It was impossible for eighteenth-century English law to be simply transplanted. That law was the product of a complex class-ridden society, and neither the society nor its rules could be dumped unchanged into the Australian bush. Nor was there an uncontested notion of English law which could have been parcelled up and sent to the colonies, let alone a single interpretation of it. Ambiguity, social difference and distance, in short, made legal originality possible.

Originality and colonial conditions

Original Australian law did not come about at once, or in isolation from colonial circumstances. Attitudes to law evolved slowly. Debates over the precise status of law were conducted at every level of social and political life in the Australian colonies. Legal and imperial officials in England had conflicting views about it, and so too did colonial governors, judges and lawyers. Most officials, of course, were very deferential towards the law—only Bligh dared to say, 'damn the Law; my will is the law, and woe unto the man that dares to disobey it.'[1] Almost all officials recognised that they were formally required to follow the laws of England, but wittingly or not, they often failed to do so. Diversity increased when ordinary people, convicts, settlers, local-born and Aborigines, carried on their lives in the light of social norms which frequently clashed with the norms prescribed in the official law, and the result was a new mixture of laws, which owed as much to local circumstances as to the inherited traditions of English law.

The official version of Australian legal history tends to occlude this because the formal law has it that all the Australian colonies were 'settled'. As a result, they inherited all the English law in force at the time of first occupation by Britain, so long as the law was 'applicable' to the colony's circumstances. English (not Scottish) law was believed to be the birthright of the British, 'the genuine offspring of that spirit of equal liberty which is the singular felicity of Englishmen'.[2] This common law position was reinforced in 1828 for the eastern Australian colonies, when the imperial parliament stated that all the laws in force in England in 1828 were automatically in force in New South Wales and Van Diemen's Land as well, 'so far as the same can be applied'. This phrase, like 'applicable', is such a loose term that in skilled hands it can mean almost anything. Even at the formal level then, there was room for local innovation, for originality and independence.

And it was needed because some English laws were unsuited to local conditions. The common law held, for instance, that those who had been condemned to death for felony were subject to attaint: they were dead in law, unable to hold property, give evidence or sue in the courts. For the first 30 years in New South Wales, however, most convicts were treated as if they had a right to own property and the freedom to sue.[3] They were also permitted to give evidence; if they had not been, the courts would have been unable to operate. In important ways, convicts even ran the legal system, because for many years the only qualified lawyers were attorneys who had been transported for forgery or perjury. This decision to ignore the common law allowed the Australian colonies to develop as places of remarkable formal equality. This legal divergence came to an apparent halt in 1820, when the English rule on felony attaint was declared to be in force in the colonies. By then, however, it was too late to exclude emancipists from the economy, and convicts were too entrenched to be excluded from society. For the next 20 years the local courts continued to struggle with this issue, moving uneasily between formal English law and local practices.

THE COMMON LAW REASSERTED

The drastic change to the law of attaint in 1820 was one sign of the beginning of a closer adherence to English common law, partly caused by the arrival of professional judges and more respectable lawyers than the disreputable convict attorney George Crossley. Most of the new lawyers were determined to follow accustomed legal procedures of England, rather than what they saw as the looseness and irregularity of local practices. This trend was reinforced by the adoption of positivist approach to judge-made law. In 1831 Francis Forbes, the chief justice of New South Wales, apparently became the first person in Australia to refer to law as a 'science'.[4] Nonetheless Forbes continued to allow considerable latitude to local legal customs, and popular beliefs about law entered into formal law in many of his judgments.

By contrast, other judges, such as William Burton in Sydney and Benjamin Boothby much later in Adelaide, thought that local law was tainted by corruption or error, and any variation from English law should be crushed. This was an extreme version of the positivism which ruled legal thought in Australia until the late twentieth century (and which still does, in the eyes of many conservative lawyers).

Positivism, imperial loyalties and what was later dubbed 'cultural cringe' came to form a powerful combination against the exercise of judicial innovation in Australia. But they never crushed it entirely. From 1788 onwards, there were judges who wanted to adapt English law to local traditions as well as those who wished to follow it slavishly. Not even the Privy Council, which remained in control of some aspects of Australian law until 1986, was able to crush anti-imperial trends entirely.

LAWS WITHOUT PRECEDENT

However, while judges, from about 1820 onwards, moved the law closer to English law, legislatures in Australia moved in the opposite direction by creating laws without English precedents. Until responsible government and the imperial *Colonial Laws Validity Act* of 1865, colonial legislatures were entitled to pass laws only if they were consistent with the received laws of England. Nonetheless, despite this formal restriction, the colonial legislatures passed many innovative Acts in these years which were repugnant to well-established English principles. Judges and imperial officials tacitly approved these laws by not challenging them. Imprisonment for debt, for instance, was abolished in Australia decades before similar legislation was finalised in England. Special laws were also passed to restrict bushrangers, despite the fact that these Acts conflicted with English notions of personal freedom. Likewise, radically democratic mining laws were enacted in the wake of the Eureka stockade incident. These laws were considered necessary to meet local circumstances, even if they did not receive the support of ultra-Anglophile judges. Boothby continued to strike down local Acts even after responsible government came into force in South Australia in 1857, but his antics led to the passage of the *Colonial Laws Validity Act*, which stated that the colonial parliaments could amend or repeal any English laws except those deliberately imposed on the colonies by the imperial parliament. The latter restriction on the formal powers of Australian colonial and state legislatures remained until it was abolished by the *Australia Acts* in 1986. Of course the British government was also able to refuse royal assent to Australian legislation, and it occasionally did so, even up to the eve of federation. Socially progressive legislation, such as equal divorce laws, were sometimes blocked in London, but so too were some overtly racist bills, such as those on immigration. On the whole, though, very much more was allowed through than blocked by imperial officials.

The colonial statutes show that formal Australian law has often been led by the conduct of the Australian people, albeit not always in directions of which we can be proud today. Australian law frequently had a strong racist tinge. Anti-Chinese laws had strong popular support, and for the first 50 years of European occupation it was not even clear whether Aborigines were British subjects, and so entitled to the same protection and regulation as white colonists. By leading to the neglect of many very brutal acts, the law's ambiguity on this question left open the possibility of unpunished massacres. These actions, however, fell under 'the law' in the sense of a pattern of conduct, even if one based on unofficial views of legality.[5] Changes in formal law often came from the law breakers themselves as well. The clearest example of this is of squatters wandering onto what was then believed to be vacant crown land and taking possession of it for grazing. Eventually they convinced the British government to legalise their trespass. They gained licences and then leases, creating by their agency a land law which had no precedent in England. Even when popular actions did not result in changes to formal law, Australian law often took on a distinctive character because in operation it absorbed some of the values of those who used it. Convict women, for example, frequently used the law quite differently from so-called respectable people.[6]

THE MULTIPLE IDENTITIES OF AUSTRALIAN LAW

From its beginning Australian law differed from the law of England, despite its many similarities and its dependent position. The more we study nineteenth-century Australian law, the more differences we find between it and English law, and the more we find diversity among the colonies. Legal historians now reject the positivist trickle-down theory of law, under which law is assumed to be made solely by judges and legislators. They realise that law is not just made in the legislatures and the court rooms, but also in the streets, the markets, out in the bush, wherever people act on an assumption that they have a right to do what they do. That is nowhere more obvious than in the case of the indigenous laws of Australia, those of Aboriginal peoples, which have never been eradicated. There is not one rule of law in Australia but many, a perception which has been hidden from us by 200 years of imperialism and pseudo-scientific legalism. The most pressing task for legal historians now is to look beneath these masks at the multiple identities of Australian law and its creators.[7]

NOTES

1 Atkins' evidence in Ritchie, J. (ed.) 1988, *A Charge of Mutiny: The Court Martial of Lieutenant George Johnston for Deposing Governor Bligh in the Rebellion of 26 January 1808*, National Library of Australia, p. 161.

2 Blackstone, quoted by H. Brougham 1828, *Hansard*, House of Commons, 7 February, col. 202.

3 This began with *Cable (Kable) v. Sinclair*, July 1788, Court of Civil Jurisdiction, New South Wales Archives Office 2/8147.

4 *R. v. Farrell* (1831) 1 Legge 5, at 9.

5 See Milliss, R. 1992, *Waterloo Creek: The Australia Day Massacre of 1838, George Gipps and the British Conquest of New South Wales*, McPhee Gribble, Melbourne.

6 See Byrne, P. 1993, *Criminal Law and Colonial Subject: New South Wales 1810–1830*, Cambridge University Press, Melbourne.

7 On the themes in this chapter, see Kercher, B. 1995, *An Unruly Child: A History of Law in Australia*, Allen & Unwin. The same themes are discussed in Kercher, B. 1995, 'Homer in the Australian Alps: Attitudes to law since 1788', *Australian Journal Legal History*, vol. 1, no. 1. There are many studies of distinctive features of Australian law, including Buck, A. 1987, 'The logic of egalitarianism: Law, property and society in mid-nineteenth century New South Wales', *Law in Context*, vol. 5, no. 18; Gava, J. 1989, 'The revolution in bankruptcy law in colonial New South Wales', in *The Emergence of Australian Law*, eds M.P. Ellinghaus, A.J. Bradbrook & A.J. Duggan, Butterworths, Sydney; Castles, A. 1991, 'The Vandemonian spirit and the law', *Tasmanian Historical Research Association Papers*, vol. 38, no. 105.

12 Australian political thought

Gregory Melleuish & Geoff Stokes

Australian political thought has been far more creative and original than the existing literature suggests. In this chapter we argue that there is a significant body of Australian political thought whose existence has been generally overlooked, and whose attributes have often been misrepresented. Australian political ideas are often regarded as mere political commentary, or as the ideological (meaning dogmatic) expression of base material interests, or simply as aggregations of popular views as described by the term 'political culture'. Such views follow the pattern set by the influential historian W.K. Hancock (1961 [1930], p. 52), who claimed that Australia had produced no original contributions to the 'science and art of government'. Yet, as the overviews by Loveday (1979), Collins (1985), Brugger & Jaensch (1985) and Walter (1988) have shown, the historical record cannot support such unqualified judgments. This essay considers some conceptual reasons in support of a more positive view of Australian political thought, describes a number of general ideological tendencies influencing Australian politics, and indicates the intellectual origins and orientation of a number of key Australian political thinkers.

Intellectual frameworks, practices, styles of argument

Until the 1950s the professional academic practice of political theory was of relatively little importance in Australia. Before that time, any analytical or historical study of political ideas usually was undertaken in departments of philosophy or history. Theoretically based programmatic and policy work was also conducted in departments of political economy and later economics. For most of its history, political theory in Australia has been produced largely outside the institutions of higher learning, and it has reflected the culture of those sites where it was produced—which is to say that its primary concern has been that of political practice. Even many major Australian intellectuals who worked as academics, including V. Gordon Childe and G. Elton Mayo, disparaged abstract theory of the sort practised in universities in favour of a form of intellectual activity integrating theory and practice. Childe (1981, p. 183), for example, attacked academic obscurantism, and his particular heroes in the development of European civilisation were the metal workers who combined the virtues of both scientist and craftsman (1981, pp. 100–6).

The key to understanding Australian political thought, therefore, lies in recognising the intellectual frameworks within which political ideas were generated, the sorts of practices to which they were meant to relate and the styles of arguments which were used. This involves an appreciation of the issues which attracted public attention at a particular time, and an understanding of the sorts of circumstances and cultures in which individuals and groups developed ideas to deal with those issues. It is this very interaction of ideas, circumstance and practice that has created the originality of Australian political thought.

The political issues that became significant in Australia during its first 175 years related primarily to the position of Australia as a settler society within an expanding and then contracting British commercial empire. Even after 200 hundred years, now that some of the earlier problems have declined in importance, the legacy of the imperial experience continues to shape not only the dominant political issues in Australia, but also the political ideas used to come to terms with them. Historically, such issues possessed an immediate and practical significance demanding responses which could solve urgent problems. Originality in Australian political thought may be found in how distinctive Australian problems were conceived, and in the ideological responses to them.

Perhaps the most enduring issue was that of settler appropriation of the land and the question of how to deal with the original inhabitants, the Australian Aborigines. After the transportation of convicts had ended, British settlers needed some broad ideological rationale for coming to Australia and taking possession of its productive capacities. In general this was achieved in terms of an empirical and normative account of the spread of European civilisation over the globe, and assumptions about the inevitable benefits, such as science, commerce and good government, which followed in its wake.

Such an account was founded upon an evolutionary conception of the development of the human race and a belief that British civilisation stood somewhere near the highest point of that evolution (Reynolds 1974a & 1974b). It also relied upon representing the indigenous people as lower in the scale of humanity than those found elsewhere in the British Empire. By this means their claims to land could be ignored and the legal doctrine of 'terra nullius' given full effect. Except perhaps in South Africa, the ideology of racial superiority was probably more powerfully developed and imposed in Australia than in any other comparable settler country, such as the United States or Canada, where indigenous rights to land were often recognised in formal treaties. In response, Australian Aborigines have begun to draw on the rhetoric of identity and universalist ideals of self-determination and developed their own distinct political thought (see Stokes forthcoming).

In many respects, the Australian colonists adapted the speculative histories of the Scottish enlightenment to meet local circumstances (see Melleuish 1989). That agriculture was represented as an advance on pastoralism (which in turn was an advance on hunter-gathering) was a matter of great political significance for nineteenth-century settlers. Not only could it be used to justify the dispossession of the Aborigines but it could also form the foundation for a political argument favouring the free selector at the expense of the pastoralist squatters. During the 1840s and 1850s constant debate occurred over the relative merits of agriculture as opposed to pastoralism (Goodman 1988). Theories of social evolution came to form an enduring part of the ideological resources of Australian political thought. They offered to some a distinctive social vision which suggested the rightful place of Australian colonists in the history of civilisation, and the means by which this should be maintained. For many commentators, Australia needed to be a particular sort of society if it was to remain in the vanguard of human progress. In general, this meant moving on from agriculture to some sort of industrial and urban social order; only in this way could Australia consider itself a legitimate heir to European civilisation. Perhaps the most recent and crudest representations of this kind may be found among those affirming the importance of mining in the promotion of an Australian civilisation (see Harman 1981; Page 1993).

Various forms of agrarian ideology, however, have remained powerful even in the twentieth century as part of an ideology of state development. Agrarianism contributed to the emphasis given to agriculture and the retardation of industrial development in Queensland (see Bulbeck

1987). Currently, it remains evident in the Catholic anti-industrialism of B.A. Santamaria (1993) and in the anti-suburbanism of the rural commune movement and some literary figures. What is striking, however, is that in Australia, agrarian programs were largely absorbed into the policies of the major political parties, whereas in the United States, agrarian populism remained the concern of a pressure group outside them (Gollan 1965).

For reasons of defence and economic security, Australians also needed to develop a satisfactory sense of their place within the larger world order. Basically there were two ways of achieving this aim: through bonds with an empire or by becoming a independent nation. Many Australians sought both routes and saw no contradiction in this. As the children and grandchildren of British settlers, Australians retained a strong attachment to the lands of their ancestors. They adopted the ideal of British nationality, that is, the national identity of members of the British isles considered largely in the context of empire. British nationality, however, was something quite distinct from English, Scottish, Welsh and Irish nationality, and it existed in addition to these other nationalities. Consequently, there was nothing unusual in an Australian nationality evolving alongside this British nationality. W.K. Hancock (1961, p. 39) was not far from the truth when he wrote of 'independent Australian Britons'.

One problem inherent in Australian nationalism was that it emerged in tandem but often in conflict, with the British identity. Political argument, such as that which appeared in the *Bulletin*, recognised the tension between the two nationalities. While there were those who sought to repudiate their Britishness in the name of their Australianness, there were others who saw Australia as the place to recover the true Britishness which had been lost at home. Nevertheless, it must be emphasised that these ideas about nation, empire, and later, multiculturalism arose out of a practical necessity to solve the question of what kind of society Australia should become. For a country which has encouraged successive waves of immigration, the shifting ideological resolutions of such issues will be a constant source for the creative development of Australian political thought, as, for example, in the 1980s and 1990s when the question of multiculturalism emerged to challenge and force a reconsideration of the national identity question (see, e.g., Kukathas 1993).

The circumstances of Australian settlement and economic development also affected the particular gender orientation of Australian nationalism. Whatever its urban literary sources, the image of the typical Australian as the 'bushman' was coloured in powerful masculinist tones. These images, brought to notice by Russel Ward (1966) and criticised by Marilyn Lake (1986) among others, provide the staples of an Australian political thought. Lake's historical reconstruction of a vigorous feminist politics indicates the extent of alternative conceptions of masculinity, and thereby an alternative set of Australian political values which may be drawn upon, rejected or adapted as the conditions require. In this regard the very masculinity of Australian nationalism has helped to provoke the creation of a vigorous and distinctive Australian feminism.

ARTICULATING THE INHERITANCE

Predictably, many settlers wished to preserve as much of the institutions and culture of their place of origin as possible. But there are a number of political traditions at work in any particular country, and individuals usually inherit these traditions in an informal and unstructured way. As inhabitants of a settler society, Australians often had to articulate more clearly the ideas contained in these traditions, and make them more explicit than perhaps they had been in Britain. The task of producing written constitutions for the Australian colonies brought many of these issues to the fore. Arguments for Australian colonial interests had to be couched in terms which would be recognisable to the imperial administrators and parliaments they hoped to persuade.

In the debates over responsible government in the 1840s and the 1850s, disputes arose over what the British inheritance really was (Hume 1994, pp. 33–5), debates complicated by the fact that the United States offered an alternative model of Anglo-Saxon political society. Australians were therefore forced to articulate through their political and legal institutions an interpretation of their political inheritance from the British world. In so doing they developed many of the key ideas, such as pluralism and populism.

Part of the political inheritance from Britain was a parliamentary system embodying democratic principles. But because of its rigid class structure, and the fear of the potentially disruptive consequences of extending the suffrage, British governments had resisted any radical implementation of democracy. Australian debates, however, demonstrated an acute awareness that, in the absence of hereditary social classes, the colonial social structure was markedly different, and that this allowed greater room for the successful construction of more thorough-going democratic institutions. Much time and effort were spent questioning the nature and implications of democracy in Australia. Was it an ideal form of political order which would enable every individual to develop his or her potential? Or was it a form of politics which encouraged individuals and interests to advance themselves at the expense of the common good? A variety of Australian contributions to the political theory of democracy can be found scattered in newspapers, books and pamphlets devoted to practical political questions, to discussions of national character and to the educational issues (see Melleuish 1994).

In a settler society, far removed from its metropolitan origins and the direct restraints of civilisation, there was widespread concern that the social order might fall apart. Such sentiments led Australian colonists and their descendants to place a premium on social harmony as the foundation of the political order. Australia has never been a land in which the virtues of rugged individualism have been much valued, and this is reflected in the dominant traditions of cooperation evident in Australian social liberalism. Nor has the labour movement been primarily oriented towards achieving its goals by class war or violence (see, e.g., Matthews 1993).

The influential Australian liberals and the socialists adopted distinctly reformist political strategies which reflected a belief in social cooperation and pluralism (see, e.g., Eggleston 1941; Burgmann 1943). Accordingly, the priority given to social harmony meant that security has ranked more highly as a political objective than individual self-expression. The utilitarian principle of the greatest good for the greatest number has tended to override concerns for individual rights. These values also favoured strong programs of state intervention, such as courts of arbitration and conciliation to encourage, and where necessary enforce, cooperation (see Higgins 1915). At the local and the national levels, direct state involvement in economic development, as with the funding, construction and operation of railways, served these broader social purposes.

INSTITUTIONAL LOCATIONS

The other significant influence upon the character and evolution of political thought in Australia has been the institutional locations of those who articulated political ideas. For much of the nineteenth century and after, the few universities in Australia were small in size, paid positions for those who would engage in political theorising were scarce, and teaching received priority over research and writing. In addition, Australia lacked a rentier class in which leisured intelligentsia on independent incomes pursued ideas as a source of pleasure. Instead there were men and also sometimes women in law or journalism who deployed political ideas but not in the form of grand theory. Particularly in the nineteenth century, journalists and lawyers were largely responsible for developing and publicising those political ideas which dealt with the questions raised by the Australian experience.

For young men of ability the law was one of the few professions they could pursue if they wished to exercise their talents and continue to live in Australia. From the practice of law the road often led into politics, as in the careers of Edmund Barton, Samuel Griffiths and H.B. Higgins. Both W.M. Hughes and W.A. Holman, who began as leaders of the labour movement, took up the study of law. It is not surprising that political ideas and institutions in Australia should have felt the imprint of a legal frame of mind (see Davidson 1991). The legalist ideology of the past has been a dominant element in Australian political thinking, and at the level of the High Court of Australia, is only just giving way to a new realism.

The other way in which young men and some women could exercise their intellectual powers was journalism. The socialist William Lane, on the *Boomerang* and the *Worker*, the feminist Louisa Lawson, with her magazine the *Dawn* (see Lawson 1990), and the young Alfred Deakin, working for David Syme's *Age*, are prime examples of this. During the nineteenth century, newspapers were the principal public forums for the analysis and dissemination of social and political ideas, and one can find in their pages, especially in the leading articles, a remarkable sophistication and capacity to deal with political concerns. When there were major public questions, such as the constitution question of the 1850s, that of free selection, or white Australia, the newspapers contained a range of articles dealing with the underlying issues.

Many nineteenth-century Australian political thinkers either operated newspapers or worked as journalists. Select examples include the republicans Daniel Deniehy and John Dunmore Lang and the Chartist, Edward Hawksley. In eastern Australia, the three most notable newspapers disseminating political ideas were the *Sydney Morning Herald*, the *Age* and the *Bulletin*. For some 30 years, from the mid-1850s, the *Sydney Morning Herald* was edited by two remarkable editors, John West followed by Andrew Garran (see Walker 1972). Both had theological training, and both used the newspaper to enunciate a clear vision of free-trade liberalism. In Melbourne, David Syme made use of the *Age* to argue for his form of liberalism founded on a policy of protection. Both Deakin and C.H. Pearson wrote for the *Age* advocating a range of liberal ideas and policies. Pearson's book (1894) *National Life and Character* could be credited with supplying the ideological foundations of the white Australia policy. Strong connections between political theory and economics could be found in both the *Sydney Morning Herald* and the *Age*. In a settler society seeking to establish its industries, these newspapers advocated two competing versions of a future Australia and different economic strategies for achieving them. For the editors, the issue of free trade versus protection was one of great practical import and it is not surprising that political thought in Australia should have assumed an economic hue to match its legalism.

Although the *Bulletin* is remembered today first as a literary magazine, in its prime it dealt with the major political and economic questions of the day (see Lawson 1987), articulating a powerful vision of Australia and its place in the world which was founded on race and the ideal of an independent Australia.

PRACTICAL POLITICAL THEORISING

Much political theorising in Australia not only embraced the value of practice as a consideration within theory itself, it also concerned itself with practical questions. It responded to the immediate problems of the political and social order. Hence V. Gordon Childe's (1964 [1923]) classic, *How Labour Governs*, attempted to come to terms with problematic aspects of the organisation of the labour movement, not as a theoretical exercise, but in the hope of resolving some of those problems. H.B. Higgins was active at all levels in Australian politics, but was conscious of the ideals and values he was attempting to put into practice in the institutions of arbitration and conciliation (e.g. see Higgins 1915). Much of Elton Mayo's work (e.g. 1920) was inspired by what he saw as the failings of the arbitration system and the hope of rectifying those failings. Similarly, Frederic Eggleston (1932) wrote *State Socialism in Victoria* to explain how state intervention had not had the desired results in Victoria. Both studies had relevance for readers beyond Australian shores.

Contrary to its general conclusion, W.K. Hancock's *Australia* (1961 [1930]) itself represents a summary of this practical style of political theorising in Australia. In his discussion of Australian politics, economics, civilisation and national character, Hancock developed a style of political analysis owing much to Machiavelli in its emphasis on achieving results as opposed to expressing purity of political intention.

Through its appropriation by a succession of popularisers, Hancock's analysis became a form of political ideology at the level of popular culture (Connell 1968). It was used by journalists and others to express a particular political understanding of Australia, and was read as such by large numbers of Australians. Manning Clark's six-volume *A History of Australia* can be seen as a Manichaean form of political thought, one which attempts to clarify the meaning of history so Australians could be warned of the recurring perils they might have to face in the future.

There are numerous examples of political problems being the spur to political theorising in Australia. The Second World War provided the context for theorising on the theme of postwar reconstruction (e.g. see Campbell 1944). More recently the policies of multiculturalism, the judgment in the Mabo case, the republican movement and the ideology of economic rationalism, to name but a few, have encouraged many Australians to develop distinctive arguments about these issues. Writings on these topics are the product of those 'organic' intellectuals whose task it is to articulate and transmit ideas to a broader public (Walter 1988, pp. 240–1). The works of these political activists, journalists and editors are central to any informed appreciation of Australian political thought. Such writings are not universalist in intent, but they often draw upon universalist themes, generally of European origin. It would be a mistake to dismiss the content as mere political commentary or political culture.

Australian political thought has been characterised by a vitality and a diversity as Australian political thinkers have avoided slavishly copying other people's models, preferring to adapt ideas intelligently to solve Australian problems. Political thought in Australia has developed in response to, and as a crystallisation of, political practice. A prime aim has been to clarify and solve those problems which were considered vital to Australians. In most cases the major political thinkers have drawn upon universalist theories and adapted them to what they have perceived to be distinctive Australian contexts, such as those of its social structure and national character, as well as its geography and place in the Asia-Pacific region. Their intellectual resources have included knowledge about ancient Greece and Rome, modern European philosophy and history, as well as select interpretations of British heritage and borrowings from North America. It is in this unique combination of interpretation and advocacy that the distinctiveness and originality of Australian political thought may be found.

ACKNOWLEDGMENT

The authors would like to acknowledge the research assistance of Jeremy Chenoweth and the financial support of the Australian Research Council which facilitated research for this paper.

REFERENCES

Brugger, B. & Jaensch, D. 1985, *Australian Politics: Theory and Practice*. Allen & Unwin, Sydney.

Bulbeck, C. 1987, 'Colin Clark and the greening of Queensland: The influence of a senior public servant on Queensland economic development 1938–1952', *Australian Journal of Politics and History* 33, no. 1.

Burgmann, E.H. 1943, *The Regeneration of Civilization*. Robert Deyson & Co., Sydney.

Campbell, D.A.S. (ed.) 1944, *Post-War Reconstruction in Australia*, Australasian Publishing Co., Sydney.

Childe, V.G. 1964 [1923], *How Labour Governs*. ed. F.B. Smith, Melbourne University Press, London.

—— 1981 [1941], *Man Makes Himself*, ed. S. Green, Moonraker Press, London.

Collins, H. 1985, 'Political ideology in Australia: The distinctiveness of a Benthamite society', in *Australia: The Daedalus Symposium*, ed. S.R. Grabaud, Angus & Robertson, Sydney.

Connell, R.W. 1968, 'Images of Australia', *Quadrant*, vol. 12, no. 2.

Davidson, A. 1991, *The Invisible State: The Formation of the Australian State 1788–1901*, Cambridge University Press, Melbourne.

Eggleston, F.W. 1932, *State Socialism in Victoria*, P.S. King & Sons, London.

—— 1941, *Search for a Social Philosphy*, Melbourne University Press, Melbourne.

Gollan, R. 1965, 'American populism and Australian Utopianism', *Labour History*, vol. 9.

Goodman, D. 1988, 'Goldfield/golden fields: The language of agrarianism and the Victorian gold rush', *Australian Historical Studies*, vol. 23, no. 90.

Hancock, W.K. 1961 [1930], *Australia*, Jacaranda, Brisbane.

Harman, E.J. 1981, 'Ideology and mineral development in Western Australia', in *State Capital and Resources in the North and West of Australia*, eds E.J. Harman & B.W. Head, University of Western Australia Press, Nedlands.

Higgins, H.B. 1915, *A New Province for Law and Order*, Government Printer, Melbourne.

Hume, L.J. 1994, 'Foundations of populism and pluralism: Australian political writings to 1860', in *Australian Political Ideas*, ed. Stokes 1994a, University of NSW Press, Sydney.

Kukathas, C. (ed.) 1993, *Multicultural Citizens: The Philosophy and Politics of Identity*, Centre for Independent Studies, Sydney.

Lake, M. 1986, 'The Politics of respectability: Identifying the masculinist context', *Australian Historical Studies*, vol. 22, no. 86.

Lawson, O. (ed.) 1990, *The First Voice of Australian Feminism: Excerpts from Louisa Lawson's The Dawn 1888–1895*, Simon & Schuster, Sydney.

Lawson, S. 1987, *The Archibald Paradox*, Penguin, Melbourne.

Loveday, P. 1979, 'Australian political thought', in *The Pieces of Politics*, 2nd edn, ed. R. Lucy, Macmillan, South Melbourne.

Matthews, R. 1993, *Australia's First Fabians*, Cambridge University Press, Cambridge.

Mayo, E. 1920, 'Australian political consciousness', in *Australia: Economic and Political Studies*, ed. M. Atkinson, Macmillan, Melbourne.

Melleuish, G. 1989, Justifying commerce: The Scottish enlightenment tradition in New South Wales, *Journal of the Royal Australian Historical Society*, vol. 76, no. 2.

—— 1994, 'Utopians and sceptics: Competing images of democracy in Australia', in *Australian Political Ideas*, ed. G. Stokes, University of NSW Press, Sydney.

Page, G. 1993, 'Rugged nostalgia: The political rhetoric of H.M. Morgan', *Quadrant*, vol. 37, no. 12.

Pearson, C.H. 1894, *National Life and Character: A Forecast*, 2nd edn, Macmillan, London.

Reynolds, H. 1974a, 'Racial thought in early colonial Australia', *Australian Journal of Politics and History*, vol. 20, no. 1.

—— 1974b, 'Progress, morality, and the dispossession of the Aboriginals', *Meanjin*, vol. 33, no. 3.

Santamaria, B.A. 1993, 'Rural exodus: a road to disaster', *Weekend Australian*, 31 July–1 August, 24.

Stokes, G. (ed.) 1994a, *Australian Political Ideas*, NSW University Press, Sydney.

—— 1994b, Conceptions of Australian political thought: A methodological critique', *Australian Journal of Political Science*, vol. 29, no. 2.

—— (forthcoming), 'Citizenship and Aboriginality: Two conceptions of identity in Aboriginal political thought', in *The Politics of Identity in Australia*.

Walker, R.B. 1972, 'Andrew Garran: congregationalist, conservative, liberal reformer', *Australian Journal of Politics and History*, vol. 18, no. 3.

Ward, R. 1966, *The Australian Legend*, 2nd edn, Oxford University Press, London.

Walter, J. 1988, 'Intellectuals and political culture', in *Intellectual Movements in Australian Society*, eds. B. Head & J. Walter, Oxford University Press, Melbourne, pp. 237–73.

13 Australian Utopias

William Metcalf

The experience of colonial Australia inspired many dramatic and highly original attempts to visualise and then bring into existence an ideal society, free from oppression and exploitation.[1]

Australia's most important and influential nineteenth-century Utopian writers were Catherine Spence of Adelaide, who wrote *Handfasted* (1879) and *A Week in the Future* (1888 but set in 1988); Henrietta Dugdale of Melbourne, with *A Few Hours in a Far Off Age* (1883), set in a matriarchal, feminist future Australia; William Lane of Brisbane, Australia's foremost Utopian intellectual, who wrote *The Workingman's Paradise* (1892), contrasting working life in Sydney with a Utopian rural Queensland; David Andrade of Melbourne, author of *The Melbourne Riots and How Harry Holdfast and His Friends Emancipated the Workers: A Realistic Novel* (1892), in which rural communism in Australia spreads across the world; Austin South of Brisbane, who wrote *In Those Days, or, Life in the Twentieth-Century* (1893), set in a perfected Brisbane of 1995; Samuel Rosa of Sydney, with *The Coming Terror, or, The Australian Revolution. A Romance of the Twentieth-Century* (1894); and Horace Tucker of Melbourne, the emotive, bucolic writer of *The New Arcadia, An Australian Story* (1894), a science fiction Utopia set in the countryside of Victoria. Of these writers Andrade, Lane, Rosa and Tucker all went on to implement their Utopian, communal dreams.

Early religious Utopias

The earliest recorded attempt to establish a Utopian commune in Australia was in 1839 when Johann Frederick Krumnow, a visionary

Christian mystic, came from Germany to South Australia. He tried to establish a Moravian Brethren-style commune near Hahndorf but his would-be charismatic leadership was rejected by those he sought to lead, and he was excommunicated by the Lutheran Church.

Australia's first successful Utopian experiment was Herrnhut, established by German fundamentalists in 1853, near Hamilton, Victoria. Their charismatic leader was the same Johann Krumnow who had ignominiously failed 14 years earlier in South Australia. The 50 Herrnhut members shared all money and property, although power was retained by Krumnow. They built stone houses and a large stone church, and supported themselves through raising sheep, and selling milk and other farm produce. More than 300 Aborigines sought protection at Herrnhut. Not surprisingly, Herrnhut received a bad press, one account claiming that a 'community of wives' and other sexual 'outrages' were allowed. In spite of contradictory evidence, Krumnow was depicted as a self-indulgent despot who duped and exploited his fellow communards. This was Australia's first example of 'cult-bashing'. When Krumnow died in 1880, Herrnhut was sadly depleted. Leadership of the remaining members was taken over by a female member, Frau Elmore, but she was unable to re-inspire her fellow communards. Australia's first Utopian commune collapsed and their 641 hectares of land were sold in 1897, after 44 years of operation.

COMMUNAL UTOPIAS

Between the establishment of Herrnhut in 1853 and the start of the 'Aquarian Age' in about 1970, 48 Utopian communal groups were established in Australia with a combined membership of about 9000. If we widen our definition somewhat, during this period we can find another 262 social groups with some element of Utopian communalism, having about 25 000 participants. And if we move past those Utopian groups which came into existence and look to those which remained only a dream, we find unrealised plans to involve about another a quarter of a million Australians. Since 1970 Australia has seen a flowering of Utopian social experimentation with about 20 000 Australians living communally in the mid-1990s, although several times that number are associated with the much broader communities movement.

While William Lane and the 700 Australians who joined him in the New Australia experiment in Paraguay are reasonably well known, few Australians know much about the many other groups which developed in the 1890s, largely under the influence of Lane's unique brand of Australian Utopianism. The first completely Australian Utopian venture was The Alice River Cooperative Settlement, established in 1891 when 72 shearers formed a commune near Barcaldine, Queensland. Their rules were modelled on the New Australia constitution drawn up by William Lane. Without title to the land, they laid out Liberty, Freedom and Union Streets, and built huts, a library and reading room, kitchen and dining room, toolshed and piggery. They cleared ten hectares, planting vegetable gardens and a vineyard. Many worked on neighbouring properties, but all income went to a common fund. They did not recognise private property. The commune prospered but by late 1893 only twelve members remained, most of the rest having joined William Lane in New Australia. This communal experiment ended in 1907.

In 1892, the Reverend Horace Tucker, Utopian visionary and author, established seven communes in rural western Victoria: Jindivik, Wonwondah East, Red Hill, Moora Moora, Kilfera, Horsham and Croydon. Seven hundred families with more than 2000 members lived on these communal settlements. In early 1894, just as it seemed that these communes were prospering, they began to collapse. Members left primarily because of the better financial and practical support available to those taking part in the Victorian government-sponsored and more individualistic village settlements scheme. In 1896, this communal experiment formally ended, probably as much because of Tucker's mediocre leadership as due to the lack of irrigation and poor land on which the communes had been located.

In South Australia, 1770 people joined the thirteen government-subsidised communal 'village settlements' started between 1894 and 1895. Gillen, Holder, Kingston, Lyrup, Moorook, Murtho, New Era, New Residence, Pyap, Ramco and Waikerie were along the Murray River between Renmark and Morgan, while Nangkita was 50 kilometres south of Adelaide and Mount Remarkable 250 kilometres north.

Murtho was the most Utopian and prosperous of these communes, its organisers advertising (The *Voice* 16 March 1894) that they would be 'similar to the New Australia organisation, viz the land and other means of production to be held in common, personal effects to be the property of individuals'. Unfortunately, the Utopian enthusiasm of Murtho's members was combined with very limited agricultural expertise, so their farming success was limited. Nearby, Lyrup commune's chairman boasted that the commune's members would show the world 'what can be done under good socialistic and communistic principles'.

Lyrup would achieve 'what political economists in all ages have longed to see inaugurated' (*Adelaide Register* 21 February 1894, p. 7). Lyrup's rules were the first to be formally approved, and were generally adopted by the other village settlements. No money was used internally, and common ownership was practised. Any outside wages were to be turned over to the commune. But in 1902 the Act which established these communes was repealed, the communes were disbanded and the land was sold as private farms.

In New South Wales, three communal settlements were established with government support in 1893 and 1894: Pitt Town, Wilberforce and Bega. Pitt Town's board of control stated (NSW Legislative Assembly 1893) that 'the principle of the settlement shall be purely co-operative, and all settlers shall be required to work . . . for the common benefit of all members'. New members had to study 'the nature of a co-operative enterprise and to subscribe to the principles of co-operation and to a communal discipline' (NSW Legislative Assembly 1896). Few members had any agricultural experience, being mainly unemployed Sydney workers, but by October 1894, they had planted 1800 fruit trees and 18 000 grape vines, cleared 200 hectares for agriculture, erected 65 kilometres of fencing and dug 16 dams. A sawmill and church were erected, a dairy started and 120 small houses built. Members, however, were in constant dispute, mainly about individualism versus communalism. In June 1896, communalism ceased, with only seven members still on site. Pitt Town, with 500 residents, is the largest communal venture so far to have existed in Australia.

In Queensland, twelve large communes, with about 2000 people on a total of 28 310 hectares, formed in early 1894, again with limited government support. Three communes were south of Roma: Excel Pioneers, Nil Desperandum and Obertown Model. Three were near Chinchilla: Industrial, Mizpah and Monmouth. Three communes were established north east of Gayndah: Bon Accord, Byrnestown and Resolute. As well, Protestant Unity was south of Gympie, Woolloongabba Exemplars near Noosa and Reliance, near Springsure.

They started off well, full of Utopian enthusiasm, but during their first year problems arose at all communes, ranging from lack of agricultural expertise to interpersonal conflicts. By the end of 1894, their earlier political and media support had evaporated, and the communards were politically and socially isolated. The *Queenslander* newspaper, which had been supportive, turned against them, asserting that 'socialism in "New Australia", as well as old Australia, has practically failed, as everyone who has read history or his Bible, ought to have known it would fail . . . Individualism is society's only adequate protection against the loafer . . . communism . . . spells pauperism, and the encouragement of the spirit of mendicancy' (26 January 1895, p. 153). In redoubtable, vitriolic prose the editor concluded: 'it may be hoped that the government will refuse to perpetuate the folly of co-operative groups by giving them more money, except possibly for absolute rations, until their members can be drafted off to other employments or to the benevolent asylum'.

As problems within all twelve communes increased, The *Queenslander* stated in June 1895 that 'average human nature is not the material for a millennium yet; and those who fondly dream of Utopia must be content to live in dreamland' (29 June 1895, p. 1211). The combined population of these communes had by then dropped to 1260.

In February 1896, all these Queensland communes were wound up and the legislation was altered to allow members to apply for individual leaseholds over portions of their communal land, with the result that 83 ex-members selected about 5000 hectares. The 'abject failure' of the 2078 Queenslanders who took part in these twelve communal settlements is part of Queensland's folklore although the failure of these communes has probably been exaggerated.

In Tasmania one Utopian commune, known as Southport, was established with 60 residents on a government grant of 800 pounds in 1894. The conservative Women's Guild, which established this Utopia, drafted 41 rules to guide daily life. These rules were personally invasive, in a classic Victorian-era attempt to raise the moral tone of the working classes. Daily life at Southport was harsh and unrewarding, and communalism clearly did not work. In April 1895, after only six months' operation, communalism was abandoned and a ballot held among settlers for individual allotments. In 1898 Southport was abandoned.

THREE UTOPIAN EXPERIMENTS

Perhaps Australia's three most interesting, albeit idiosyncratic, Utopian experiments were Kalevan Kansa, Holy City, New Jerusalem and Poynduk.

Kalevan Kansa was established in Queensland in 1899 by Matti Kurikka, a Utopian socialist who came from Finland with 78 followers. He sought to establish a Utopian social order in which all social evils could be replaced by harmony. Kurikka, along with 27 male followers, moved north from Brisbane, while the women and children stayed behind. The men lived communally near Chillagoe, where they cut railway sleepers, planning to save their money to buy good seaside land. Kurikka was a poor administrator so their collective money was wasted and members suffered. In early 1900, in a desperate attempt to realise his dream, Kurikka convinced his followers to accompany him on a lengthy march to establish his Utopian Kalevan Kansa on the Gulf of Carpentaria. 'Matti Kurikka, a profoundly religious man, at times could hardly have resisted the image of unifying and saving his people by leading them to salvation as Moses had done for his people' (Cormick 1989–90, p. 21). Not surprisingly, they nearly starved to death. By July 1900, this Utopian experiment had collapsed with Kurikka leaving to establish another Utopia in Canada, while many of his followers settled in Queensland's Nambour area.

A breakaway group of Plymouth Brethren came from England to Kyneton, Victoria, in 1900 to establish a millenarian commune known as Holy City. They were under the leadership of Dr Dalziel, a retired physician from Edinburgh who received angelic visions, and who regularly communicated directly with God. Holy City's main building was Ermstowe, a sixteen-room mansion which not only housed Dr Dalziel and his family, but also served for prayer meetings and as a communal centre. In 1909, Dr Dalziel left Kyneton to await the Second Coming of Christ which, direct revelation had now led him to believe, would be in Jerusalem, not Kyneton, Victoria. After he left, Holy City lost its identity, and gradually his Utopian followers moved away or blended into the wider community.

In 1902, New Jerusalem, a 'Jewish-Christian' community, was formed 40 kilometres east of Narrogin in Western Australia. In 1905, 70 communal members lived on 4000 hectares, with 400 hectares under crops. Their leader, James Fisher, received direct revelations from Jesus Christ, accompanied by visions of angels, foretelling that 'the true religion of God has been sleeping for the last 1800 years but is now going to bud forth with fresh vigour and . . . [at Utopian New Jerusalem] all mankind will be united in one fold of love and happiness' *Western Mail* (26 August 1905, p. 28). New Jerusalem, however, rapidly lost its Utopian ideals and uniqueness, and after Fisher died members blended into the local community.

Perhaps Australia's most imaginative and creative, although bizarre, Utopian proposal was Poynduk, a Jewish Utopian commune in Tasmania. It was planned and described in great detail in 1940 by a wealthy young Australian, Critchley Parker. Poynduk would develop a wide range of secondary industries and would become 'the Paris of Australasia'. In this Utopia, there would be a form of olympic games to be known as 'Pacific Fair', involving not only sports but also poetry and public speaking contests, and musical performances. In addition, Parker planned a university, with 'distinguished scholars', which would provide scholarships for 'Tasmanians as well as Chinese, Japanese, Javanese, Indians, Burmese, Arabs, Malays, South Americans and African negroes . . . [so] that the community may uphold the principles of racial tolerance and international brotherhood' (Rubinstein 1990, p. 60). Management would be based on that of USSR-style collective ownership. Parker firmly believed that his Utopia 'will so amaze the people of Australia that the little settlement in Tasmania will be the leaven that will completely change the economic and financial system of Australia' (Gettler 1993, p. 123). Poynduk received the formal backing of the Tasmanian government. Critchley Parker, however, died in 1942 while exploring the area he intended for his Utopian colony, so Poynduk never eventuated.

LATER DEVELOPMENTS

In the late 1960s, a variably Utopian, countercultural and back-to-the-land movement started in Australia. The disparate participants first identified themselves as a solid social movement when 10 000 of them came together for the Aquarius Festival, at Nimbin, New South Wales in 1973. Since then, thousands of attempts have been made at Utopian experimentation, ranging from small urban communes to large and long-lived intentional communities, such as Tuntable Falls, Crystal Waters, Wytaliba and Bundagen. However, most Utopian schemes have failed while still only an idea. Long-lasting Utopian intentional communities are relatively rare, given the number of attempts which have been made.

Contemporary participants in Australia's intentional communities are predominantly middle-aged, with as many over 50 as under 30 years old. Forty percent have tertiary qualifications and 20 percent work as professionals, mainly in 'human services' sectors. These communal groups are scattered across Australia, but with concentrations in the 'rainbow region' between Lismore and Murwillumbah, New South Wales, the Bunbury to Albany area of Western Australia, and Queensland's Sunshine Coast hinterland.

THE REPRESSION OF AUSTRALIAN UTOPIANISM

Why is the history of Australia's Utopian experimentation so poorly known? If we look in most general histories of Australia we find only a few references to William Lane, and then as someone who sold out his mates and left Australia, as if his influence went with him to Paraguay. In most histories with more of a left or labour orientation we find slightly better coverage, but still rather scanty. Verity Burgmann's history, *In Our Time*, at least gives some coverage to the Utopian aspects of the 1890s, but still mainly as a side issue, even though probably more Australians were involved in Utopian communes than in the Labor Party until the middle of the decade. Ross Fitzgerald's detailed history of Queensland, the state which was in many respects the cauldron of Utopian experimentation in Australia, discusses Lane at length but is silent on the thirteen communes, involving about 2000 people which Lane inspired in Queensland. All the so called 'labour (and Labor) histories', in which one would perhaps expect to read of these Utopian experiments, provide details *ad nauseam* of the shearers' strikes, the tramways strike et cetera, but rarely a word about that *other* labour response—Utopian communalism.

Why such a deafening silence about Australian Utopianism?

Australia's labour movement in the late 1880s and 1890s was divided between the 'meliorists', who saw parliamentary representation and trade union muscle as the way to improve the lot of oppressed workers, and the 'radicals', who argued that the only way forward was to create a dramatic new social order—a Utopia. Those who sought to create a new social order, a Utopia, lost out, their schemes being defeated by a host of factors ranging from poor land to political opposition from numerous critics of both right *and* left. The reformists, working within the system, who were striving for parliamentary representation, legal reform and an arbitration system, slowly succeeded. History is written by the winners. Utopianism was not only defeated by pragmatism within leftist circles, but it came to be written out of Australia's social and cultural history.

Nonetheless, Australia's history is rich with the creativity of Utopian visionaries and their imaginative social experimentation. Australian Utopian writers, such as Spence, Lane, South and Tucker, while part of a European Utopian socialist tradition, offered original insights into the Australian condition, as well as developing original ways to overcome oppression and exploitation. Moreover, the numerous Utopian experiments made in Australia, past and present, show just how imaginative and dynamic 'ordinary' Australians can be in creating their own social and cultural reality. To this extent, recovering the history of Australian Utopianism has implications for creating Australia.

NOTES

1 Further information and references on Australia's Utopian history as well as detailed case studies of contemporary communal groups can be found in W. Metcalf 1995, *From Utopian Dreaming to Communal Reality*, University of NSW Press, Sydney.

REFERENCES

Cormick, C. 1989–90, 'Matti Kurikka and a Queensland Utopia', *Blast 11*, summer, p. 21.

Fitzgerald, R. 1982, *From the Dreaming to 1915: A History of Queensland*, University of Queensland Press, Brisbane.

Gettler, L. 1993, *An Unpromised Land*, Fremantle Arts Centre Trust, Fremantle.

NSW Legislative Assembly, 1893, *Votes and Proceedings*, vol. 2, p. 998.

NSW Legislative Assembly, 1896, *Votes and Proceedings*, vol. 5, pp. 766–7.

Rubinstein, H. 1990, 'Critchley Parker (1911–42): Australian martyr for Jewish refugees' *Journal of the Australian Jewish Historical Society*, part 1.

14 Australia as Asia

David Walker

No analysis of Australia has attracted as much comment and as many sales as Donald Horne's *The Lucky Country*. From its first appearance in 1964 the book and the implications of its catchy title have been the subject of regular commentary, often enough by Horne himself. Most of the attention has focused on whether or not Australia could be considered lucky and the meanings that Horne attached to that term. However, for all the commentary generated by the title, some of the most arresting observations in Horne's portrait of Australia in the 1960s relate to Asia. The book opens with snippets of conversation from several Asian settings: Hong Kong, Taipei and the Philippines. Horne not only claimed that his trip through the 'Far East' in 1963 enabled him to see Australia more clearly, but he returned believing that 'Australia was worth a book'. It was a carefully judged piece of provocation to suggest that the Asian interest in Australia made the place worth writing about. Raising the stakes a little higher, he went on: 'In the future it might be of interest to know what the huge continent was like in those early days in the nineteen sixties before it was peopled from all over Asia.' The prologue ended with the comment that 'Australia in its present form may cease to exist' (Horne 1964, p. 10).

Horne's Asia was at once the recollection of a trip, a travel experience, replete with its itineraries, discussions and meetings, and a narrative device, introduced to dramatise Australia, to sharpen interest in its future. By its proximity to Asia, Horne suggested, Australia acquired a new interest, it became a place worth looking at more closely, a place worth a book. It was also a place being talked about in Asia. Wherever he went in Asia, Horne found someone saying something about Australia. These somethings were sometimes shrewd and well informed and at other times bizarre and unpredictable. But Horne maintained that Australia and Asia were linked, nevertheless, by a growing buzz of conversation. We had been noticed.

If it was the business of the writer to dramatise Australia, there was a lot to be said for introducing a narrative of disappearance. While Horne was by no means the first to introduce into Australian writing the theme of people from Asia entering the continent and changing it beyond recognition, his account of the disappearing nation was shaped by pleasure to be had from contemplating the emergence of a better Australia. Horne welcomed an Asia that would provoke, challenge and question Australia; an Asia that would push an underperforming country to plot a more independent and imaginative future for itself. This was the Asia that Australia had to have.

IMAGINING ASIAS

In imagining their Asias, Australian intellectuals have been both active agents and, given their geopolitical perspective, unintentionally original. For at least a century Australian intellectuals have created Asias designed to frighten or persuade Australians to get their house in order. It was considered all the more urgent to make Australians 'wake up' to the responsibilities of nation-building, because it was widely understood that Asia itself was undergoing sweeping transformations. From the late nineteenth century, public figures were quick to refer to the 'awakening East' and its implications for the region. One of the big issues confronting the new Commonwealth in its first decade was northern development and in particular the future of the Northern Territory, which had been a South Australian responsibility since 1863. After protracted debates in the federal parliament, the Commonwealth assumed responsibility for the Northern Territory in 1911. Throughout the debates supporters of the transfer warned that an empty and undeveloped north might well provoke crowded Asia into establishing its own northern settlements. Sir Joseph Cook spoke for many of his parliamentary colleagues when he warned that the 'Asiatic shadow is becoming bigger every day by reason of internal developments, and the awakening that is taking place . . . ' (Cook 1909, p. 5128).

While disgruntled opponents of the Northern Territory Acceptance Bill did all they could to discredit the notion that Asian nations might want to invade Australia, they recognised that the adroit manipulation of invasion fears was a powerful weapon. Alfred Deakin wielded it with as much skill as any in federal parliament when it served his interests to do so, as proved to be the case with this Bill. There were occasions on which the threat of Asian invasion had its uses and needed to be cultivated for political ends. 'There would be no chance of this Bill passing', one member asserted, 'if it were not for the bogey of invasion'.

ASIA AS A CHALLENGE

The threat of losing Australia's empty north to Asia, the threat of disappearance, was also, as in Horne's case, a call to imagine a new future for the nation. There was nothing quite like the threat of losing the country to provoke an analysis of how it might be defended, not only in military terms, but as a distinctive community and as a nation that deserved an opportunity to make its mark on the world stage. It is also clear that the need to live in relatively close proximity to awakening Asia lent a certain drama and intensity to the Australian situation, it conferred a special status on Australia as a continent set aside for the development of the white race. The more awake Asia became, the more alert Australia would need to be. It was a distinctive perspective with its own biases and possibilities. While the dangers of this predicament were obvious enough, so too were the benefits to be had from a more alert and watchful citizenry.

In the 1920s there was a steady push for an ever larger population from across the continent and not least from a Sydney group calling itself the Millions Club.

In the October 1923 issue of its magazine *Millions*, there appeared a cartoon which showed an Australian male asleep against a tree, hat over his eyes, legs folded and seemingly without a care in the world. He is lying on a map of Australia. There are five other males representing India, Java, Indo-China, China and Japan looking down upon the sleeping figure. Each of them has a caption at his feet showing the population of his country. All wear a resentful expression as they glare down upon the somnolent figure below them. The cartoonist left no room for doubt that the sleeping figure's air of arrogant detachment from the problems of the world was offensive and dangerous. To be off duty with watchful Asia about was the height of folly. If this fellow was meant to be guarding the continent on behalf of his race, he was making a very poor job of it. The message was clear: Asia's proximity, its huge populations and its resentment of empty Australia provided every reason for Australians to become especially alert, watchful and internationally aware. It would hardly misrepresent the purposes of the cartoon to suggest that its creator wanted Australians to become Asia-aware.

The idea that the geopolitical challenges of Asia's awakening would test the quality of Australian nationhood goes back to the 1880s. It was there in full measure in William Lane's *Boomerang* serial, 'White or Yellow? The Race War of AD 1908'. In most of Australia's Asian invasion literature, including Lane's serial, precise accounts of the motives and tactics of the enemy are not a high priority. Enemies certainly needed to look plausibly threatening, but their importance lies not so much in what they represent, but in the responses they evoke from the Australian population. In determining where the strengths and weaknesses of the nation lay, there were some broad areas of agreement. Rural populations were credited with a firmer patriotism and greater fighting capabilities than were urban populations. Men were thought to be more reliably anti-Asian than women. Politicians and their parliaments, state and federal, were thought to be compromised, slow to react and lacking in vision. By and large, those who speculated upon geopolitical threats from Asia at any time from the 1880s to the First World War, saw the core of Australia's defence coming from rural males. The defence of the nation, it was often maintained, would become the responsibility of the bushman. In short, Asia's awakening helped raise the stocks of the bushman and his reputation as the embodiment of the national ideal.

It is a mistake to see threatening Asia as a wholly negative construction, because it contributed to Australians' understandings of their own identities. The dynamism, restlessness and energy commonly attributed to awakening Asia, particularly Japan, were qualities which critics often wanted to see in Australia. Up until the 1920s, it was commonly assumed that Australia could carry a population much nearer two hundred million than a miserable four or five million, concentrated in a few coastal cities. While critics who condemned Australia's emptiness often focused on the population question, there was more often than not a deeper concern about a people who seemed too indolent and unambitious, too attached to the pleasures of life to realise the potentialities of their continent. Nearby Asia could be invoked to teach these people some of the stern realities of life.

Dr Richard Arthur, who commented extensively on population and invasion fears in the decade before the First World War, conveyed such frequently ambivalent attitudes when he speculated on what the Japanese might have done with Australia. 'Scatter a score or two millions of these industrious little people over the great continent', he advised, ' . . . and one can conceive how this land would hum with industry and wealth production' (Arthur c1910). The Japanese are represented as a kind of human fertiliser that instantly turned barren regions to productive use, and while Arthur's tone is certainly patronising, he also seemed convinced that there was almost nothing the amazing Japanese could not accomplish. While the Japanese performed miracles on cramped islands with limited natural resources, Australians crowded into cramped cities, doing little or nothing, so it was commonly argued, with a continent of unparalleled potential.

The appeal to threatening Asia can be seen as part of an unfolding examination of what it might mean for Australia to be part of Asia. Despite this history, extending back over at least a century, there is a tendency today to see the discovery of Asia as a recent and singular event. Asia comes as a revelation to prescient beings whose task it is to waken the sleeping nation to the dawning of the new world. For Lane, the new world looked distinctly alarming. Almost exactly a century later another lonely visionary discovered Asia, although in his case the new day looked more promising. In 1988, Prime Minister Hawke announced that it was time for Australia to become 'Asia-literate', not because ignorance would weaken our security, the message underlying Lane's call for Asia literacy, but because it would diminish our access to Asian markets. Fear of military vulnerability had been replaced by concern about our economic vulnerability. Though the new message about Asia emphasised the trading opportunities available to Australia, there were still distinct echoes of the old, punitive message that Asia could inflict real damage—this time by locking Australia out of its markets.

From the final decades of the nineteenth century, the rise of Asia was increasingly presented as a looming reality in world affairs, as disruptive in its likely effects as floods and volcanoes proved to be in the world of natural disasters. It was also well understood that Asia as a natural disaster about to burst upon the world might well have a devastating effect upon the continued existence of European Australia. There was also a growing conviction that the focus of world power was shifting to the Pacific. For Australia to have a ringside seat was no doubt a mixed blessing and particularly as it was thought to be within Asia's power to end Australia's brief life as an independent nation. Yet the growing interest in the Pacific did mean that Australia was noticed and was a factor in world affairs. While Asian developments might have aroused apprehension, they also lent a certain gravity, even glamour, to the predicament of being a European power in an increasingly Asian setting.

In much of the invasion speculation that arose between the 1880s and the 1930s, Australians were assured an important role in stemming 'the rising tide of colour'. Asia was drawing Australia into the world and while there was much to fear in this development there was also an anticipatory frisson at being assigned a lead role on the world stage. Besides, these Pacific possibilities had all the hallmarks of a major story. They made Australia at once interestingly vulnerable and strategically critical to the white races, not simply a tiny, rather pointless outpost of Europe. And our proximity to Asia permitted Australia to make its own contribution to the encounter between East and West, which was already being widely proclaimed as the story of the century.

Speculation about an impending 'clash of colour,' widely circulated through the writings of popularising race theorists like the American Lothrop Stoddard, and encapsulated in phrases like the 'the yellow peril,' ensured that explosive Asia was an ideal subject for manly pessimism. It inspired conspiratorial exchanges among the cognoscenti as they drew deeply on their cigars and circulated the port decanter in the Millions Club. If it was a fact that there was a coming racial smash, that fact travelled through a medium of rumour and innuendo. Someone might have noticed something in the cable news or heard something from the ministry. While there was no knowing what the Japanese might have been up to, there was invariably a fellow prepared to swear that spies accompanied the Japanese squadrons. These communications often achieved their perfected form in cryptic revelations of the kind that appeared in A.W. Jose's *The Romantic Nineties*. Jose cited a prominent banker who in 1913 told him that Australia would soon be a colony of either Germany or Japan (Jose 1933). That was enough to suggest that at the big end of town grave matters were under discussion. This micro-story had just the right mix of certainty and mystery. This Asia was man's talk.

ASIA AS OPPORTUNITY?

There is more to be said by historians about Australia's encounter with Asia in both its negative and positive manifestations than is often supposed. The story of a fledgling nationhood, endangered by its proximity to the turbulent social upheavals of Asia, is considerably enriched because it also permitted, even demanded, an ongoing audit of the nation's capabilities. Were Anglo-Saxons improving or declining? Was the climate a boon or a curse? Was there enough strength in rural Australia to offset what were widely regarded as the degenerative impacts of urbanisation? Assuming a threat, what were the nation's strengths and weaknesses? Would the fellow asleep under the tree awake in time? Would those seeking to draw attention to developments in Asia prevail over those who dismissed Asia's significance? Would the white races draw together in a union of strength? Viewed as a threat, Asia could be readily seen as a new and demanding test of the agency and strategic intelligence of Australians, of their knowledge of the world and their value as a nation. If it came to the point, were Australians worth preserving?

The common view, particularly favoured by politicians, that Asia has been a closed book to Australians is false. When Prime Minister Hawke reflected upon the importance of Asia to Australia, he showed no interest in putting his views in context. On the contrary, in a 1993 interview with *Window*, a weekly Hong Kong news magazine, he insisted that the discovery of Asia was something that he had managed all by himself. He claimed to have been 'overwhelmingly responsible for the vision of Australia as part of Asia'. He had insisted that Australia's future lay in 'enmeshment with Asia' in the face of scepticism and opposition. There could be no more abrupt dismissal of the attempts to explore the meanings of Asia which, for all their twists and turns and fevered speculations, had been going on for at least a century.

Asia has been a regular presence whenever Australians turned their attention to the kinds of future that awaited them. In 1895 Mr E. Jerome Dyer, at the invitation of a number of Melbourne's leading organisations in the world of business and public affairs, addressed an audience on 'Australia and the Asian-Pacific' where which he spelt out in substantial detail the considerable trading opportunities that awaited Australia in the region and particularly in Japan. In what was to become an increasingly familiar appeal to Australia's Asian future, so familiar that even a prime minister heard it a century later, Dyer predicted that 'the time may not be far distant when the importance we attach to European markets will be more than evenly shared by those Eastern countries'. For Dyer, Australia's Pacific location was not a military or defence problem, not a question of the rising tide of colour threatening to inundate Australia, but a providential opportunity to open new markets (Dyer 1895). A decade later an audience of Sydney business men were told that Japan would become Australia's major trading partner in an address which painted a glowing picture of the complementarities in trade between Australia and Japan.

Some of these trading possibilities were realised in substantial wool sales to Japan in the 1930s, though this development was abruptly curtailed by a trade diversion policy which asserted the need to put the empire first. One sign of the expanding interest in Asia in the 1930s among Australian intellectuals was the publication in 1935 of *Australia and The Far East: Diplomatic and Trade Relations* by Angus and Robertson in conjunction with The Australian Institute of International Affairs. In his foreword T.R. Bavin noted that the 'Far East' though distant from Europe, 'was within a few days by sea, and a few hours by air, of our coasts'. Though Asia had become 'the focus of some of the world's most difficult and threatening international problems', Bavin hoped for the development of a community of Pacific experts who would contribute to a resolution of the complex international tensions which threatened the region. He was confident that Australia was well placed to contribute expertise to regional forums (Clunies-Ross 1935).

The focus of the 1935 volume was on Japan, China and to a lesser extent the Netherlands East Indies and British Malaya. Of all these countries, Japan was seen as the key to Australia's future in Asia. That Japan loomed so large was a comment both on the recent growth in trade between the countries and on the reputation that Japan had won for itself in world affairs, particularly from the end of the Russo-Japanese war in 1905.

Australia and The Far East raises the thorny question of what constituted Asia in the Australian imagination. There was the 'awakening East' and threatening Asia, the Asia of diplomacy and trade, and the Asia of the empire, particularly the Asia of the shipping routes which took Australian travellers to the old country via Colombo. In commenting on what he called the travelling classes, Richard White noted that they drew a distinction between the 'foreigners' one encountered in Europe and the 'natives' of the non-European world (White 1987, p. 441). For the traveller, Colombo was a routine stopover. What Australians found there depended a great deal on the timing of the visit, their frame of reference and their preoccupations. The novelist and entrepreneur Randolph Bedford, on a visit before the First World War, found confirmation that mixed-race communities were a calamity that Australia should avoid; the historian Kathleen Fitzpatrick, visiting with her mother in the 1920s, was so preoccupied by the Europe she had just left that she saw almost nothing at all; in the 1930s, essayist and academic, Walter Murdoch, felt that he had encountered both the 'mysterious East' and the beginning of the end of British rule.

ASIA AND THE IDENTITY OF 'AUSTRALIA'

By the 1950s Australia was coming under increasing pressure to change its policies towards Asia and in particular to relax the immigration restrictions imposed by the white Australia policy. One of the weapons used by opponents of the immigration policy was to depict Australia as a narrow and fearful community, closed to the outside world and particularly to Asia. One of Donald Horne's purposes in *The Lucky Country* was to encourage a suburban and unambitious people to start to think about Asia in a more systematic way. For those who wanted to see Australia develop policies that were more receptive to Asia, there was a logic in emphasising how closed this community had been. There was every reason for them to pile up the evidence for this being either an unrelievedly anti-Asian culture or a culture which knew nothing about Asia and was in no hurry to learn. It was, and to an extent remains, a predictable tactic for those who urge us to know more about Asia to document or infer a history of ignorance that needs immediate remedial action.

Yet there were those who developed interests in Asia that merit closer scrutiny. One of the most promising lines of inquiry is the substantial literature of Asian travel. Melbourne writer James Hingston made an extensive journey through Asia in 1879 to 1880, which became the basis for his witty and idiosyncratic *The Australian Abroad*, a generous, inexhaustible travel book. Allowing for the hyperbole that surrounds press notices and reviews, it is clear that Hingston's book was a great success in England and America. Hingston was frequently compared with Mark Twain as a travel writer, often to the American's disadvantage.

Hingston was a formidable cultural tourist. He entered Asia with familiar prejudices against the degenerative impacts of tropical climates and with the view that modern Asia was a shadow of its grand past. But Hingston was nevertheless willing to be impressed and often was. He was swept away by the beauty of Japan, its cultural richness, its vitality and the honesty of its people. He considered Japan's climate the nearest to perfection in the world, from which, no doubt, he believed all other blessings flowed. Though he was not primarily concerned with buying and selling, Hingston also recommended Japan to the 'mercantile traveller', but insisted that the country would be just as suited to the needs of the artist in search both of new scenery and new techniques in the decorative arts. But it was the spiritual wealth of Asia that impressed Hingston most. He had travelled a part of the world that had allegedly made two-thirds of all history, and cradled all existing faiths worthy of the name (Hingston 1885). Hingston had imagined Asia and packaged it for the traveller. He has had many followers though few peers in the years that have followed.

Alfred Deakin was among those who had read and approved Hingston's *The Australian Abroad*, as well he might, for they shared an interest in Asia as the cradle of the world's major religions. In matters of faith, Deakin wrote: 'The East remains mother and mistress of all.' As a young man, Deakin had been attracted by the spiritualist movement and had developed a quite intense fascination with India. Some of the appeal was certainly to an exotic India, though that merely contextualises his interests rather than disqualifies them. Of India and its associations Deakin wrote:

> some words are enriched by historic memories . . . and present themselves before us with a glamour greater than that of romance. Such a magic name is India, before which the throng of unimpressive words falls back as if outshone by a regal presence, clothed with 'barbaric pearl and gold'.

In his 1923 biography of Alfred Deakin, Walter Murdoch noted that Deakin's visit to India in 1893 was brief, 'but the preparation for it had been spread over many years of study; he knew the history of the country as few Englishmen know it' (Murdoch 1923). The trip resulted in two publications on India, *Temple and Tomb in India* and *Irrigated India*. Sir Charles Dilke, a considerable traveller himself, claimed of *Irrigated India* that no 'European traveller has ever shown a higher appreciation of the beauties of the Indian cities'.

Towards the end of that volume Deakin presented an issue which has a very contemporary ring to it. Since geography had brought Australia and Asia 'face to face, it may yet bring them hand to hand, and mind to mind. They have much to teach other' (Deakin 1893, p. 16). Deakin was setting a high standard in urging Australians to approach Asia as both pupil and teacher. Yet his comments also express something of the complex particularity and originality of the Australian responses to Asia. We looked at the world differently and responded to different creative pressures. There was the inheritance that membership of the British Empire conferred, which for the Australian was at once a matter of being among the rulers and among the ruled. There was an appreciation of 'the East' as the source of spiritual and philosophical truths which had profoundly influenced what it meant to be human. And there was the growing awareness of the geopolitical implications of Australia's proximity to Asia. Deakin no doubt achieved a heightened expression of these competing Asias and their implications for Australia, but in doing so was responding to cultural pressures, contradictions and opportunities common to a range of Australian intellectuals. What was meant by 'Australia' and what was meant by 'Asia' were not unrelated questions.

The evidence marshalled in this chapter is modest. However, it suggests that over the course of a century Australia has evolved distinctive and in many instances richer, more creative and more inquiring responses to Asia than our histories might suggest.

References

Arthur, R. (n.d.) *The Question of Questions for Australians*, reprinted from the *Australasian Review of Reviews*, c. 1910, Richard Arthur papers, Mitchell Library, State Library of NSW, Sydney.

Clunies Ross, I. 1935, *Australia and The Far East: Diplomatic and Trade Relations*, foreword by T.R. Bavin, Angus & Robertson with the Australian Institute of International Affairs, Sydney.

Cook, J. 1909, *Northern Territory Acceptance Bill (No. 2)*, Representatives

Deakin, A. 1893, *Irrigated India: An Australian View of India and Ceylon*, E.A. Petherick, Melbourne.

—— 1893, *Temple and Tomb in India*, Melbourne.

Dyer, E.J. 1895, 'Trade with the East: The proposed Japanese Treaty', *The Age*, 22 October. p. 5.

Hingston, J. 1885, *The Australian Abroad on Branches from the Main Routes Round the World*, William Inglis, Melbourne.

Horne, D. 1964, *The Lucky Country: Australia in the Sixties*, Penguin, Melbourne.

Jose, A. W. 1933, *The Romantic Nineties*, Angus & Robertson, Sydney.

Murdoch, W. 1923, *Alfred Deakin*, Constable, London.

White, R. 1987, 'Overseas', in *Australians 1938*, eds Bill Gammage & Peter Spearritt, Fairfax, Syme & Weldon, Sydney.

15 Celebrating Australian music

Bruce Johnson

An examination of the academic literature suggests that there is really only one aesthetically significant Australian music tradition. Studies of 'Australian music', 'Australian composition', 'Australian composers', have over many years constructed a canon dominated and legitimated by a tradition constructed in nineteenth-century Europe out of Eurocentric high art music. It is a tradition created by and for a white European bourgeoisie at a time when their standards of taste and artistic value were so dominant as to be presented as 'universal'. Musical practices which did not conform to those standards were consigned to the domain of such areas as folklorism and ethnomusicology.

White settlement in Australia coincided with the apogee of white, Eurocentric, bourgeois imperial dominance. This settlement was established as a prison in which the trustees had a paternalistic obligation to protect their charges from criminal and savage tendencies—a circumstance which has generated an attitude to popular culture which is very different from that in the United States. In Australia, particular emphasis was placed on the civilising influences of 'the arts', but conceived in a very restricted sense. Any cultural activity which does not conform to that tradition has had an unusually difficult time gaining respectful recognition in Australia.

As a result, the 'discourse of excellence' in relation to Australian music has excluded the overwhelming majority of Australian music-making. It has diminished radically the rich plurality of this expressive practice and its sites. The diverse and abundant music actually produced and consumed in Australia is not registered in the 'definitive' accounts of significant music practice. Most Australian music-making is dismissed as various picturesque practices reflecting ethnicity (local or transplanted) rather than aesthetics, or, in the case of pop, it is seen as a phenomenon of the political economy. As I shall go on to illustrate, this does not simply erase most of the music-making practices in Australia as sites of aesthetic experience. It also occludes the astonishing diversity of such practices. The privileging of European canonical notions of musical form banishes beyond the realm of the aesthetic music which is shaped by different formal traditions. It must be emphasised that this means most of the music made by human beings: most of the music made in a multicultural society. But this privileging also recognises only a very limited number of music forums—above all, the concert hall performance centred on a score. Again, most of the world's music-making, including Australia's, occurs outside that forum. It is a forum which imposes intimidating restraints on notions like originality and diversity. The score and the regimented concert hall allow virtually no scope for democratic and ethnically diversified channels of originality, such as improvisation, ecstatic reciprocity between audiences and musicians, and a creative harmonisation of music and the richness of specific local social materiality. Concert performances of 'high art' music are special events, architecturally, acoustically, and aesthetically divorced from the chaotic, unruly uniqueness of life in a particular place at a particular time, of Australian life as it is experienced and produced at a given place and moment. Banishing the rich uniqueness of those moments as they are articulated musically masks the diversity of that life and conceals the musical originality which that diversity generates.

MUSIC AND AUSTRALIAN IDENTITIES

Because the representation of music in Australian scholarship ignores most of our musical experience, it has radically undervalued the contribution music has made to the construction of 'Australia'. Relative to other art forms, there is little of the sound of music in our definitions of Australia. Publishers' catalogues and bibliographies confirm that studies of Australian cultures and identities are overwhelmingly dominated by the examination of verbal and visual narratives. Yet of all the arts, music is arguably the most pervasive in everyday life. In June 1991 the Australian Bureau of Statistics (ABS) surveyed households on their attendance at venues over a twelve-month period. In that time 4 442 500 persons attended libraries, 2 886 800 attended art galleries, 2 151 300 attended non-musical theatre, and 8 219 100 attended music concerts, musical theatre, dance concerts (*Attendance at Selected Cultural Venues, Australia, June 1991*, ABS Cat. 4114.0). These formal recreations, however, are only a very small fraction of our experience of music. Music saturates contemporary urban life, and is inescapable for creatures lacking earlids. We can decide not to read a newspaper in a bar, but we cannot decide not to hear the piped music. It is in lifts, restaurants, sporting venues, airports, waiting rooms, on telephone hold, in theatre, television, film. If we are trying to isolate definitive aspects of modern urban experience, the ubiquity of music is one of them. It is not simply the amount of music that makes it important, but its unparallelled power as a way of articulating identities at every level from the individual to the national. 'The musical event . . . evokes and organises collective memories and present experiences of place with an intensity, power and simplicity unmatched by any other social activity' (Stokes 1994, p. 3).

Obviously there are many kinds of music. Much of it is covered through such loose but somehow recognisable categories as 'classical' and 'pop', and there are formal spaces in which they are enjoyed—concerts, discos, festivals. But there are other forms of music which don't quite fit these categories, such as hymns, country, folk, jazz, school songs, the durable Victorian parlour repertoire, brass bands. And there are forums in which music is experienced which generate collective and regional identities with profound intensity, but which receive no recognition in music studies: street marches, political rallies, sports stadiums, 'ethnic' clubs, domestic celebrations. These are sites at which the dynamic multiplicity of Australian identities and their roots are proclaimed through music which can generate the most powerful emotions. That multiplicity is the outcome of infinite permutations of parameters: gender, class, age, place, profession, race, ethnicity. The racial and ethnic diversity of Australian society is among the most visible of any country. It is a diversity reflected in the astonishing range of regional cuisines which we can enjoy in our restaurants. The distinctive 'flavour'—Greek, Thai, Indian—is also frequently defined through piped or live music. What often emerges is a music with an inflection unique to Australia, as unique to the specificity of this moment and place of consumption as the cuisine which, in the opinions of many international gourmets, is one of the most exciting in the world because of that unique blend of diverse sources. So with the music.

Yet this richness and the sites where it is displayed are barely noted in studies of Australian music. There are various reasons for this silence. Some are to do with the dominant aesthetics, others relate to the power of the mediations. There are several combinations of ways in which different kinds of music activity are delivered and promoted, presented, talked about, supported. Classical music is presented and talked about in ways that differ from pop music. Pop music is delivered mainly through media technology (radio, video, recordings, CD ROM, Internet). Because of the distance between the producers and the consumers (audiences), the mediations are immensely powerful. They control what we may hear. Rugby songs and local church music are experienced much more directly. The producers and the consumers are closer to being identical than in most other forms of music. This is the least mediated form of music experience, yet it is also the least recognised. People write about the growing popularity of *a capella* music and think in terms of conventional performance conditions, but never refer to our largest and most frequently performing *a capella* groups—sports spectators. This reminds us of the power of the mediations in giving authority to cultural activities. Could it be that the greater the distance between the producer and the consumer—that is, the more elaborate the mediations—the more importance our society attaches to music? The mediations are the 'centre' and music experience is on the 'margin'.

Perhaps more than any other of the arts, music provides a vehicle through which we experience and define our day-to-day lives and, in so doing, register the multiplicity of Australian identities. Yet when we come to look at authoritative ways of talking about music, we find that it is this richly variegated everyday-ness, the most direct experience of music, which is left out in favour of the internationalism which is praised as 'universal' in art music, and condemned as 'homogeneity' in mass-mediated pop. The inextricable connections between music and daily life are very much the subject of ethnomusicology, but the subject of ethnomusicology is also most frequently the music of someone else—another tribe or race or place, whose picturesque otherness is largely confirmed precisely by the way their music activity is woven into everyday life. The same essential, hygienic connection between music and our own everyday lives remains almost invisible in the standard studies, which ascribe the highest importance to a completely different relationship between ourselves and music.

THE NEGLECT OF AUSTRALIAN MUSIC EXPERIENCE

Where is the recognition, let alone valuation, of our local music culture with its ambience of the everyday, the music which embodies our distinctive individual and collective specificity? There is a most curious relationship between studies of Australian music and Australians' experience of music. The *Australian Directory of Music Research* (Sydney, 1978), covering work up to February 1977, Deborah Crisp's *Bibliography of Australian Music* (Armidale, 1982) and the annual directories carried in the journal of the Musicological Society of Australia reflect a longstanding disparity between Australian music studies and Australian music experience. The pattern is reproduced in areas of government policy formation and arts subsidy (Johnson 1995c, pp. 12–13). There is a shift towards increased emphasis on our vernacular musics in the 1996 *Register of Theses in Australian Music* produced by the University of Melbourne's Centre for Studies in Australian Music. Nonetheless, the fundamental pattern persists. It is noteworthy, for example, that among the more than 150 studies of 'composers' and the dozen studies of 'instruments' listed, none is outside the 'high art' tradition. The nineteenth National Conference of the Musicological Society of Australia, held in Melbourne in July 1996, produced a range of papers that disclosed a suddenly increasing recognition of everyday music. It is clear that we are entering a paradigm shift in music studies. There is inevitably an interval between this, however, and its emergence into public visibility and influence. The Australian National Academy of Music's program impassively excludes all vernacular forms—popular, folk, multicultural—from its category of 'Australian music'.

The standard ways of defining Australian music still have very little to do with how Australian music overall is expressed. The 'canon' centralises musical traditions which serve a tiny minority of Australians (including myself, though not to the exclusion of other tastes). Australian Bureau of Statistics documents tell us that attendances at classical music performances in Australia in 1991 numbered only 986 000. In a group surveyed in 1991 regarding leisure patterns, only 2 percent (the smallest category) attended classical music concerts during the relevant period. Among various categories of 'cultural venues', the lowest national participation rate was for classical music concerts (8.2 percent), while the third-highest—and the highest for people with full-time employment—was for popular music concerts (Johnson 1995c, p. 1). On the basis of these figures, the canonical accounts of Australian music exclude the experience of music in performance of the great majority of Australians.

What is left out by this account is the originality of Australians and their agency in constructing Australian identities. One of the arguments mounted by high-art apologists is that it is the commercialism of some kinds of music that makes it trivial in relation to the criteria of artistic and cultural value. This view cuts us off from some extraordinary and unique achievements of Australian culture. Australian jazz musicians, for example, have played a most important—in some ways incomparable—role in the articulation of twentieth-century Australian identities both locally and internationally. While the standard history of Australian music dates the onset of musical modernity after mid-century, jazz had already sounded the call as early as 1917. It was the anthem of that twenties feminist, the flapper, and women were prominent in innovative improvisatory practices which signalled the arrival of the modern. Jazz, of course, was and has remained at the forefront in improvisatory practice, long before it was being rediscovered by composers locked into the text-centred traditions of high-art music. Jazz's Dada-esque violation of the conventions of Eurocentric art music was allied with a modernist call to 'make it new'. Jazz was also the incidental music for the 'Angry Penguins' and the Contemporary Art Society, two of the most significant sites of artistic radicalism in the first half of the century. [1]

The influence of Australian jazz internationally also stretches the imagination of canon-based historians. European historians and critics attribute to Australia a distinctive jazz style to an extent accorded no other country outside the United States. The 'Australian jazz style' is noted, collected and imitated internationally, including by musicians in the United States. From Graeme Bell's European tours of the forties, to the Australian Jazz Quartet's American successes in the fifties, to the acclamation accorded musicians like Bernie McGann, Australian jazz musicians have made their mark, not simply by successful imitation of their sources, but by national distinctiveness. This is so much the case that, uniquely among our musical forms, Australian jazz musicians have actually changed the course of their music's history in other countries.

Graeme Bell is regarded as the father of the jazz tradition in Czechoslovakia as a consequence of his work there in the forties. Much as young Australian musicians revere the seminal work of American jazz musicians, Bell's recordings were still being described as 'the Bible' by young Czech musicians when he was invited back 50 years later as the guest of the government of the Czech Republic. The members of the Bell band introduced an exuberant music into postwar Europe that generated a new spirit of optimism among those who heard them play. Their impact on youth was so great that when the communist regime came to power it was forced to review its assumptions about the possibilities of centralised cultural engineering. The Australian musicians inspired several generations of artists in Czechoslovakia, giving momentum to radical theatre and performance, and to what became known as the Prague Spring, one of the most significant liberalising moments in the history of European communism. Australian jazz musicians also changed the course of popular music in the United Kingdom, transforming the social function of British jazz, deliberately changing and expanding its audiences in a way that laid the foundations for the arrival of rock and subsequent developments in English popular music.[2]

No other Australian musical form has exercised this kind of international influence. Yet the Australian music canon and its scholarship have provided scarcely a glimpse of these achievements. And I have focused here on only one of a great many music genres whose contributions to our cultural identities have been largely ignored. More recently, in a period of increasing sensitivity to multiculturalism, it is the unique syncretism in vernacular music which has been prominent in signalling diversity, rather than the peak art music organisations, which have shown relatively little resonance to the distinctive variety of Australian society in the nineties. Perusal of current and recent seasons of, for example, the Sydney Symphony Orchestra and the Australian Opera, or of the curricula of Australian Conservatoria, give virtually no hint of the distinctive variousness of Australian society and its music. In 1995 the Australian Opera gave 236 performances of 18 operas, of which only eight performances were of the single Australian work in the program. This is not to express disapproval of these music programs, but to note simply that in spite of their lion's share of the funding and discourse, they do not happen to register very much of the rich and unique embroidery of contemporary Australian society. On the other hand, as we move towards areas of music which are less privileged in terms of funding and academic legitimation, we also gain an increasing sense of the jostling diversity which constitutes Australia's unique presence in a global community increasingly homogenised by mass mediations. It is in the informal sites and vernacular genres I have exemplified above that we find the unusually harmonised blend of genres and ethnicities that makes Australian culture 'original'. At the level of 'community music', in groups where salsa fuses in creative tensions with Balkan, flamenco with gamelan, bouzouki with bush band, rock with Aboriginal, and jazz with Javanese, an original music is emerging which articulates the unique and unruly realities of Australian culture in the late twentieth century. Where a tribal site like a sports ground, a school fete, a music festival, a street market, a ballroom dancing class spontaneously creates a new community that draws together and re-articulates identities rooted in Asia, the Americas, Europe, Africa, the Pacific—there we find newly compounded musical utterances that not merely reflect but construct new identities specific to contemporary Australia.

A RICHER VIEW

To disclose these new and distinctive realities as they proclaim themselves musically, it is necessary to recognise the ways in which musical experience articulates the conditions of life and belief at any given moment in any given place. The idea that music is a finished text with an inherent meaning, that remains fixed no matter what the enfolding social dynamic, still has a disproportionate degree of authority in the context of developments in the study of other expressive forms and of popular music. Likewise the idea that these meanings are fully intelligible to formalist analysis (or indeed any one master discourse) can only bring about frustration and irritation on the part of the scholar when he or she encounters music as a social practice.

Individual and collective identities, including nationhood, are processes, not products. They are infinitely dynamic, and if we wish to understand how music contributes to the unfolding of these processes in continuous renewal, we will learn little by trying to lock it into discourses about formal perfection, permanence, universality. Music as a practice is always affected by the specific circumstances of performance. This is why it can be so sensitive as a register of cultural experience. This is especially so of improvised musics performed in the less regimented venues of pub, club, street, mall. It is difficult to capture such music through the more traditional discourses of musicology, yet it is what cannot be captured in that way that is most immediately expressive of the particular moment in the processes called culture and music.

To increase our understanding of that dynamic we need to continue to bring 'art music' into the realm of social materiality, as a marker of community, of class, of gender, of politics in its broadest sense. At the same time let us shift pop into the aesthetic field. See it not simply as an alienating product of a global marketing structure, but also how it is reappropriated as an aesthetic experience by its consumers. This would help to disclose the artificiality of many of the aesthetic distinctions which marginalise vernacular music. The formal differences between a multimedia, audience-interactive performance which describes itself as avant-garde and karaoke night at the Bondi Hotel are not so clear if we resituate them in our conceptual framework. Is the standing ovation given to a visiting virtuoso in the Opera House such a different phenomenon from the arms waving like a wind-stroked cornfield at a Ween concert at Eastern Creek? They are both tribal rites, acts of collective bonding through music participation.

To gain a richer view of Australian music we also need to give more recognition to a range of sites of musical experience that are rarely recognised in the standard studies but are part of the fabric of everyday life, such as the walkman and the car radio. Our daily actions also belong to music-making—humming, whistling, adjusting the rhythm of our walk, tapping a steering wheel. Instead of trying to resolve the ambiguities between music-making and -listening, we need to attempt to generate an aesthetic that maintains their integrity. For these ambiguities break out of the established aesthetic moulds and resonate with the uniqueness of the collective and individual lives they expresses.

Before music means something, it is a sound in the ear, a component in a soundscape. It is accompanied by traffic noise, social conversation, poker machines, the ringing of telephones, aircraft, the tinkling of glasses and crockery. Even a recording, made in the most immaculate acoustic environment, is most frequently heard in conjunction with other domestic sounds—these become part of the experience. However distasteful this may be to a musicologist, the overwhelming majority of our experience of music is as part of the soundscape of the everyday. Soundscape studies provide one of the alternative discourses through which some of the blindspots of established music analysis in Australia may be overcome. To address music as part of our daily experience of sounds provides insights into the distinctive character of that experience. An emphasis on the larger sensuous context of music activity helps us to understand ecstatic dimensions of it that more strictly semiological or formalist approaches miss (see Johnson 1994).

To sum up, at the centre of music studies in Australia there has been a massive hole, into which our common experience of music disappears, with all its originality, uniqueness and enriching diversity. Academically approved ways of writing about Australian music have in the past left vast areas unmapped, above all, the everyday realm of music as it is actually experienced by most people. As a consequence, we are only now beginning to learn about the place of music as a terrain of individual and collective agency and self-definition.

NOTES

1 On the connections between jazz and various forms of modernity, see Johnson 1987, especially pp. 3–13 and Johnson 1995a; on women and improvisation, see Whiteoak 1993, e.g. p. 180.
2 On the 'Australian style' see Clunies-Ross 1979; on Australian jazz in Europe and the UK, Johnson 1995b.

REFERENCES

Clunies-Ross, B. 1979, 'An Australian sound', in *Australian Popular Culture*, eds P. Spearritt & D. Walker, Allen & Unwin, Sydney.

Johnson, B. 1987, *Oxford Companion to Australian Jazz*, Oxford University Press, Melbourne.

—— 1994, *Soundscapes: Essays on Vroom and Moo*, Department of Folk Tradition, Helsinki.

—— 1995a, 'Towards a new cartography—rethinking Australia's musical history', in *One Hand on the Manuscript: Music in Australian Cultural History 1930–1960*, eds N. Brown, P. Campbell, R. Holmes, P. Read & L. Sitsky, Humanities Research Centre, Canberra.

—— 1995b, 'Australian Jazz in Europe: A case study in musical displacement', *Perfect Beat—The Pacific Journal of Research into Contemporary Music and Popular Culture*, vol. 2, no. 3, July.

—— 1995c, 'Jazz and the cultural politics of Australian music', *Context* 10, summer.

—— 1996, 'Directions in popular music studies', *Perfect Beat—The Pacific Journal of Research into Contemporary Music and Popular Culture*, vol. 2, no. 4, January.

Stokes, M. (ed.) 1994, *Ethnicity, Identity and Music: The Musical Construction of Place*, Berg, Oxford/Providence, United States.

Whiteoak, J. 1993, Australian approaches to improvisatory musical practice 1836–1970: A Melbourne perspective, dissertation, Department of Music, La Trobe University, Victoria.

16 A secret history

McKenzie Wark

What was Australian postmodernism?[1] I think it's an interesting time to ask. Particularly in the light of that famous speech Don Watson, the historian and speech writer to the former prime minister, Paul Keating, gave at Mieta's in Melbourne, 'A Toast to the Postmodern Republic'. Whatever shape the republic takes, he said, there will be

> something unstructured, if not . . . deconstructed about it . . . I'm only just game enough to say it: it might be the first postmodern republic, and I mean that in the nicest possible way. I mean a republic that exalts the nation less than the way of life. Whose principal value is tolerance rather than conformity, difference rather than uniformity (Watson 1993).

He's talking there about what in the early eighties were marginal concerns, found in the little magazines and art gallery catalogues. In the early nineties they became, for a moment at least, rhetorical options for the nation. Possible grounds for creating notions of Australian culture and identity. This is not unprecedented. The literary critic A.A. Phillips coined the now popular expression 'cultural cringe' in an essay for the Melbourne-based quarterly *Meanjin*. Donald Horne, editor of the Sydney-based magazines the *Observer* and the *Bulletin*, gave us the 'lucky country'.[2] With Watson, as with Phillips and Horne, critical essay-writing became a resource for thinking the nation's creativity, and thinking the nation creatively.

To me there was a sly irony hidden in Watson's creation of a notional 'postmodern republic'. One of the major themes of postmodernism in the eighties was that creativity results from the appropriation and recombination of existing elements in culture that speak through us, rather than some kind of spontaneous act of romantic genius. Watson seemed to be borrowing and collaging together ideas current from postmodern thought itself. If those postmodern currents had made much of the fragmentation and multiplication of identities, then Watson rose to the challenge of finding a way to make that very plurality the premise of an essentially Australian identity. Only one cannot appear to bestow tolerance and difference from above, as Watson does in his speech. And that is not just my reading of the kind of theoretical underpinnings Watson offered for prime minister Paul Keating's version of the republic. The electorate seemed to think so too. With the victory of John Howard's coalition, all that returns to the margins from whence it came. With the departure of Keating and Watson, someone else will be writing quite a different prime minister very different speeches and the postmodern republic retired to the Jurassic Park of history.

History is a republic of documents. I've hoarded several milk crates full of documents that are bones of a postmodern life, if there was such a thing. I've always wondered what I would ever actually do with these parched white remainders. I think now they are perhaps meant for carving an image of a certain cultural moment that had its day and will have to wait now for another time, to come again. And so—a secret history of my postmodernism. Which is certainly not Don Watson's, although there may be some obscure Caledonia where they are cousins. In this chapter I want to perform a bit of personal archaeology about the rhetorics and practices of postmodern culture in Sydney in the eighties. What I have to offer are perceptions of certain events. Not necessarily the most important or representative. Just events. It's what Greil Marcus calls a secret history, 'the result of moments that seem to leave nothing behind, nothing but the mystery of spectral connections between people long separated by place and time, but somehow speaking the same language' (Marcus 1989).

Marcus was looking for the subterranean connections underlying a history of the punk insurrection of the late seventies. A historical configuration that Marcus sees as embodying the 'demand to live not as an object but as a subject of history—to live as if something actually depended on one's actions' (Marcus 1989). The moment that interests me comes after this, and embodies, if anything, a different desire. That insurrectionary moment had its effects in Sydney city culture.[3] Punk subjectivity left its traces. And yet the postmodern moment dwelt in the lees of this last failure of the project of becoming, of becoming the subject of history.

IRONY

The spirit of Sydney postmodernism is a spirited irony. It is about the displacement of cultural elements from the customary order in such a way that it makes that order transparent, so that we can self-consciously examine the order of culture as something created rather than natural, an effect of power rather than divine necessity. Actually, it goes one better—it is the doubling or folding of irony into itself in a situation where irony has begun to proliferate throughout all of the surfaces of contemporary culture. As Catharine Lumby writes:

> What if the role of the artist and the status of the art object were so uncertain that there was no longer a status quo to disrupt? Indeed, where would the possibility for ironic gesture lie when irony had become the status quo? In such a situation, irony might be said to have had its revenge—to turn on those who wield it—and collapse into complacency (Lumby 1996a, p. 20).

What lies at the end of this thought is a certain vertigo: the artist or the writer might be the object, not the subject of the creative act. 'The makers are no longer in control of the ironic possibilities. Rather, it is the objects themselves which mock us for our attempt to fix their aesthetic meaning and value' (Wark 1994, p. 225). What might have brought about such a situation? The proliferation of media 'vectors'—the trajectories along which information moves—undermines the established orders of representation. Whether celebrating or deploring it, critics to the right and left agree that this makes the old verities of cultural order appear somewhat shaky. Once-fixed points of cultural identity and value appear subject to flux. Which leads one troubled postmodernist to a somewhat irksome question: 'What if the vector becomes so ubiquitous that every point becomes mobile, and every point becomes interconnected with every other point? What will become of us' (Lumby 1996a, p. 20).

In such a situation, irony is no longer something that a writer can confidently claim is simply an affect of her or his creative and subjective will. Irony becomes objective, produced by the media's effect on the public sphere, which now undermines itself to the point of disrupting its circuits of meaning, its partitions of good sense and good taste. 'Do not adjust your set. That black thing in the centre of your screen is the hole the public sphere made on the way out.' Or as Eric Michaels put it, in a suitably parodic style:

> Andy Warhol became famous in the 1960s for saying that, in the new electronic age, everybody would be famous for five minutes . . . Never noted for his mathematics Warhol's prediction may require a recalculation:

> if you take the number of radio and TV transmitters operating everywhere in the world and multiply this by the number of total broadcast hours each, and then divide by the total world population, the result might indicate that by, say, 1982, everybody, everywhere, had had their five minutes. The precise date when this happened, I submit, marks the beginning of the postmodernist moment. At that point, we were required to come to some new relationship between texts and audiences (Michaels 1994, p. 180).

Given that this is a story about irony, it will come as no surprise that everyone who had anything to do with postmodernism distances themselves from it. Postmodernism is nothing but a crate of empties left over when the party ends. But perhaps it's time to redeem them. One could write a whole essay on what the postmodern isn't, and wasn't. By the mid-nineties, it had become a favourite bogey of the tired old 'new left' and the wearisome old 'new right', who erased their differences and became a culture of reaction precisely in their wilful refusal to understand what the new moment entailed. They got by on a series of graceless parodies to the effect that the postmodern was a mindless 'relativism', a recline into 'nihilism' or a celebration of the 'popular'. In so doing, they proved themselves even less artless victims of the postmodern condition of the public sphere than the self-styled postmodern ironists. Their artifice lacked not only substance, but grace. Although in the case of David Williamson's plays and sermons, there was no shortage of force.[4] And of course they missed the point—that the postmodern, as an aesthetic strategy responding to a condition of the proliferation of signs, was a revaluing of all values, which means overturning the table of assumed and established taste, preferably with a flourish. The postmodern is not an inversion of the relationship of high culture to pop, but a series of tactics meant to displace it so that one can begin to evaluate afresh. A second caveat has to do with the odd fact of writing about postmodern 'creativity', creatively. One of the original pomo moves was to declare orginality dead, and create instead only in the mode of appropriating from the past. But that, I think, was part of the value of the moment: to propose that there was indeed nothing at all creative about conventional modes of understanding and valuing creativity itself. And so a creative version of the idea of 'creativity was created out of its opposite—appropriation.

I warned you about the irony . . .

IN THE MARGIN OF MARGINS

In a fit of absent-mindedness, the Visual Arts Board of the Australia Council funded what will turn out to be the most daring, original and necessary literature of the eighties. For it was in the little art magazines that I now hoard in my milk crates, like *Art & Text*, *On the Beach* and *Tension*, where Australian sensibility reinvented itself.

The Oscar Wilde of Australian art in the eighties was without doubt Paul Taylor, editor of *Art & Text*, writer, curator and all round hustler of what would become the postmodern sensibility. Taylor had the cunning and the wit to see Australian culture as a valid site for the production of a truly contemporary art, and as an exemplar of the emerging taste of the eighties. If this was to be a time when art grew self-consciously subtle and subtly self-conscious about its borrowings and relations with its own past and with popular culture, then Australia's peripheral vision of the global art world was the postmodern in a can.

The postmodern moment was about the conscious exploitation of one's irredeemable status as an object of history, not least of cultural history. Rather than jamming, interrupting, breaking with one's cultural matrix, the strategies for making culture would instead quite consciously play on memory, citation, pastiche, on the wit of knowingness about the past, not its carnivalesque overturning. Rather, what Catharine Lumby called, 'the aesthetics of surrender' (Lumby 1985). Or as Ted Colless and David Kelly said in their aleatory 'Lost World' essays published in *Art & Text*, 'No longer the victimised outsider but the continuum of the insider, disillusioned, dispassionate, left alone in a world well lost' (Colless & Kelly 1983). What for Colless and Kelly demanded a wistful melancholy Taylor was quick to spot as an opening for a rhetorical gambit with more purchase, more power. Australia, he said, 'can be called a culture of temporary culture because of its enormous and all-pervasive skills in setting up and dismantling its own cultural programs and its metaphors of cultural progress and aspiration according to their momentary efficacy' (Taylor 1994).

That it borrows even its avant-gardes from elsewhere is for Taylor just part of the expediency. Australian culture hasn't necessarily 'come of age'; rather, it is the beneficiary of a worldwide loss of confidence and nostalgic yearning for lost Utopias. Here we have an early version of the argument that Australian culture is always and already postmodern. Flung out on the antipodes, always on the 'other foot', not able to get on the good foot—nothing for it but to plunder all the cultures beaming in via satellite, from James Brown to Roland

Barthes, or preferably a bit of both—with Warhol on the side. Its unique creation is a culture of appropriation, not of creativity. Our creativity is appropriated, always derivative of elsewhere. But our style of appropriation is a unique creation. That is the original irony of Australian culture. In this moment when the dominant metropolitan cultures give up the ghost of acting as the subject in history, Australian culture comes into its own, having always been a culture of 'effects' rather than 'causes'.

Searching for a signal event in both local and global time, Taylor nominates the 1956 Melbourne Olympics as an emblem of an era of consumerism doubled by its televisual simulacra. He speaks to and for and from a generation that grew up in television's shadow. In the shadow of silent majorities, aggregated as consumers of spectacle but otherwise devoid of consensus.[5] Those of us born into TV's warm embrace, as something already part of the landscape, would never see the world the same way again. The doubling of perception in this relentless flow of images from elsewhere would work its way into our dreams and thoughts. The role of both art and criticism would be to make apparent this doubling of the world in endless flows of images. And beyond that, the cold fact of the endless making of the appearance of the world as relentless images could be teased out. Postmodernism thus had two projects. One was historical, to explain this moment in perception when images proliferate through the media and work their way into the landscape. The other was conceptual, to show how perception is always created in the act of perceiving, that it makes the object that it sees.

Taylor was a brilliant wit with a remarkable eye. And he was fully aware of the way power worked through art and its institutions, as his later New York writings show.[6] Like Wilde he worked the 'politics' into the wit to the point where the wit was the politics.[7] To champion the aesthetic as something distinct from moralising sermons is of course a moral position in itself. A position that favours the infinite freedom that opens up when images and words reflect on themselves and reveal endless possible new worlds beyond the limits of the one we think we know.

Fresh landscapes

Taylor hangs his case for an Australian postmodernism across the gap between two canonic films: *On the Beach* and *Mad Max*.[8] Ross Gibson, one of the editors of the little magazine called *On the Beach*, wrote one of his finest essays on *Mad Max* for *Art & Text*. Gibson reads the *Mad Max* series, and in particular the third film, as a story about a new relationship to landscape. In the wake of the early explorers like Mitchell and their will to dominate the landscape, and moving away also from submission to a landscape that is curiously empty yet spiritualised in Patrick White's *Voss*, Gibson sees in *Mad Max* a place where one can 'begin again', assembling fragments of image, sense, memory and self. 'In a culture that is beginning at page one, all available signs and artefacts might be counted temporarily equal' (Gibson 1985).

Like Taylor, Gibson plays with the image of a culture of failure. But in the wreckage of received ideas that came to dominate or sublimate the landscape, lies a new field of possibility—a democracy of objects. Gibson reads Max as a mythic reincarnation of Sturt, Eyre, Leichhardt and Voss, where the failure of conquest becomes the triumph of conquering the will to conquest. Gibson sees in Max a figure that goes beyond the noble failure of the subject in history, in this case the colonial subject acting in the land. Here at last is the image of a figure who will begin again. 'Now Max is simply moving with the continent, reading it a little more cannily, growing from it' (Gibson 1985).

This idea of a practice of reading the country also appears in the work of Stephen Muecke, particularly in his collaborations with Aboriginal storyteller Paddy Roe and painter Krim Benterrak, and in Eric Michael's extraordinary experiments with arming the Warlpiri community at Yuendumu with video cameras. In both cases the notion of a practice that is highly aware of its own jerry-built and partial nature, yet which can relate different cultures to each other and to the land, in the shadow of ever more global corporate and media relations, finds a place for itself in the desert.[9]

STYLE AND POWER

'We hear a lot these days about superficial style obsessed postmoderns: but the smart young things about town have very little to teach the Left about the politics of authoritarian control through style. We're the ones, after all, who installed a ruthless surveillance system monitoring every aspect of style . . . the fact that some stylish kid might be striking nihilistic poses in the latest exhibition catalogue is quite frankly the least of my worries.'[10] That was Meaghan Morris—the thinking person's survivor of the Libertarian push in 1985—on politics then. By opening up the whole question of the rhetoric of speaking, Morris was one of the people who opened the door to an even more self-consciously ironic style of writing. But Morris was always aware of addressing at least two kinds of reader. On the one side she is conducting the free thinker's ongoing war with the authoritarian elements of the left. These are the readers to whom she has offered the tactical concession about 'nihilism', ten years before it will occur to David Williamson to use it as a term of abuse. On the other hand, she is also addressing those 'superficial style obsessed postmoderns' and reminding them of the way the shimmer of images are still woven from a taut fabric of power.

The 'nihilistic poses' referred to might very well have been those of Ted Colless, whom I think was and remains the critic's critic, if not exactly as widely known as his arch and elegant writings demand. For Colless, the critic invents the very possibility of the aesthetic image and its autonomous being in the world through the struggle to produce it in language. Time and again, Colless conjures up images and concepts of astonishing and lucid beauty, and reminds us that we see and are astonished by the light only because of the impenetrable shadows from which the image and the word are cast.

The Error of My Ways, Colless's collected essays, begins by conjuring up a young Ted watching TV:

> Before the grey, spectral smears of late 1950s television, I sat innocent but expectantly through the Disney Mousketeers' jitterbug-like dance routines. I was waiting for the little pleated dresses to spin out and up above the girls' black knickers. The delight was purely phenomenal: only fleeting impressions of a firmness, fullness of the bottom or hip as the fulcrum for an energy that tipped the world. No thoughts of the origin or destiny of that vitality, let alone the content of such revelations of physique and movement. Later in the evenings, from the same screen luminous flying saucers would loom out of the drear pearl skies over a black and white American town as if they were coagulations of the material energy of television itself (Colless 1996).

From the Mouseketeers Colless fashions the beginnings of an essay, or a way of writing essays, about perception itself. This has nothing to do with 'relativism', but everything to do with scepticism, in the tradition of Michel de Montaigne's judicious, ironic, prudent use of doubt.[11] The issue is perception. And it has nothing to do with a celebration of 'popular culture'. Like Paul Taylor, Colless writes for the generation of aesthetes for whom television and pop are a necessary landscape of perception. But if the media really have swallowed up the public sphere and turned it, willy-nilly, into a fathomless mediasphere, then one cannot take for granted that there is a solid place to ground one's speaking position, as a critic, an intellectual, as anything. One has to begin ironically, by displacing one's self from the certainty of simply writing from some romantic notion of creative inspiration. One has to create a new way of creating, one that begins by taking its distance from any such assumptions. One begins again, from page one. And like the only true and original heretic, one starts from knowing that one knows nothing.

This is what the postmodern writers of the eighties took from Meaghan Morris—the self-conscious grounding of criticism in its own reflection on itself and its particular speaking position, in the moment (Wark 1992). Writing has to provide its own rhetorical platform, rather than simply assume a moral authority or a claim on the real. What writers like Colless, Lumby or Taylor left behind in Morris is the reflexive gesture back to the new left and its aura of moral and political certainties. That is a historical moment consigned, before our time, to the dustbin of history. They had May '68, we had Countdown. They had the Chicago 7, we had the Brady Bunch.

FLOWERS FOR THE CINEPHILE

It was as if a parody of John Docker's generalisations about the differences between Melbourne and Sydney were being staged when Adrian Martin came to town for a 1986 conference on culture, art and politics.[12] The Melbourne boy wanted to talk about 'the big picture', typical Melbourne stuff about the intellectual's responsibilities. Catharine Lumby gave the classic Sydney answer: that the big picture usually looks after itself and pays very little attention to a mere writer, but what concerns the writer is writing and writing's style. 'Perhaps really excellent writers have developed the knack of getting things wrong, flawlessly' (Lumby 1986).

I think there may be a peculiar undercurrent connecting Sydney Freethought, the Libertarian 'push' and Sydney postmodernism. Where John Anderson talked about pluralism, the pomo term was 'difference'.[13] So when Adrian Martin squared off against Catharine Lumby there seemed to be some secret history at work that was and remains a secret even to the participants. All the same, Martin played a key role in defining a postmodern sensibility that was more genuinely populist than could ever arise out of the cloistered halls of the University of Sydney's Power Institute, from which sprang both Colless and Lumby. Martin was a product of screen culture, of WEA film nights and post-punk do it yourself super-8 film nights at Melbourne's Clifton Hill community centre. He was, and remains, a cinephile (Martin 1988). And there's a common ancestry in terms of the push there in John Flauss.

The significance of Martin's writing is that it was the most elegant expression of a practice of beginning again in a democracy of cultural objects, rather than being merely a theory about it. Martin's writing is like a pop de Montaigne, making surreal leaps between Pasolini and Krazy Kat, Walter Benjamin and Arnold Schwarzenegger, Mizoguchi and Clint Eastwood. Even his nuttiest associations have an uncanny knack of seeming right on the money. Here is a sensibility that has trained itself, through the self-discipline of writing, to follow the lineaments of cultural experience, not the arbitrary conventions of 'interdisciplinary' criticism, and certainly not the middle-brow snob's idea of 'high culture', as if this were something self-evident and immutable. 'Surreal' and 'nutty' are favourite Martin adjectives. He looks in culture high and low, and he finds in everything those moments when culture reveals itself as a mass of arbitrary codes, borrowed conventions, hokey narratives that reveal shiny horizons of madness, sex and death in spite of themselves. Like Ross Gibson's essays, Martin's collection, *Phantasms*, reveals a reader of profound wit. Enemy of formalism and moralising, he reconciles the theoretical and the popular in prose. What Lumby objected to was Martin's insistence on framing such a practice 'Melbourne style', in a grand idea of the intellectual's mission in relation to culture, rather than 'Sydney style', in a preoccupation with the formal problems of the practice of writing itself. Another way of looking at it is that between them they embodied two possible readings of Meaghan Morris, the engaged public intellectual, or the formalist critic.

The irony is in how it turned out. Ten years later, Martin is in danger of making the 'big picture' into a residual, repetitive sign of itself, disconnected from anything other than the lovingly detailed criticism he practises, particularly in his Radio National voice essays on cinema. On the other hand, Lumby developed her style of critique into a critique of style that works across a wide range of contexts, from journalism to academia to public policy. In her book *Bad Girls: The Media, Sex and Feminism in the Nineties*, she makes the postmodern reflection on styles of speech and writing one of the bases of a feminist critique of the media. It is also a media-savvy critique of what feminism owes to what Morris called the 'politics of authoritarian control through style' as practised by the '68-inspired radical left (Lumby 1996b).[14]

What had been a wilful exercise in producing one's self as a finely tuned mediator of the objects and signs of a world awash with proliferating images became in itself a part of that flow of images, freely appropriated by others for quite other purposes, from Don Watson's celebration of the pomo republic to David Williamson's attack on pomo nihilism. Or perhaps most appropriately, Tony Moore's ABC TV documentary, *Bohemian Rhapsody*. Perhaps it is an appropriate fate for a movement that reconsidered creativity as appropriation, that it, in its turn, has been appropriated in such different ways. Meanwhile whatever will be post-postmodernism stirs again, in the little magazines and art catalogues.[15] Or perhaps, most appropriately, on the World Wide Web.

NOTES

1 Frow, J. 1991, *What Was Postmodernism?*, Local Consumption Occasional Papers. An excellent essay, but Frow is not particularly well attuned to pomo with an Australian accent.

Some of the essential texts for thinking about the peculiarities of the Australians are collected in Grosz, E.A. *et al.* (eds) 1986, *Futur*fall: Excursions into Post-Modernity*, Power Publications, Sydney; Hansford, P. (ed.) 1993, *Wit's End*, Museum of Contemporary Art, Sydney; Frow, J. & Morris, M. (eds) 1993, *Australian Cultural Studies: A Reader*, Allen & Unwin, Sydney. The latter is particularly useful for demonstrating why postmodernism and cultural studies are not the same thing.

2 For the context of the 'lucky country' and the 'cultural cringe', see Docker, J. 1974, *Australian Cultural Elites*, Angus & Robertson, Sydney; Rowse, T. 1978, *Australian Liberalism and National Character*, Kibble Books, Melbourne.

3 See Hayward, P. (ed.) 1992, *From Pop to Punk to Postmodernism*, Allen & Unwin, Sydney; and Potts, J. & Wark, McK. 1995, 'Play That Funky Music White Boy', *Communal/Plural*, no. 4, Sydney.

4 The media carried on a very one-sided debate against postmodernism in 1995 and 1996. See Faust, B. 1995, 'Unthrifty writers', *Australian Rationalist*, no. 38; Wark, McK. 1995, 'The new mysticism', *Australian Rationalist*, no. 39; Williamson, D. 1996, 'Universal moral soldier', *Bulletin*, 2 April. See also Williamson, D. 1995, *Dead White Males*, Currency Press, Sydney, which includes Keith Windshuttle's favourable review.

5 Two key books here are Debord, G. 1983, *The Society of the Spectacle*, Black & Red, Detroit; and Baudrillard, J. 1983, *Simulation*, Semiotext(e), New York. The former is by the leader of the revolutionary avant-garde movement, the Situationists, and the latter is in many respects its ironic inversion, although both Debord and Baudrillard owe an obvious debt to Henri Lefebvre's work, such as his 1991, *Critique of Everyday Life*, Verso, London.

6 See Taylor, P. 1995, *After Andy: Soho in the Eighties*, Schwartz City, Melbourne.

7 Ellmann, R. (ed.) 1982, *The Artist as Critic: Critical Writings of Oscar Wilde*, Chicago University Press, Chicago. There is also a strong connection between irony, postmodernism and camp—the connecting thread between Wilde, Warhol and

Taylor, and part of the reason for the violent distaste for all three displayed so consistently by their more muscular critics.

8 *On the Beach* 1959, directed by Stanley Kramer, was based on the novel by Neville Shute. *Mad Max* 1979, *Mad Max 2* 1981 and *Mad Max: Beyond Thunderdome* 1985 were all directed by Dr George Miller.

9 K. Muecke, S. & Roe, P. 1984, *Reading the Country: Introduction to Nomadology*, Fremantle Arts Centre Press; and Michaels, E. 1994, *Bad Aboriginal Art*, Allen & Unwin, Sydney.

10 Morris, M. 1988, 'Politics now', in *The Pirate's Fiance*, Verso, London, p. 178; originally published in 1985, *Intervention*, no. 20, the issue which includes my extended reply to it, 'The last post'.

11 de Montaigne, M. 1995, *The Complete Essays*, Penguin, London. See also Ross Gibson's brilliant essay on the essay, and the essay-films of Chris Marker, in *South of the West* (1992) Indiana University Press, Bloomington.

12 Docker, J. 1986, *op cit*. The conference was Manuf(r)acturing Australia. Papers from it by Adrian Martin, Ross Harley, Catharine Lumby and McKenzie Wark appear in *On the Beach*, no. 10, 1986.

13 Anderson, J. 1982, *Art & Reality*, Hale & Iremonger, Sydney; Baker, A.J. 1979, *Anderson's Social Philosophy*, Angus & Robertson, Sydney.

14 If there is a fatal irony about eighties postmodernism, it is that its fate, in the end, was determined by neither of these self-styled and self-styling options. What determined the fate of eighties pomo and consigned its chalky remains to dusty milk crates was something that Meaghan Morris saw coming, if nobody else did—that the temporary culture of little magazines, art spaces and quasi left-wing movements that were the autonomous space it inhabited would give way to a more rationally ordered and 'disciplined' cultural life. The institutions of the media, the subsidised art world and the academy absorbed postmodernism into its feature pages, catalogue essays and reading lists.

15 See, for example, Chapman, C. 1996 *Adelaide Biennial of Australian Art*, AGSA, Adelaide.

REFERENCES

Colless, E. 1996, 'Folly', in *The Error of My Ways*, Institute of Modern Art, Brisbane.

Colless, T. & Kelly, D. 1983, 'The Lost World 3', *Art & Text*, no. 12/13, summer, reprinted in Colless, E. 1996, *The Error of My Ways*, Institute of Modern Art, Brisbane.

Gibson, R. 1985, 'Yondering: A reading of Mad Max Beyond Thunderdome', *Art & Text*, no. 19, October; reprinted in Gibson, R. 1992, *South of the West*, Indiana University Press, Bloomington.

Lumby, C. 1985, 'Videodrome: The aesthetics of surrender', *Frogger*, no. 19, November.

—— 1986, 'Speech impediments', *On the Beach*, no. 10.

—— 1993, 'Smiling sabateurs', in *Wit's End*, ed. Pamela Hansford, Museum of Contemporary Art, Sydney.

—— 1996a, 'Media culpa', *21*C*, no. 2.

—— 1996b, *Bad Girls: The Media, Sex and Feminism in the Nineties*, Allen & Unwin, Sydney.

Marcus, G. 1989, *Lipstick Traces: A Secret History of the 20th Century*, Harvard University Press, Cambridge.

Martin, A. 1988, 'No flowers for the cinephile', in *Islands in the Stream*, ed. Paul Foss, Pluto Press, Sydney.

Michaels, E. 1994, *Bad Aboriginal Art*, Allen & Unwin, Sydney, originally 1987, 'My essay on postmodernism', *Art & Text*, no. 25.

Taylor, P. 1994, 'A culture of temporary culture', *Art & Text*, no. 17, summer.

Wark, McK. 1992, 'Speaking trajectories: Meaghan Morris, Antipodean theory and Australian cultural studies', *Cultural Studies*, vol. 6, no. 3, October.

—— 1994, *Virtual Geography: Living With Global Media Events*, Indiana University Press, Bloomington.

Watson, D. 1993, 'A toast to the postmodern republic', *Island*, no. 55, winter.

17 Cultural undergrounds and civic identity

Wayne Hudson

The time has come for Australians to think of themselves as complex, cosmopolitan people. Doing so, however, will involve acknowledging the advantages as opposed to the disadvantages of 'distance', the opportunities made possible by living in multicultural cities with access to multilingual broadcasters, and the rich complexity of Australian cultures—a complexity currently often buried by stereotypes.[1] In this chapter I attempt to show that a greater sense of the complexity of Australian cultures can be related to a stronger sense of Australian originality and a richer understanding of Australian civic identity. I conclude by drawing out some implications of my argument for the writing of Australian history.

I

Australians have been educated to search for uniquely Australian features of their cultural life, but it is possible that an obsession with the unique and the distinctive has led us to misconstrue and also to underestimate our originality. Certainly Australians have been slow to recognise the complexity of their cultural life, including the diverse, heterogeneous and conflicting sources which made its originality possible. Here the case of Australian intellectual life is particularly interesting, not least because it is comparatively neglected.

Although there are now clear signs that more self-confident Australian intellectual cultures are flourishing, Australians have still not recognised their own intellectuality or the achievements of their most important intellectuals. There is still no intellectual history of Australia.[2] The major collections of papers have not been properly studied or, in many cases, even catalogued; and the books that have been written have not always been given the credit they deserve. Instead, Australian academics have sometimes hidden behind very wide social anthropological definitions of 'intellectuals' which, while they may not be overtly elitist, are compatible with the suggestion that Australians are not conspicuously innovative or creative in the realm of ideas. To be fair, Australian intellectuals themselves do not always help much, especially when they pretend to be as ordinary as possible. However, even in contexts such as art and technological design, in which Australians are beginning to celebrate their originality, there is little recognition as yet of crucial features of the social and cultural arrangements which made this originality possible.

A few years ago, with David Carter, I interviewed a number of distinguished Australian intellectuals.[3] We found that the intellectuals concerned were distinctly nervous about claiming to be intellectuals in any strong sense, and that they did not know how the presence and absence of crucial knowledges had helped them achieve originality. This put us on notice that major features of cultural life in Australia were not yet well understood. Subsequent interviews suggested, predictably enough, that the originality of Australian intellectuals was often related to well-read schoolteachers, who changed the horizons and expectations of the people concerned, and to bookstores and little magazines. They also suggested that the originality of Australian intellectuals was sometimes related to unusual trajectories which landed them in international cultural capitals, such as Paris, London and New York, without the benefit of a strong grounding in the relevant European knowledges—and that the absence of these knowledges paradoxically often helped the Australians achieve original and independent stances. Finally, and most striking of all, they suggested that the originality of many of these Australian intellectuals was related to involvement with *cultural undergrounds* which were not well known to other Australians.

The notion of cultural undergrounds denies the transparency assumed in Australian cultural history and subverts the idea that Australians participated in a common culture which everyone knew about. It goes against the received notion of an 'Australian society' with egalitarian aspirations by implying that many Australians desired to be other and different from the bulk of their fellow citizens. It also emphasises an element of reserve and even secrecy which is at odds with how Australians have chosen to fantasise about themselves. Of course, the term 'underground' is used freely, implying that powerful cultural streams flowed across Australia which were not visible to or accessed by everyone. It cannot be taken literally since in many cases these streams were visible and on the surface. The point is that the cultural resources found in these 'undergrounds' were not visible or accessible in depth to Australians not linked to them, so that advanced discussions of such resources often tended to take place in coteries of people linked to the undergrounds rather than in public.

The presence of cultural undergrounds makes it easier to explain the tendency for Australian intellectuals to hide their learning in public and to deal with other Australians on the basis of exchangeable identities while maintaining other richer identities which are not necessarily exchangeable. Some Australian intellectuals, for example, have access to Orthodox or reformed Jewish undergrounds. In that capacity they speak Hebrew, travel to Israel and practise the cabbala after the age of 40. But none of this is easily exchanged with non-Jewish Australians. Other Australians have links with the Society of Jesus, meet members of the order from many parts of the world, and have books on philosophical and theological topics on their bookshelves with which other Australians are not familiar. Such Australians have read Rahner and Lonergan; they may have even visited key Jesuit centres, such as Boston College or Fordham University. But they do not discuss these matters at the office or among their peers. In the same way in the past many Australians were linked with communist parties in other countries. They listened to foreign language radio broadcasts and received periodicals from those countries, had libraries of philosophical and political books, often in foreign languages, and frequented particular pubs and bookshops where recent developments were discussed. For example, the New World bookshop in Sydney stocked an astonishing range of books on art and literature from Eastern European countries as well as communist materials in many languages.

Today other Australian intellectuals read esoteric Buddhist philosophy from China, Japan or Korea, and spend time in Buddhist monasteries. Still others are anthroposophists and delve among the four hundred volumes of esoteric lectures left by the Austrian clairvoyant, philosopher and scientist Rudolph Steiner. Such intellectuals often have private libraries of anthroposophical books on everything from music to projective geometry to physics, and once again the crucial fact for Australian cultural history is that these are books which other Australians have not seen. The examples can be multiplied at various cultural levels to include the Swedenborgians and the Christian Scientists, who also have their own journals and publishing houses. Once the Lutherans, the Mormons and the Freemasons are included, the number of such people and their strategic location becomes obvious. Yet in each case the crucial lore is not in the public domain in the sense of being well known to other Australians. Of course, it can be argued that such people are small in number and unrepresentative. This may be true, but their number and influence is much greater than has ever been recognised, at least outside the pages of Jill Roe's magnificent study of theosophy in Australia (Roe 1986).[4]

What is striking, though not necessarily unique to Australia, is that these underground knowledges tend not to circulate in the public culture generally. This is significant because Australian intellectuals not linked to undergrounds often rely on vernacular or non-tertiary knowledges outside the area of their professional expertise, whereas those linked with undergrounds are more likely to be familiar with tertiary perspectives across a wide area, partly because such knowledges circulate in the undergrounds. As a result, the low-cultural-capital style of most Australian intellectual life is both misleading and possibly harmful. Whereas in New York or London one could discuss Russian poetry, the philosophy of Spinoza, and various performances of major works of Western music with a numerous class of educated people, in Australia this would be more difficult, and many intellectuals would not take up such references at a social function. The fact that in Australia underground knowledges do not circulate widely means that Australian intellectuals linked to one underground easily underestimate the knowledges available to other Australian intellectuals. It is not simply that relatively few Australian intellectuals admit to knowing the history of astronomy in detail, just as hardly any non-Jews are prepared to discuss the Baal Shem Tov. The noncirculation of underground knowledges also impacts on our sense of place. Thus hardly anyone in Australia has an adequate idea of the materials held in private libraries in Brisbane. In Sydney or Melbourne the suggestion that major holdings exist in Brisbane is greeted with incredulity, whereas there are considerable collections of French, German, Russian, Chinese and Korean books, not to mention scholarly holdings in Syriac and Arabic.

Now all this is relatively new and subversive of stereotypes which downplay the cultural resources to which Australian intellectuals have access. Of course, it is only a beginning and does not do justice to, for example, changing patterns in different decades or variations from one part of the country to another. Nor does it take account of women's networks or of gay and lesbian subcultures, even though these also sometimes function as cultural undergrounds. Nonetheless, focusing on cultural undergrounds implies a different approach to originality in Australian intellectual history: an approach which relates this originality to complex cultural resources and to specific absences, rather than to mystical emanations of a unique single identity out of 'the land' or 'the place'. In doing so it qualifies any narrowly geographic conception of 'Australia' and implies that negative stereotypes derived from a reactive nationalism may have led us to underestimate our originality in many different areas.

II

I now relate these tentative conclusions to multiple identities and the need for a stronger Australian civic identity. To emphasise the role of cultural undergrounds helps us to appreciate the complexity of Australian cultures and the criss-crossing networks they contain. Once we think of Australians as culturally complex people who inhabit diverse cultural spaces, only some of which are public, then it is not difficult to imagine that we might need to explore networks of multiple identities rather than to search for unique and distinct characteristics in isolation. This is not because distinct and unique characteristics do not exist, but because without some sense of multiple identities we may not be able to appreciate when and how Australians deployed these characteristics. In this sense it is crucial to study what Australians *did* with their multiple identities. This argument holds for Aborigines as well as for Australians of Asian and European descent. It is equally valid for Sir Henry Parkes and Anita Keating.

An emphasis on multiple identities is not new in Australian history, but there are very few attempts to relate the porous character of plural identities to originality. To appreciate the change of perspective, it is enough to turn back to the standard histories of Australia and to notice how little sense of Australian originality comes through and how few multiple identities are recognised. Even elementary points about the British, the Irish, the Chinese and Aborigines all being motley crews are not adequately discussed, although there is better specialist work in the case of Aborigines. And the link with originality is seldom made. There is also remarkably little acknowledgment of the fact that large numbers of Australians are bi- or multilingual, especially when what is at stake is a characterisation of the intersection of cultural fields, and not merely aggregated statistics of those who speak a so-called 'second' language.

An emphasis on multiple identities also makes it possible to combine plasticity with a sense of constraining cultural determinacy.

Clearly constructivism of the type Richard White appeared to argue for in *Inventing Australia*, will not do, as White himself now substantially concedes (White, chapter two). Indeed, White now finds the theme of multiple identities in his earlier work. He also emphasises a 'materialist' strand in his work which is compatible with much that I have said in this chapter. Indeed, the complexity of Australian cultures obviously includes the cultural resources brought to this continent, and a new Australian history might appear if these resources were acknowledged more openly and better integrated into general cultural histories. Thus the Afghan presence, the role of Germans in north Queensland and the importance of specific Jewish settlements are not just colourful additions to a British–Irish story. They changed who the British and the Irish in Australia were, not least through intermarriage.

These cultural resources and the way they are appropriated here also shape the clues Australians seek to follow up when they are overseas. To illustrate this, let me refer to my own early life in Arncliffe, a largely working-class suburb of Sydney. In my family no one talked of London, and there was very little sense of doing anything in an English way, although there were Welsh-speaking visitors to the house. There *was* conversation in the house about Jerusalem and Russia, as well as tales about the American South, where my grandfather had taken two degrees. There were also stories of a one-eyed Russian nobleman who got himself to Sydney. Above all, there was a local public library and a shop selling second-hand comics and paperbacks, which made it possible for me to read comics about the Korean war and a paperback about Two Gun Cohen and the communists in China. Hence it is perhaps not surprising that when I arrived in Britain for the first time I had already travelled in Russia, China, and Japan and chose to work there with a Montenegran nobleman and an ex-communist Pole on a German Jewish philosopher. The mixture of hubris and ignorance reflected my Australian upbringing in Sydney. It could not have been less British.

Multiple identities, however, are not merely plural identities, for our multiplicity goes to the way in which each particular identity is held and promotes interactions between them, including erosions of essentialist identities. Nonetheless, the writing of Australian history will only be able to assimilate this insight in stages, and with appropriate sensitivity for the part played by specific named identities, despite the diversity from which they were constructed. In a longer term perspective the search for single Australian identities, including ethnic identities, may be simplistic, not least because evolved human beings often lose their passport identities and become more original in the process. This implies that Australia is created by how those who came here changed after arrival. In a short-term perspective looking beyond single identities has merit, even if the difference between plural and multiple identities is not always pressed. This is especially the case because the pretence to single identities often conceals cultures which are not common, including elements of them which could be. Thus many Australians know what happens when relatives visit from the old country, whatever country that happens to be, just as they know proverbs and children's songs which they do not use with other ethnic groups. Irish Australians, in particular, know whole worlds of feeling which are not mentioned when the company is 'mixed'. The tendency to conceal actual language use also throws a pall over the past. Many younger Australians do not realise that even in the 1950s many Australian intellectuals spoke French, sang in Latin, or read one of Italian, German, Russian, Greek or Hebrew. They also do not know that the Cockney term 'mate' was used ironically by middle-class people as part of a public cultural script, acted out partly perhaps because they could not share their love of the Latin mass or Anglican evensong.

Once again the effect is not only to conceal the existence of various ethnicities, but to conceal multiple identities all around us, and the originality they have and could make possible. This tendency to conceal cultural complexity also makes it difficult to keep in mind at particular dates, for example, 1850 or 1914, who the 'Australians' were. It is also crucial to understand that Greeks or Maltese who came to Australia became fusions of several identities, as they discovered when they returned to visit Greece or Malta. Even Australians of Anglo descent soon discover that many of their sympathies differ from those of the English: that they are keener on the Germans, that they like 'Europe' more—and so on.

Against this it can be argued that a single Australian identity is emerging, that younger Australians often feel defined precisely by Australia as a single place, and speak increasingly in a single accent. There is considerable truth in this, but it needs to be qualified by an analysis of social strata and by studies of immigrant communities. Moreover, it may be that conflicting processes are occuring at the same time. It may be that some of of those currently in positions of influence have escaped from the multiple identities of their parents. This does not affect my argument since one of the things you can do with multiple identities is to give them up in a bid to assimilate with a single exchangeable identity. And to some extent this has happened. It is much less clear that people who are not in positions of influence have assimilated to the same extent, whether they be Aborigines in Brisbane or Greeks in Melbourne. It is also far from clear that younger Australians are as monocultural as the objection suggests. Indeed, studies of popular music and eating habits suggest that they are not. To this extent, new multiple identities may be supplementing or even replacing older multiple identities tied to ethnicity.

An emphasis on multiple identities qualifies both nationalist and one-sided multiculturalist approaches to Australian identity. It is controversial because it strikes at the vitalist strand in Australian nationalism from Henry Lawson on, which claims that Australians are typically original *when* they embody the spirit of 'the land' or 'the place'. This vitalist strand derives from a romantic irrationalist cult of *Heimat* encompassing both 'land' and 'place', which still dominates most Australian discourse about identity and is often projected, without adequate qualifications, onto the spirituality of Aborigines. It is also reinforced by a rhetoric of 'post-colonialism'[5] which implies that it is wicked to adopt the cultural mores of the colonial power, and crucial to negotiate identity around the specificities of the country in which you actually live. For post-colonial critics it is not who you are, but where you are that matters. Both the vitalist and the post-colonial approaches contain obvious good sense; they also preserve the nativist will to independence and originality, which in the Australian context deserves to be respected. Nonetheless, they are naive when considered from the standpoint of world history, as though Chinese, Parsees, Jews and Armenians were bound to give up those aspects of their culture which do not derive from the local palm trees. They also overlook the exact form and meaning of 'colonialism', in Australia, including the differences between the regimes established in the Australian colonies and those found in the West Indies or Bengal. Finally, they collapse cultural identity into what is allegedly appropriate to the local 'society', as if the inhabitants of the Roman colonies in North Africa were dim to build theatres and aqueducts when they should have been creating a new culture organised around camels and deserts. However, it is not clear that multiple identities are incompatible with an original response to the particularities of the Australian landscape, or, for that matter, polity. On the contrary, they may enhance it, as the cases of the Australian wine industry and Australian cuisine both demonstrate.

A greater sensitivity to multiple identities may also help to clarify neglected aspects of Australian civic identity by showing how Australians were original in their agency, and how far and why our civic identity permitted agency and originality. Indeed, multiple identities could promote a richer view of Australian civic identity which discovers negotiations between multiple identities, from Botany Bay to Eureka to Federation, in the history of the women's movement, and within twenty ethnic communities. This perspective could also usefully inflect the way Australian history is taught in schools[6] so that even popular understandings of the Australian past are pluralist rather than covertly essentialist. An emphasis on genuinely multiple identities may also help to articulate a polycultural Australia, as opposed to an Australia of multiple but distinct cultures assigned by tribes. Until recently Australian opinion-formers have often been supportive of versions of multiculturalism that have lacked clearly defined accounts of Australian civic identity. They have sometimes used the language of pluralism to support a basically nonpluralist cultural politics, which allocates people to their community and culture of ethnic origins. Today multiculturalism needs to be rethought[7] in a way which does not retreat from the advantages of affirming cultural difference, but which affirms the case for a strong civic identity, while recognising multiple porous or pervasional identities as a central ingredient of an expanded and differential conception of Australian citizenship.[8] A sense of belonging may be compatible with nuanced relationships to multiple particular identities, a theme explored in recent feminist debates.[9]

An emphasis on a strong civic identity need not imply a return to a hegemonic monoculturalism. On the contrary, it can emphasise multiple identities as part of Australian civic identity. Moreover, it can do so not only as a way of doing justice to past as well as present diversity, but as a way of building a distinctive Australian polity characterised by civic pluralism as a constitutive part of civic identity. In this way a proper regard can be paid to common national symbols and to the constitutive and not merely contingent contributions of groups such as the British, the Irish and the Scots, and more recently the Greeks, the Italians, the Chinese and the Vietnamese. Likewise, legitimate concerns expressed by critics of multiculturalism that being 'just Australian' has been devalued can be met both by promoting rich common cultural components and by encouraging taking up multiple identities not conferred at birth as a very Australian cultural strategy. In this way the hidden meaning of movies such as *Strictly Ballroom* could become a national cultural strategy. And significantly a policy which was historically subtle in this way would have positive implications for exports and jobs in a world which increasingly values both cultural uniqueness and global cultural portability.

III

I now turn to the implications of my argument for the writing of Australian history.

What should Australian history now become? No one is ideally qualified to answer this question. And yet it needs to be addressed at a time when the survival of interest in the past is in question and there is a crisis of 'history' in the schools as fewer and fewer Australians leave the school system with any real historical understanding either of their own country or of the contemporary world. The boom in public history in oral history, and in heritage studies does not compensate for the failure to inculcate skills and knowledges that would equip Australians for effective political and economic citizenship. In this sense, changing the writing of Australian history is about creating Australia.

After decades of self-examination, it may now be possible to detect a change of mood in Australian historical writing: a desire to establish a more positive relation to whatever the 'Australian' in Australian history means, combined with an enhanced ethical sensitivity to the need to respect difference and not to usurp the speaking positions of others. These changes are appearing after major work has been done on challenging nationalism and on exploring in depth the issues of race, class and gender. They also come after extended but inconclusive methodological debates about the demise of liberal humanism and the impact of differently disciplined writing, much of it from cultural studies. Today there is uncertainty about what comes next. Hitherto Australian historical writing has often been shaped by a desire to find a common story as a basis for Australian identity. In effect, Australian history has been burdened with a mixture of social science positivism and missionary intent. We have had overwritten Australian history; we have had Australian history as complaint; we have had Australian history as an attempt to bring about political, social and sexual change. We have also occasionally had Australian history as party trick and literary coup. We have even had theoretically sophisticated history, although in limited supply. What we have not had, in adequate quantities, is Australian history which embraces the problem of how to write pluralist history without surrendering the quest for a strong culturally articulated civic identity. Today the need for such history is acute, especially in the context of the need to project clear and distinct images of Australia into the Asia-Pacific region.

In books about Australian history the term 'Australia' is often used in ways which conceal the need for creativity. What older historians meant by 'Australia' in the context of Australian history was 'the country', 'the land', ' the nation'– even though these are all different things. In so far as place dominated, the rhetoric deployed was that of geographic romanticism, although this was nowhere acknowledged, and the actual geographic links between Australia and South America, Australia and India, Australia and South Africa were little explored. More recently, there has been some acknowledgment of the constantly re-enacted and renegotiated space labelled 'Australia'. Nonetheless, 'Australia' as a settler society to which migrants come when they are not 'Australian' in any simple fashion, does not make sense apart from actual social and cultural exchanges. And these, in turn, occur in the context of specific forms of civic identity. Australian history which fails to emphasise this occludes the civic significance of facts such as that in Australia lower middle-class norms provide many of the routines of public interaction long after migrant families have acquired considerable wealth; or the fact that in Australia Greeks and Turks live in peace with each other, while continuing to read discourses of hatred for each other from their countries of origin. To this extent, there may be some merit in the largely discredited nationalist approach to Australian history, in so far as it sought to grasp what was particular and enhancing about the fact that Australians lived in this country and not another. But 'country' here is a socio-political term. It *is* geographic, but it primarily refers to the ways life is lived in this geography.

The essays in *Creating Australia* make the case for more inclusive Australian history, but they do not attempt to determine how many 'Australias' there can be. The approach taken in this chapter suggests that the term 'Australia' is still viable as the name of a political and social space, but that it needs to be fleshed out. Certainly we need to enlarge what we mean by 'Australian' in Australian history to include Australians from every ethnic background, Australians who live in rural areas, and Australians working overseas, especially in war time. Studies of Australians in Israel, in Greece, in South Africa, in China, in Japan and in Britain are long overdue. Similarly, the exceptional status of Aborigines and other indigenous peoples needs to be addressed. This could be done by giving them first-nation status, as Henry Reynolds suggests[10], or by allowing them a specific, differentiated form of citizenship. In either case, we cannot pretend that all those who live within the continent are 'Australians' by virtue of that fact and in the same sense, and admitting this will make a single voice or subject position harder to maintain in Australian historical writing in the future.

Clearly an emphasis on multiple identities complicates any single story-line, just as it questions the ethnic and cultural indices used to pick out 'Australians'. If Australia continues to accept significant levels of Asian immigration, it is possible that struggles over the meaning of 'Australian' may become even more intense in the future. Technology is also making an impact, especially on the young. There are now computers in thousands of homes which challenge localist versions of identity. It is also hard to communicate with people in Asian countries by e-mail and not to feel virtual geographies replacing actual ones. When the virtual geography arrives next door, the impact is even greater. It is similarly not easy to stand in the room with 3000 Buddhas in the Nan Tien temple south of Wollongong and feel exclusively defined by a localist culture.

This implies that we will have to learn to approach creating Australia more sensitively. We will not be able to make our own particular identities or our own political, social and cultural preferences mandatory for others. Moreover, the point of writing Australian history will no longer be to forge a single story and to make migrants from all over the earth share a common folk memory. Perhaps, among other things, it will be about how creative agents can use their multiple identities for different purposes, while continuing to live together in civility and peace. But if so, then Australians will require a stronger set of civic committments than they currently possess. This has crucial implications for a future Australian republic. It goes to the heart of the republican political doctrine needed to make the Australian republic work.[11] At the same time it tends against the unitary tenor of the older nationalist Australian history, just as it implies that Australians should be better informed about their civic heritage, especially in the context of attempts to redefine and strengthen Australian citizenship. To this extent, it may be necessary to take practical steps to strengthen Australian civic identity, even as we make efforts to recognise and respect multiple identities in our history.

NOTES

1 Some of the most innovative work recognising the complexity of Australian cultural life has been done by non-historians—for example, by people influenced by cultural studies, such as Paul Foss 1988, *Islands in the Stream: Myths of Place in Australian Culture*, Pluto Press, Leichhardt.

2 For important additions to the older studies, see G. Melleuish 1995, *Cultural Liberalism in Australia: A Study in Intellectual and Cultural History*, Cambridge

University Press, Cambridge and B. Kennedy 1995, *A Passion to Oppose John Anderson, Philosopher*, Melbourne University Press, Melbourne.

3 Among those interviewed were Elizabeth Gross, Meaghan Morris, John Docker, Kevin Hart, Ann Freadman, John Frow, Simon During, Paul Patton, John Honner and Peter Beilharz.

4 Roe's study is much more important for the study of Australian cultural patterns than its topic suggests. Characteristically, it has not received the wide discussion it deserves. See J. Roe 1986, *Beyond Belief: Theosophy in Australia 1879–1939*, NSW University Press, Sydney.

5 On the need for for more cautious and nuanced discussion, see N. Thomas 1994, *Colonialism's Culture: Anthropology, Travel and Government*, Polity Press, Cambridge; and S. Macintyre 1994, *A History For A Nation: Ernest Scott and the Making of Australian History*, Melbourne University Press, Melbourne.

6 It is an open question how far Australian history should be presented in the social science mode, and how far allowance should be made for what has been called history as performance; see G. Dening 1996, *Performances*, Melbourne University Press, Melbourne.

7 The role of multiculturalism in Australian civic identity needs more careful elaboration. For essential discussion, see S. Castles, M. Kalantzis, B. Cope & M. Morissey 1988, *Mistaken Identity: Multiculturalism and the Demise of Nationalism in Australia*, Pluto Press, Sydney; C. Kukathas (ed.) 1993, *Multicultural Citizens: The Philosophy and Politics of Identity*, Centre for Independent Studies, Sydney; and A. Theophanous 1995, *Multiculturalism and Australian Identity*, Ilikia Books, Melbourne.

8 On differential citizenship, see W. Hudson & J. Kane (eds) *Rethinking Australian Citizenship*, Cambridge University Press, Melbourne (forthcoming).

9 See, for example, E. Probyn 1996, *Outside Belonging*, Routledge, London.

10 See H. Reynolds 1996, *Aboriginal Sovereignty: Reflections on Race, State and Nation*, Allen & Unwin, Sydney.

11 For an argument that minimalist and maximalist republicanism may be compatible, see W. Hudson & D. Carter, 'Republicans must realise a president is only the start', *Australian*, 28 July, p. 18; and W. Hudson and D. Carter 1993, *The Republicanism Debate*, NSW University Press, Sydney.

Index

MORE GOOD BOOKS FROM ALLEN & UNWIN

MEMORIES AND DREAMS

Reflections on 20th century Australia

EDITED BY RICHARD WHITE AND PENNY RUSSELL

'Modern Australia . . . has many different meanings. The essays in this collection demonstrate that historians have been involved in both constructing and challenging those meanings. Most history asks how we came to be as we are, but never is the question so immediate as when we face the twentieth century. Here we look into a mirror in which we can recognise ourselves. This disturbing feeling of closeness is the peculiar challenge of twentieth-century history—the consciousness that so many of its events are within living memory, the sense that our lives are entangled with it, the awareness that it underpins so many of our dilemmas today. The twentieth century is the repository of our collective memories and dreams.'

In this collection, thirteen accounts demonstrate what has been happening to the study of Australian History. Through these essays—on subjects as diverse as ANZAC and shopping, 1950s monarchism and forbidden comics, Hills hoists and Aboriginal politics—the reader can share the excitement of arguing about a past which shapes, and is shaped by, the lives of all of us.

1 86373 536 4

MORE GOOD BOOKS FROM ALLEN & UNWIN

AUSTRALIAN CHILDHOOD

A history

JAN KOCIUMBAS

'It may be that the land and the people are young-hearted together, and the children's spirits not crushed and saddened by the shadow of long years' sorrowful history. There is a lurking sparkle of joyousness and rebellion and mischief in nature here, and therefore in children.'

'History, yes, we learnt History, all about Captain Cook. Who the hell wanted to learn about James Cook? He was just another white man. I thought, "If this James Cook's like the Manager, I don't want to know 'im anyway!" That Manager seemed to shout at us most of the time, and if you done anything wrong you got whipped across the bum with a heavy piece of rope.'

In *Australian Childhood*, Jan Kociumbas explores the experience of growing up in Australia since white settlement. She acknowledges the resilience and adaptability of the young and re-evaluates their contribution to our past.

The first comprehensive history of childhood in Australia, *Australian Childhood* is engaging reading for students, teachers and anyone interested in Australian history.

1 86448 059 9

BELIEVING IN AUSTRALIA

A cultural history of religions

HILARY M. CAREY

Australians have been slow to appreciate the rich variety of their religious inheritance. *Believing in Australia* is a much-needed cultural history of Australia's many religions which goes well beyond existing studies of denominationalism.

Hilary Carey traces the changes in religious practice brought by waves of migration, including European occupation and the post-war growth of Orthodox, Jewish, Muslim and Buddhist communities. She also examines the slow European discovery of Aboriginal religions, the vital importance of religion for women and the recent growth of Christian fundamentalism and New Age sects.

Believing in Australia demonstrates the central place of religion in the Australian experience and offers an engaging introduction to Australia's religious history for believers and non-believers alike.

1 86373 950 5